Praise for *Someda...*

"In this wise, imaginative, and moving book, Jackie Stevenson conveys Eight Paths to Authentic Presence through compelling stories from her treasure trove of profound experiences working with equines as collaborators. Raven, a horse whose ancestors carried knights into battle, brings a wounded warrior back to wholeness. Spirit the soulful paint mare, Holly the zebra, and other members of Jackie's perceptive herd work their magic with people from all walks of life. Together, these potent tales of healing and empowerment show us how learning to live like horses can help us negotiate life's challenges, gifts, and mysteries with grace, courage, compassion, and fun!"
—Linda Kohanov, author of *The Tao of Equus, Riding between the Worlds, Way of the Horse, The Power of the Herd,* and *The Five Roles of a Master Herder*

"This book tells of CEOs and veterans, teens, and therapists becoming aware and being authentic, feeling their heartbeat through a deep connection to one of Jackie Stevenson's horses (and zebra) and their herd. She offers humorous and moving stories woven into lessons for living and learning. It is a zen experience with the smell of fresh hay and evidence of horses. Joining a herd is a total immersion and far more than joining 'friends' on social media. Put on your boots, read it and get ready for the ride of your life!"
—Richard Boyatzis, Ph.D., Distinguished University Professor, Case Western Reserve University, Author, *Becoming a Resonant Leader*

"This engaging book offers gentle insights and appealing wisdom to enable us to discover our authentic presence and purpose, and enact the best of our unique selves. Through captivating stories of a herd of horses and appreciative lessons of nature, we learn how to cope with our challenges and emerge as authentic leaders who serve the people in our lives. A delightful, evocative, and self-reflective read for those who seek to make a positive difference in our world!"
—Diana Bilamoria, Ph.D., Professor, CWRU

"Horses—and how they exist as a herd—have so much synergetic similarity to how teams in business work together to accomplish a common goal. I had our Executive Leadership Team become immersed into the herd. It took us to a raw, real state of who we are—and who we want to be. The insights and experience reshaped our thinking as individuals and as a interdependent unit."

—Jodi Berg, Ph.D., CEO VitaMix

"*Some Day We'll Live Like Horses* invites us to awaken to a new state of consciousness and follow the path to a truly authentic existence. Its gift is the transformation of our ordinary life into an experience of peace, joy and connectedness with our fellow human beings and the larger natural world. Jackie Stevenson's deep relationship with her horses and her authentic presence will help readers arrive at greater self-understanding and purposefulness in life."

—Alice Kolb, Ph.D., and David Kolb, Ph.D., Experience Based Learning Systems, Inc.

"Who are you? Why are you here? What is your core? What—and where—is your why? Jackie's story of life in the herd will inspire you to authentic connection—with all of the natural system—to listen to that still small voice within that connects us all in a giant web of flourishing life. Often it is the unspoken, quiet reflection that we get from authentic connection with, observation of, and participation in the natural world—of which we are a part—that feeds us and shows us the path forward for the best possible future. Jackie shows us how to learn to attend to self, to the herd, and to the environment around us—all at once in a unified, generative systems approach. Watch as your worldview grows larger. Highly recommend this inspiring journey for anyone really seeking."

—Beau Daane, M.A., M.B.A., Director of Sustainable Development at Fairmount Santrol

"Horses and mankind have been deeply linked for millennia. This book offers a pathway for humankind to connect to the 'herd' of all living beings by discovering our individual authentic presence by deeply connecting with horses as teachers. Good luck, Jackie, with your efforts to help us remember how to be better human beings."

—Roger Saillant, Ph.D., past Executive Director at the Fowler Center for Sustainable Value at the Weatherhead School of Management, Case Western Reserve University.

"I brought my team out to Pebble Ledge some years ago and we spent two days with the herd. I had some members of the team who were quite skeptical of the approach and actually tried to back out of their attendance. Within the first morning, as we explored the behavior of the horses and their leadership styles, we had captured everyone's imagination. Of course, the fact that certain horses actually selected some of the disbelievers to spend time with during our group discussions helped with the process! The team was deeply affected by the experience and the event became part of our shared culture, and we spoke of it often for years afterward. The closeness with nature and the time to reflect our principles and ways of working together was the best investment we could have made as a team and company. My compliments to Jackie for her unique way of bringing the team and the horses together to achieve a deep understanding of self and of team behavior."

—Paul Basar, General Manager, Commercial Engine Lubricants, The Lubrizol Corporation

"I have had the privilege of spending time with Jackie's herd. It was an experience that humbled me to my core. At one point, the horses surrounded me…carefully, deliberately, slowly. It was, I realized then, a spontaneous act of protection: in that moment, they made me feel safe, safer than I had for many years. The tears came naturally. That experience and the author's words have led me back to a rhythm that resides in each of us. It is primal, simple, and timeless. And yet it is a rhythm we have mostly forgotten exists. *Someday We'll Live Like Horses* stirs that rhythm, bringing it back to life, and inviting us to do one thing above all others: Find, and honor, the 'horse' within each of us."

—Larry Ackerman, Author, *The Identity Code* and *Identity is Destiny,* Consultant and Coach

Someday We'll Live Like Horses

Authentic Presence in Leadership and Life

Someday We'll Live Like Horses

Authentic Presence in Leadership and Life

JACKIE STEVENSON
& the Pebble Ledge Ranch Herd

© 2018 Jackie Stevenson

Spirit of Leadership Services
9796 Cedar Road
Novelty, Ohio USA 44072

All rights reserved. This book may not be reproduced in whole or in part without written permission from the publisher, except by a reviewer who may quote brief passages in a review; nor may any part of this book be reproduced, stored in a retrieval system, or transmitted in any form or by any means electronic, mechanical, photocopying, recording, or other without written permission from the publisher.

Front cover by Shelley Weitz Schloss
Front cover photograph and interior horse portraits by Lynne Ellyn, Lellyn Photography
Art direction: Katherine A. Dieter
Cover & interior layout: Lesley Thornton-Raymond

ISBN-13: 978-0-692-09435-8
Printed in the USA on acid free paper
10 9 8 7 6 5 4 3 2 1

DEDICATION

Dedicated to all who through their authentic presence offer respect and loving kindness to all Earth's beings.

To my husband Herb, the love of my life, and to my children and grandchildren who bring love to life.

Some Day We'll Live Like Horses
Authentic Presence in Leadership and Life

CONTENTS

Acknowledgments	ix
Section I Pathways to Authentic Presence	1
1. A Journey to Authentic Presence	3
2. Eight Paths to Authentic Presence	13
Section II The Path of Collective Wisdom	37
Learning from the Culture of Horse and Herd	
3. Meet the Herd: The Heart of Collective Wisdom	39
Bea: Inspiring Lead Mare	
Raven: Honorable Warrior	
Sir Toby: Nobody Gets Left Behind	
Spirit: Passion and Purpose	
Bud: Humble Leader	
Chief Silver Cloud: Moving Forward	
Tess: Tiny Pony with Big Presence	
Holly the Zebra: The Courage to Show Her Stripes	
4. Honoring the Horses Who Have Passed Away	163
5. Jackie's Story: The Human in the Herd	167
6. Horses, Humans and Magic Moments	181
7. Human Guests in a Herd of Horses	197
Section III The Path of the Natural World	221
and the Call of the Wild	
8. Nature and Human Nature	223
9. Listening to the Genius of Nature	237

10.	Nature and the Wild Path to Authentic Presence	251
Section IV	**The Path of Embodied Presence**	**259**
11.	Embodied Presence–The Vessel of Our Humanness	261
12.	Embodied Ways of Being	279
Section V	**The Path of Positivity**	**291**
13.	The Positive Approach to Leadership and Life	293
Section VI	**The Path of the Eight Intelligences**	**313**
14.	The Collective Wisdom of the Eight Intelligences	315
Section VII	**The Path of Indigenous Culture**	**359**
15.	The Wisdom of Our Indigenous Way of Being	361
16.	Cross Cultural Guide to Authentic Presence	381
17.	A Journey Around the Circle of Authentic Presence	409
Section VIII	**The Path of Greeting the Emerging Future**	**421**
18.	The Collective Wisdom of the Emerging Future	423
Section IX	**The Path of the Great Integrity**	**441**
19.	Entering the Field of the Great Integrity	443
Section X	**The Journey to Your Spirit of Authentic Presence**	**453**
20.	Bringing It Together and Bringing It Home	455
Notes		**469**
About the Author		**485**

Acknowledgments

I appreciate the opportunity to acknowledge the family, community, and herds that made this book possible. While I am responsible for the ideas in this book, the inspiration, support, and encouragement, this book came from a number of people and other members of the family of nature.

First and foremost I express my gratitude to my human fam-ily. Loving gratitude to Herb, my husband and life partner, who offered unconditional support and love all through the writing journey. Herb, I thank you for encouraging me to live my dreams and believing that I could make them come true, and you being the most important dream to come true.

Thank you to our children, David, Joseph, and Jeremiah Lowe, their spouses Sarah and Steve for the privilege of being your mother and for always in all things cheering me on. I am grateful to our grandchildren Joshua, Jaren, Ethan, Natalie, and Aria, who nurture my heart and provided essential breaks from the writing by reminding me to play. I have deep ap-preciation for my parents, Mac and Shu Schloss, who offered me unconditional love and gave me the confidence to follow my heart. Thank you to my brothers Lee and Mark and sister Linda and their spouses Shelley, Shirley, and Ron who had my back during the writing process as they always have.

Gratitude to the Pebble Ledge Ranch human herd who so

with the herd, in keeping me company along the path of this book and offering their insights learned from the horses and zebra. Deepest appreciation to my human herd friends Lisa, Linda, Lourdes, Debbie, Kathy, Lauren, Leila, Leslie and so many more who always showed up with grace and good spirit.

Deep gratitude to the horse and zebra herd that on a daily ba-sis both encouraged me and challenged me to tell their story and mine in an honest and authentic way. Their horse whisper wisdom inspired the stories in this book and is responsible for essential learning that will never be able to be captured in words. Deepest appreciation to Bea, Raven, Bud, Toby, Spirit, Chief Silver Cloud, Tess and Holly, Lily, Rojo, Thunderheart, Jet Set, Tootsie Pop and El Nejar Rudan, Sundance and Trapper and all the many horses who are part of the Heart and Hoof-wide web past and present.

Special gratitude to my many teachers and mentors over the years, some I was privileged to know intimately, some from a respectful distance and others simply from their ideas in their books and lectures. Of particular value was the think-ing of David Abrams, Diana Bilamoria, Richard Boyatzis, David Cooperrider, Linda Kohanov, David and Alice Kolb, Brooke Medicine Eagle, Mary Oliver, Mark Rasid, Barba-ra Rector, Roger Sailant, Otto Scharmer, Martin Seligman, Peter Senge, Melvin Smith, Richard Heckler Strozzi and the Case Western Reserve Weatherhead School of Management Executive Education and Mandel School faculty and staff and the Gestalt Institute. I honor my primary spiritual teachers, Rabbi Arthur Lelyveld and Rabbi David Hartman, and honor the sacred teachings of Nature. The collective wisdom from all theses[x] communities of learning encour-aged my curiosity and stretched my way of thinking, feeling and knowing.

My thanks to several editors who inched the book forward, Dave Patterson who encouraged structure, David Molyneaux who encouraged a free flowing story, both of whom helped me begin the book journey.

Deepest appreciation and gratitude to Katherine Dieter, the primary editor and the publisher who with promise, purpose and positive spirit helped me bring this book home. This book could not have happened without her patience with me, and her persistence.

Gratitude to Shelley Schloss, who captured the authentic presence of the horse in her design of the book cover, and to Lynne Ellyn for her ability to capture the spirit of each horse in the photographs that appear in this book.

I hold appreciation for the thousands of people who entrusted their personal discovery and professional development to the Spirit of Leadership and the Pebble Ledge Herd. Some of their stories appear in our book and none are forgotten. All of the stories herein are true, though sometimes names have been changed to protect privacy. Among the exceptional peo-ple and their organizations that entrusted us with their work are: ArcelorMittal Steel, Akron General Hospital, Ameri-can Heart Association, American Holistic Health Associa-tion, Americare Kidney Institute, Banfield, Berea Children's Home, Cleveland Clinic, Cleveland Metropolitan School Sys-tem, Cleveland Metroparks Zoo, Cleveland Zoological So-ciety, Cleveland Rape Crisis Center, Case Western Reserve University Frances Bolton School of Nursing, Case Western Reserve University School of Applied Social Sciences, Case Western Reserve University Weatherhead School of Management, Cleveland Water Department, Cleveland State Univer-sity, Dare to Care, Edwins Restaurant and Leadership Acad-

Acknowledgments

emy, Erikson Manufacturing, FairmountSantrol, Fieldstone Farm Therapeutic Riding Center, Geauga County Youth Center, Gestalt Institute of Cleveland, Girl Scouts, Great Lakes Biomimicry, Hershey Montessori School, Hiram College, Horses and Human Resource Foundation, Hospice of the Western Reserve, Humana, Inovalon, John Carroll University, Jewish Family Service, Jewish Federation of Cleveland, Israeli Defense Force, Lake Erie College, Lake Metroparks Farm Park, Lubrizol, Luna Living Recovery, Mars, Non Violent Communication Association, Ohio Mutual Insurance, Pradco, Ravenwood Service for Families, Summa Heath Care, University Hospital Medical Center, Ursuline College, VitaMix, YHaven, and YMCA Men's Transitional Housing.

Special thanks go to Dr. Ray Hephner, DVM veterinarian, who through great wisdom, skill, perseverance and care has supported our herd to be healthy and enjoy a life of well-being. Thanks to Jared Oats, farrier, who has helped keep our horses standing steady and strong on all four feet.

Deepest gratitude to this land and each of her magnificent sunrises and sunsets, changing seasons of beauty, the living river, meadow, ledges, the 1.1 billion-year-old pebbles, the wild beings big and small, and the consistent heartbeat of the earth. I bow to the wild that revealed what was possible and challenged me to trust in the impossible. Appreciation for the moments of peace in the meadow of challenge along the river of calm under the hemlocks perched on the ancient glacier rock outcroppings. Gratitude for all the sacred life beings and forces for reminding me of my humble insignificance as well as my essential place in the family of all life. I am simply in awe, appreciation and gratitude with radical amazement at the wonder of life.

I

Pathways to Authentic Presence

Chapter 1
A Journey to Authentic Presence

*"Someday we'll live like horses,
free reign from your old iron fences.
There's more ways than one
to regain your senses.
Break out of the stalls and
we'll live like horses."*

—"Live Like Horses," lyrics by Elton John and Bernie Taupin.

A zebra chasing bubbles, a pony drumming, horses helping people heal, leaders listening from within, a herd running free—just another day at Pebble Ledge Ranch.

Opening to the unexpected and to everyday miracles, we can shift our perspective, moving toward a reality far beyond our expectations, beyond what we believe is possible. I believe that all of us have the ability to turn the ordinary into the extraordinary when we live with authentic presence.

Finding our herd and following our unique path of purpose, we have the capacity to do remarkable things and live a re-markable life. Walking or galloping together in a common direction, we can make a positive difference in our lives and the lives of others.

This is what inspired me to discover what "authentic presence" is for me and to invite others on this journey of passionate dreams and purposeful destiny with horses and nature as our guides.

I am reminded of this every morning as one horse or another greets me with a welcoming nicker and the whisper of sweet horse breath. They are the true horse whisperers and without words they offer us a deep sense of inner peace and possibility, courage and confidence. "This new day, anything is possible," they seem to say. "Simply listen from the place of inner knowing where dreams become reality."

Our authentic presence is already within us, the challenge is to own it; it's about showing up in life fully and truthfully. What matters is being real, living with meaning, making mindful decisions and taking purposeful action. Our authentic presence is our unique signature. It contains everything about us—our strengths and our challenges, our conscious and unconscious knowing. Our authentic presence determines how we engage in relationship with others and ourselves. It is reflected by the alignment of who we are, why we are, and how we are in the interconnected network of life.

All of us have the ability to turn the ordinary into the extraordinary when we live with authentic presence.

Nature, horses and the wild operate from an authentic, inherent and collective intelligence and they can guide us to that place of wisdom within ourselves, if we let them. In relationship with nature, in the company of horses and other beings of the wild we can slow down, quiet our mind, and open our hearts to connect from a place of authentic and innate knowing. It is a practice of loving kindness learned and earned by

A Journey to Authentic Presence

a positive sense of self and by compassionate engagement and relationship within the world.

From this expansive way of being authentically present we can find our unique voice and allow something vitally important to emerge. Like horses in their herds and all families of nature in the wild, we can move beyond our current reality, create the conditions for our best possible future to emerge, and then be there to greet it. This is the journey into authentic presence.

I believe this is why passionate seekers, curious people, and reluctant adventurers are drawn to meet the horse herd that lives at Pebble Ledge Ranch, in the forestland and hills of northeast Ohio. Some people come to the ranch to solve problems in their professional and personal lives. Others arrive to strengthen their leadership and teamwork abilities. Some come to heal emotional wounds. Some people are sorting out complex relational dilemmas; others are seekers at a cross-roads in life looking for answers to decide which way to go. People of all ages arrive here seeking a more playful and fun life and to discover creative and meaningful solutions to nor-mal life challenges. Some folks are wandering about look-ing for their herd and place of belonging. Many people are blessed with knowing they belong, and experience their life as wondrous. Most, whether they know it or not, are at the ranch to evolve and strengthen their ability to flourish in their lives, and to help others do the same. People that transform the lives of others intuitively come here to this sacred land and herd of gentle-hearted horses and one courageous zebra to transform their own lives.

Pebble Ledge Ranch, my home and the home of the herd, sits at the edge of where a glacier moved across this land 350 million years ago and carved its character. Today, the land continues to carve the character of the people who come here to discover themselves and their place in the world. Amidst glacier rocks are beautiful pebbles, 1.1 billion years old, carried here from the Arctic through Canada, and this gave our ranch its name. Picking up one of the milky quartz pebbles, you miraculously hold life in your hand—in the form of a pebble that is 1.1 billion years old. Walking this sacred land and holding the ancient story of the earth we can discover the story we want to leave behind for the generations to come.

Here you can wander along deer paths where many native peoples walked and follow a river running through the land where wildlife and people found drinking water and food. Here nature's open system thrives and lives intelligently in harmony and balance. Canadian geese visit to get ready for their flight north or south, turkeys raise their young, strutting across the meadow in a line on their daily walk, coyotes sing in a collective howl and owls call to each other back and forth across the forest.

The paths hold the memory of the footprints of many beings that have walked this land, including human beings. At the northern border is part of what was old Interurban Railway, and part of the path of the Underground Railroad, where brave people and families who were enslaved walked this path on their way to freedom.

Walking the spirited path of authentic presence is also an individual and collective journey to freedom. As each of us releases what has held us captive we walk freely. We take our place within the interconnected family of all of life, which is the source of our authentic self and best emergent future. Being fearless, not afraid to be who we really are, and being fiercely brave enough to do what we are meant to do, we discover our destiny.

A Journey to Authentic Presence

Amidst the interconnected culture of wildlife, Pebble Ledge ranch is a place that a herd of seven wise elderly horses and one lively young zebra call home.

I am an ordinary woman living an extraordinary life. My daily routine as a responsible caretaker of the horses, steward of the land and as a family and community member offers both challenge and opportunity to practice living with conscious awareness, with choice, and with reverence for life. I have the amazing privilege to live and learn at Pebble Ledge Ranch with the herd of horses and Holly the zebra. My husband and I care for this land, a place that has been a home to wild beings, to many cultures over the ages and to generations of life yet to come.

For me the journey into authentic presence is a lifelong practice of being in touch with my true inner self, knowing what deeply matters to me, and reflecting that in how I live. It is pursuing a life that has joyful meaning and actively contributes to the goodness and well being of all. Authentic presence is a journey of honesty and integrity, being our unique selves and not who others or we think we are or should be.

Authentic presence carries the responsibly of entering into meaningful dialogue, vital interactions and genuine relationship with others. It is the choices and informed decisions we make and the actions we take when our inner self is in alignment with our outer actions. To live and lead with authentic presence requires a connection with yourself, knowledge of what is most important to you and the capacity to follow your life's purpose, heart's desire and sensibility (sense-ability). It is an emergent search for unique individual identity and equally an exploration of collective identity. Our authentic presence is made up of interactive relationships and emotional investments. It is a search for belonging and it is a connection with something greater than our self. Our authentic presence is experienced in relationship with others and through a collective identity of shared meaning, purpose and evolving spirit. The exploration of authentic presence is an opportunity to open to conversations with others about what deeply matters, why it matters and how we might choose to be and become in leadership and in all life.

I have been challenged, like all of us, by unexpected curves and obstacles that I had to get over, around or through on my life's path. The challenges and choices we make carve our character and are opportunities to go deeper into our hardiness and heartiness, our humility and humanity. We may not be able to change outside circumstances but as we change from the inside the outside responds to our inner movement. Moving toward our challenge crafts inner character, prepares us to live with deeper awareness and intention, and can strengthen our ability to grow more fully into the person we are capable of being.

In my wanderings over the years and in my quest to discover the spirit of authentic presence, eight pathways emerged to guide my personal journey. These pathways might prove to be a resource for you as you encounter your most important personal and professional life questions, as you look inside yourself rather than outside for answers to your essential questions. These eight pathways serve to remind me to trust the wisdom of the inner self, to focus on what is of greatest value and for the highest good. The pathways challenge you to find your true self, your herd, your purpose and the place to which you belong.

Eight Paths to Authentic Presence
1) The Path of Collective Wisdom: Learning from the Culture of Horse and Herd
2) The Path of the Natural World and the Call of the Wild
3) The Path of Embodied Presence
4) The Path of Positivity
5) The Path of the Eight Intelligences
6) The Path of Indigenous Culture
7) The Path of Greeting the Emerging Future
8) The Path of The Great Integrity

Untapped human potential lives within all of us. Finding it may be difficult because we are surrounded by external information, noise, and technology. Sometimes we lose ourselves, lose the pathway to our own inner knowing. We lose the way of being authentic that can guide us through life's complexity and unknown terrain. In the quiet open space of nature and the authentic presence of the horses we can better discover our true human identity.

Each day we create consequences that we do not intend. We can become aware of the consequences of our choices and actions. We can begin to take responsibility for the power of our influence and explore a more expansive way of being con-sciously human within the more-than-human family of life.

Finding ourselves and creating alliances with like-spirited people and beings, we can move forward, like the horse herd, with innate intelligence toward a positive horizon. We can create a responsible human culture as members of nature's in-terconnected system of collective intelligence. We can transform ourselves and the systems in which we operate as we open-heartedly tend to the emerging future while being fully in love with present life.

As humans engaging in relationships of mutuality with other members of nature's family we can experience a deeper sense of belonging to nature's herds and to the community of Earth.

Someday We'll Live Like Horses

In no way are we horses, nor do we try to be them at our ranch, but we can learn from them how to be better human beings and leaders in our lives.

At the ranch people build on their own strengths, face their challenges, and begin to find out who they are when they are most in rhythm with themselves. Without the daily internal noise that is typical in most people's lives, what they listen to at the ranch is the wind and quiet breath of the horses. What they hear is the silence within themselves and the deeper, wiser voice inside.

The song recorded by Elton John and Luciana Pavarotti chal-lenges us to someday live like horses, taking down fences, removing the barriers that exist inside of us and between us. In doing so, we may live more freely and joyfully. I believe this is one of the lessons that horses and nature teach us.

If we all lived like horses—in an inclusive herd with posi-tive regard for one another, confident in ourselves, respectful of personal space, playful and trustworthy, protective of the herd, and forward-moving—our lives would be more authen-tic and joyful.

Members of the herd—horses and one courageous zebracame to the ranch from highly diverse backgrounds. The

A Journey to Authentic Presence

stories of their lives, past and present, are fascinating tales about magical moments and relationships that continue to develop between humans and herd as the emphasis turns from the roles of horses in a human world to that of humans in the horses' world. Telling their stories I can share their horse sense and wisdom to inspire people to discover their sense of best self. I know how horses benefit human life. I have yet to discover how humans benefit horse life and I am committed to listening for an answer.

This book, inspired by horses and nature, is an invitation to listen for your answers and to take your own journey into your authentic presence. As leaders in our families, places of work and communities, at the heart of authentic presence is the challenge to learn what really matters to you, why you do what you do, and how to fulfill that promise. Join the journey into the world of horse and herd to learn about you. Someday we'll live like horses regaining our senses and breaking free.

A zebra chasing bubbles, a pony drumming, a horse helping people heal, leaders listening from within, a herd running free...

We are on a journey. So much wisdom awaits us. "May the horse be with you."

Chapter 2
Eight Pathways to Authentic Presence

"One simple image... We are continually building more and more healthy networks of relationships in the world amongst people of all sorts and with the larger natural world as part of the web of life. How can human beings live in a way that we are continually nurturing networks of relationships that promote well- being, health and vitality and a future we all would want to live in."
—Peter Senge

The Path of Collective Wisdom: Learning from the Culture of Horse and Herd

The path of collective wisdom is a remarkable, lived experience of horses and herd and people at Pebble Ledge Ranch. The horse herd lives as naturally as possible. It is an interconnected living social system in attention, intention and in action. Observing and interacting with the herd has been primary to my understanding the path of collective wisdom.

Members of the herd that graze at Pebble Ledge Ranch play an essential role in human life. They are teachers of universal life lessons on inclusiveness, collective intelligence, shared leadership, multiple perspectives, being present and creating conditions for the best possible future to emerge. The herd brings common sense ability, the ability to sense what is essential, and offers horse sense, the ability to respond for the benefit of all the horses and for herds for generations to come.

The horses demonstrate for us how to gather collective wisdom and how to live in ways conducive to life. Horses operate as a self-organizing living system that builds on what works and what lasts. The herd collaborates to survive, to improve and to reach its potential thereby ensuring the viability of its next generation. Their ability to co-create a dynamic way of living together in harmony with their environment contributes to their most promising future. The herd evolves to survive through generations by integrating the unexpected, operating from collective intelligence and creating conditions for the best possible future to emerge.

Observing horses in their herds and engaging with them in their world we can observe our human social systems in our businesses, families and communities with fresh eyes and from new perspectives.

Horses in their herd operating as a generative learning system can be models for how organizations, corporations or families can live and thrive through the generations.

We work together at the ranch, people and horses side by side. We observe the herd's habits, participate in the life of the herd and directly experience the lived lessons they create for us to be more of our best authentic human self. They teach us how to be part of an intelligent collective, show us how to share leadership and to live with a mindful awareness. In the good company of the horses we are reminded to appreciate the wholeness and holiness of life.

Eight Paths to Authentic Presence

In the silent presence of the horses and the natural classroom of the field in which they live, deep and powerful personal core questions emerge for almost all humans who engage with our horses.

Why am I here, and what is my purpose? What is it that I love?

When did I lose myself and how can I find me? Who is my tribe and where do I belong?

Am I fully engaged in the process of becoming the person I want to be?

Am I living in an environment that defines me or am I creating an environment to be me?

How can I live my life with more joy and meaning? What does it mean to be alive?

How can I participate in a collective community to create well-being and success for all?

Asking these questions, listening deeply from the source within, observing and reflecting on the world around us, we experience our authentic presence. Engaging in honest inquiry, learning from collective intelligence and directly experiencing the journey of life is a first step on the path to discovering authentic presence.

At Pebble Ledge Ranch, we have released our horses from their harnesses and created the best conditions for our horses to travel their path of authentic presence. Much of what I have learned in my quest for authentic presence revolves around the personal understanding of my purpose, and asking, "Why is it important to choose how I act? Why is it important for all beings to live with respect, dignity and freedom? Living these questions builds the relational field at Pebble Ledge Ranch.

We treat the horses with respect, trust, positive regard and loving kindness. We do not do anything for the horses that they can do for themselves and we do not make decisions for them they can make for themselves. We provide them with essential resources and support them with the freedom to be self-supporting. They can then develop the confidence and skills necessary to best care for themselves and each other. This horse sense translates to human sense as people observe and engage with the Pebble Ledge herd.

Horses that are bought, sold, separated from their companions and isolated by walls and from nature, struggle to maintain their natural herd ability. But as soon as you turn horses back out into the field of the natural world to simply be horses, they begin to remember about being a herd, how to adapt physically, survive relationally, and to thrive optimistically. Living authentically and in harmony, horses become a natural herd that is collaborative, inclusive, and joyful. People who live in environments where they are unable to live in rhythm with who they are lose spirit and struggle to exist. People who live in conditions of poverty of the body and of the soul struggle to live free. Living interdependently like a herd, living more tribally and joyfully like free-spirited horses, maybe we can live purposefully and productively into our best humanness and human kindness.

The more we as humans support the horses and each other to be mutually interdependent, while respecting independence, the more the horses remember about being horses and the more people remember about human kindness. The response is much like those of native people who have forgotten a lot of their tribal dances, but they start to remember by dancing.

Horses can help us remember to be better human beings in our organizations, in our homes, in our communities, and in relationship to the earth. In the awesome presence of these majestic beings, we meet ourselves in an expanded sense of freedom and awe. In relationship with horses, we touch spirit and we experience the grace of being human.

The path of collective wisdom guided by the horses offers families, teams, communities the opportunity to experience collaboration, cooperation, courage and care. People experience what it means to belong, be included and matter. They discover the value of leadership that belongs to all and is expected of everyone.

This, and an intuitive knowing that there is something personally important for them to learn, draws leaders and teams, soldiers and seekers, and a variety of other diverse individuals to join the horses at Pebble Ledge Ranch in "Spirit of Leadership" programs. In our hearts we know why we are here at the ranch and in life. The choices and decisions we make and the actions we take determine our present, our destiny and our legacy.

If "someday we lived like horses," not as horses, but as people who lived with collective wisdom and concern for future generations, we might discover more effective ways to be in harmony with each other and planet Earth.

The Heart and Hoof-Wide Web

> *"Deeper down, we feel kinship with all other people. We share a tremendous amount in common simply by being human. We often call this 'our common humanity.' We can respond to all forms of life, since we are living creatures. We are part of the earth, and kin with everything on it. Every atom in our bodies has been part of this planet for eons, flowing through life in all its forms, including its winds, seas and lands."*
> —Thomas Malone, MIT

Horses are connected to each other over long distances and through generations. They share information through the resonance of their heart and the connection to the pulse of the earth through their feet. I call this the "Heart and Hoof-Wide Web."

The horses share emotional resonance through their hearts and information from their unique perspective in the herd. This collective wisdom is shared and the herd responds moving forward as one towards a common purpose. Tapping into this collective intelligence they have a better connection to their present situation and can make the best decisions for the future of the herd.

The Worldwide Web, our global connection, is fragile and its technology can be hacked, interrupted or shut down by out-side sources. The Heart and Hoof-Wide Web within us is a lim-itless internal source of information and connection, which is resilient and is secure from external disturbance. Horses, as well as humans and all nature, are an interconnected liv-ing system, which can communicate and share information to help prepare for and adapt to change.

Eight Paths to Authentic Presence

We all have the ability to access the heart and hoof-wide web. Simply bring to heart and mind someone or some being with whom you wish to connect. As we invite them into our hearts and minds they become present to us. I often bring my mother who died over ten years ago into my mind's eye and heart and I clearly feel her unconditional love and lively presence. Often times I connect with my grandkids who live across the country in California and I easily feel their lively, loving presence. Sometimes I almost feel a tap on my shoulder or a warm feeling in my heart and I know someone is reaching out to me on the heart and hoof-wide web.

Horses have a heart that's seven times as big as ours, but they also have four other hearts; in the center of the bottom of each foot is a soft place that looks very much like a heart. As they walk, the heart in the sole of their foot touches the earth and pumps life-giving energy all through their bodies. We, in the sole of our feet, may also have a soft spot.

Many of us are longing for the call of the wild, the part of us that is fully aware and present, intuitive and passionate, naturally wise and utterly free.

As we walk on the earth with intention and awareness, we also can feel the nurturing and the benefit of grounding, balance and a felt sense of abundance that is so generously offered through the earth.

When we tap into the Heart and Hoof-Wide eb, when we listen to the collective knowing from within, memories will come back showing us how to live and thrive into the fu-ture. Living like horses, we can set aside differences, take down fences, and together create a positive reality for the good of all.

In this book, you will meet the members of the Pebble Ledge horse herd. You are invited join the herd and participate in the heart and hoof-wide web. You can listen to horses' stories and learn from their common horse sense. Within their stories, you might hear your story. You can tap into their and our innately intuitive intelligence and collective wisdom. Find your hooves and walk boldly along your path. Courageously open your hearts to your purpose and move toward your destiny. Discover your horse sense-ability as you journey forward through the field of dreams. Join the adventure into your authentic and most lovable self.

The Path of the Natural World and Call of the Wild

> *"Within...there is a wild and natural creature, a powerful force, filled with good instincts, passionate creativity, and ageless knowing. We are all filled with a longing for the wild.... The way to maintain one's connection to the wild is to ask yourself what it is that you want."*
> —Clarissa Pinkolas Estes, author, *Women Who Run With the Wolves*

Alive within us, the path of the natural world and the call of the wild are available to all of us, at all times and in all places. Whether we live in the midst of a city or in the wilderness we are part of natural environment. Nature, alive in our back yards and our places of work, enhances the quality of our daily life and human experience.

Awareness of our place in nature and relationship to the wild can inspire a larger sense of our human identity and to relationships beyond human relationship. Expanding our human identity to an ecological identity we expand our perspective of life. Integrating our human identity with a nature-based identity and a nature-centered perspective, we open to a larger and more conscious worldview. This has a direct impact on our authentic presence, our beliefs and values, and our behaviors in relationships with people and all life. As a responsible (response-able) and active participant within nature's family, we can contribute to and benefit from a more peaceful and well-balanced planet.

The rhythm of Pebble Ledge Ranch follows the path of the natural world and provides a strong context to be in intimate relationship with nature and our own inner nature. Many of us are longing for the call of the wild, the part of us that is fully aware and present, intuitive and passionate, naturally wise and utterly free. Our connection with nature and participation as an active and responsible member of life's tribe gives a stronger voice and additional meaning to our authentic presence. Accessing the intelligence of nature and the wild we can adapt effectively to changes in the environment, share and manage resources with more balance and innovate in ways conducive to all life. Reverence of nature is appreciating that as an animal, not only are we part of nature, but we are also not "higher" than nature. We are one of the earth's younger creatures. We have not been alive as long as most trees, rocks, and minerals. We came along as a species much later than many of them and have much to learn from them; they are a source of profound intelligence.

Horses sit within the larger realm of nature. At the ranch, we are not learning about horses. We are learning from horses. Touching a horse and being touched by the horse, our minds and hearts open to new and expanded possibilities. While it may be difficult for us to see into our animal being, because horses are not like us they offer us a way to tune into the best of our animal self, primitive knowing and sense-ability. Being received as a fellow animal they offer a primal way of relating and non-verbal communication in which we can reawaken some of the best and most vital aspects of our human nature.

> *Owning up to being an animal, a creature of earth. Tuning our animal senses to the sensible terrain... the pulse of this place. Becoming earth, Becoming animal, in this manner, becoming fully human.*
> —David Abrams

Research indicates that part of our being off balance as humans is a result of losing touch with nature and the wild. Reconnecting with the natural world as part of an ancient legacy helps us reconnect with our natural way of being, of who we are and can become at our best. It took a long time for humanity to manifest, but we were here 3.8 billion years ago, because some piece of human existence was here, and that legacy carries with it responsibility. As we reclaim our authentic presence, as part of nature's family, we can participate in its well-being, and, in doing so, in our own well-being.

In their quiet presence we slow down, deeply listen, and with focused attention in the moment, we can hear what most wants to be heard from within ourselves.

The Path of Embodied Presence

> *"There is more reason in your body than in your best wisdom."*
> —Friedrich Nietzsche

How we work, play, connect with others, love, discover, learn and achieve is directly related to embodied presence. Our embodied intelligence is one of our most valuable natural resources on the path to authentic presence. Embodied Presence and our body intelligence, though often not called upon, is a domain of intelligence equal to cognitive intelligence and emotional intelligence

"Embodied presence" is the capacity to literally use our senses, to experience our physical selves, not simply our thoughts about ourselves. It is intelligence alongside of cognitive intelligence and emotional intelligence that provides us with a deeper awareness of ourselves and others, allowing us to develop a more authentic presence in leadership and in all life.

Embodied presence, our embodied intelligence and body language, communicates much more than our words convey. It provides us with a deeper awareness of ourselves, allowing us to develop an authentic presence in leadership and in life. From this deeper awareness comes the ability for deep listening, solid thinking, insightful reflecting, and effective responding. Our first language is body language, and its impact is profound.

Horses and all of nature communicate through movement, resonance and embodied presence in languages beyond the human spoken or written word. They are the true horse whisperers. In their quiet presence we slow down, deeply listen, and with focused attention in the moment, we can hear what most wants to be heard from within ourselves. This authentic communication between human and horse is a beautiful and deeply satisfying experience of connection between self and the horse, our human community and all life. Embodied presence is the ability to live and function more fully as an embodied being by physically sensing, registering and managing inner experience and outer experience in relation to the surrounding world so as to have greater awareness, range and choice.

Our body language sends, receives, and deciphers a myriad of nonverbal cues, signs and signals. Bringing our attention to this level of communication gives us immeasurable insight, and helps us decode the real meaning beneath spoken words to determine what is really going on with and between people.

Embodied presence is engaging the world from the wisdom of the senses more fully aware to the present moment, seeing life as it actually is, responding to the challenge of each unfolding moment with resiliency, honesty, integrity and wisdom.

We often have a feeling or a sense about someone but are not aware of the data that led us to that feeling. We can learn to be more aware of the body signals and sense-ability that gives us this insight so that we can use these skills for more accurate communication.

Embodied presence is a way of being and behaving that expands the ability to understand complexity, make informed decisions and inspire creativity. Embodied presence is core to being aware and available to achieve and sustain high quality work and life experience. Our embodied presence keeps us true to who we are while adapting, evolving and connecting and engaging with others.

The Path of Positivity

> *"With a firm belief in a positive future, you can throw yourself into the service of that which is larger than you are. When well-being comes from engaging our strengths and virtues, our lives are imbued with authenticity. What are the enabling conditions that make human beings flourish: positive emotion, engagement, relationships, meaning and purpose, accomplishment."*
> —Martin Seligman

The path of positivity leads to learned optimism, resiliency and flourishing. It is integral to the spirit of authentic presence and opens an expansive opportunity to find value and meaning in all aspects of our life. The horses at our ranch are the ultimate optimists. They move forward towards that which is of value to them and never look back in disappointment or dwell on past regrets. They learn from what does not work and stay focused on what does work. They lead from their hearts and are free from the mental models of negative thought. As we each transform our lives using positive thought, compassionate hearts and mindful action, we transform the systems in which we operate. The collective strength within the spirit of authentic presence expressed through unconditional compassion, loving-kindness and a commitment to the Earth and her inhabitants opens a path to a more peaceful and promising planet.

When we are authentically most at home and present within ourselves we experience life as meaningful and abundant. We experience having more than we need and needing less than we have. We share a realistically optimistic sense of the world that it is a good place and can be even better. We find life positive when we are in the flow of doing what we love or learning to love what we do. Relationships are respectful, trustworthy, have positive regard and maybe even love. Present life has value, purpose and meaning to us. We can better connect to our self, other beings and that which is higher or grander than humanity.

Our individual and collective future emerges from both the well being of our current best self and from the learning from our failures and our flaws. We can learn from our mistakes as we transform them into our lives most precious lessons. We flourish as we sense into, engage, participate and accomplish our purpose.

Being authentic informs and is informed through a positive approach, an optimistic view, a belief in the inherent goodness of our world and its people, and a sense of life as abundant.

When we live fully in the present moment and are in flow with our life purpose, we can flourish. Sharing in the wealth of interrelationship with life, celebrating as a community and participating in the creation of conditions for the benefit of all beings, life flourishes.

The Path of the Eight Intelligences
1) Cognitive intelligence
2) Emotional intelligence
3) Social intelligence
4) Body intelligence
5) Intuitive intelligence
6) Natural intelligence
7) Spiritual intelligence
8) Transformational (beyond your wildest imagination) intelligence

> *"It's not about the smartest guys in the room, it's about what we can do collectively. So the intelligence that matters is the concept of collective intelligence."*
> —Peter Senge

The path of "knowing" through the collective of eight intelligences provides diverse perspectives to inform our authentic presence and expand our range of choice and possibility. Being aware of balancing and incorporating diverse perspectives enriches our source of inner wisdom and expands our range of action. Integrating multiple intelligences expands our capacity to shift ourselves, and the social systems from which we operate, in a positive direction, adapting to change as it emerges. Essential to the learning process, which informs our diverse sources of intelligence, is active engagement in life and relationship to the natural world. Engaging from our various ways of knowing, and coming together to learn with other people and beings, and their ways of knowing, provides expanded opportunity for wise decision-making, meaningful vision and purposeful action.

Each of the eight intelligences challenges us to be open minded to allow new thoughts, open hearted to allow us to listen courageously, and open willed enough to challenge our limiting patterns so we can be receptive to positive change. Engaging in conversations with others and learning from the alive and living system of all life, we cultivate both our individual intelligences and our collective intelligence. The many ways of knowing become the source and resource from which our authentic presence matures.

*The test of a first-rate intelligence is the ability to
hold two opposed ideas in mind at the same time
and still retain the ability to function."*
—F. Scott Fitzgerald

When we gather and share our wisdom we have more than any one individual is capable of having. As we gather the collective intelligence all who contribute to the wisdom will benefit from the shared knowledge. True intelligence draws information from and encompasses a variety of ways of knowing and understanding our selves, others and the world around us.

Engaging with horses and nature and in my relationship with people I began to observe and identify eight primary forms of intelligence. Each of the intelligences offers a unique perspective, expanding our reality and supporting our being authentically present in each moment. The future that wants to emerge from being authentically present is informed by the interconnected system. Understanding our world and ourselves from the diverse perspectives of these eight intelligences reveals a path into our authentic presence.

The Path of Indigenous Culture

*"Humankind has not woven the web of life.
We are but one thread within it.
Whatever we do to the web, we do to ourselves.
All things are bound together.
All things connect."*
—Chief Seattle

As the astronauts on the first manned voyage to the moon looked backed to planet earth, there came a new, shared perception of Earth as a home and as the indigenous place of all peoples and beings.

The path informed by indigenous culture is one of balance and harmony and is discovered when we all understand ourselves to be indigenous members of the earth, the place we all call home. We can better understand authentic presence by exploring the wisdom of indigenous cultures that have existed in harmony with their world for thousands of years and through many generations. Remembering and deepening our authentic presence through our awareness of and connection to our indigenous soul enhances our capacity for understanding our true calling and the essential contribution we can bring to our modern day tribes and to all beings.

The indigenous path of balance and harmony leads us to an intimate connection to our authentic presence. This path asks us where is home? Where do I belong? What is my purpose? Who are my people and my herd? Why am I here? How am I to live?

There are many ways to think about and appreciate what it means to be indigenous. I hold with great respect and compassion the Indigenous people of the earth who identify themselves as indigenous by birthright, lineage, ancestry, and culture. I honor the rights and contributions of those who inhabited and belonged to a place or a region when people of a different culture arrived.

All people have roots in ancient indigenous culture and roots in the modern culture. We may come from different tribes, traditions, belief systems and lineage but we collectively belong to the family of life on Earth. All people come from its water and earth and an integration of past living beings. Our first and last most intimate breath comes from air. Our bodies are nurtured and warmed by the sun. Each of us depends upon the natural world for our existence and is held by gravity and other laws of nature. All living beings have a point of origin. Most have migrated from where our ancestors once lived and have adapted to and put down roots on other lands. Many of us can only remember knowledge and wisdom carried from the generations in our bones. Some of us know who are our people, culture and traditions. Nature is local to its place of origin and migrates like seeds in the wind, moving changing regrouping, adapting to new places, innovating and trying new things, letting go of what does not work or last in a generative way. We all were indigenous and nomadic living in harmony and balance with all life and we can be that again.

The connection between authentic presence and indigenous culture can be a foundation for discovering and sustaining harmony in our life. It provides a set of values and guiding principles that helps us to be in balance with our selves, other people and beings in leadership and life. Sometimes called the sacred path it challenges us to awaken the sacredness within ourselves and see the sacredness in others. Living in an indigenous relationship and interconnected to all life we are aware that our individual actions touch the whole of life. When we honor life for its authentic presence by seeking connection, respecting all traditions, caring for our habitat, and preserving our world for generations of children—a future of balance and harmony emerges.

Understanding our place in the family of nature indigenous to our planet we can choose to live in harmony and balance in ways that benefit all people and all life.

The Path of the Emerging Future

> *"The future enters into us,*
> *in order to transform itself in us,*
> *long before it happens."*
> —Rilke

The pathway of greeting the emerging future is a natural process of positive change. This path opens when we get out of the way of our limiting past patterns and fears of the future and live in the awareness and flow of the present. With an open mind, open heart and open will and with actions of unconditional acceptance of the goodness of all life we can collectively co-create conditions for the best possible future to emerge. (Based on the work of Otto Scharmer and the Presencing Institute.)

Investing ourselves in an emerging future requires that we live with awareness and respect for the abundant resource available in the present. Moving from the best possible present creates the conditions for more than what was possible in the past and opens the way for the best future to emerge. The challenge is to observe our patterns and be aware of how they both serve us and how they interrupt our ability to adopt new and more useful patterns.

The challenge is to let go of fear, cynicism, mistrust and to open to the best of what is in our present realty without judgment. From this mindful, compassionate and courageous place of simply being present with what is we can move forward and up. We can take the first small steps or bold leaps into a less known future. We can move toward what now becomes the new current reality and best possible future. We can be there to greet it.

The Path of the Great Integrity

> *"The Great Integrity is the sanctuary of all human beings. To live in the great integrity is the ultimate wisdom. The Great Integrity has given us three treasures to cherish: The first is Love, the second is moderation and the third is humility. If you love, you will be fearless. If you are moderate, you sense abundance in life, if you live in humility you will be widely trusted."*
> –Lao Tzu, The Tao Te Ching

The pathway of the great integrity is found in all spiritual traditions. In oral traditions and sacred teaching stories and through spiritual texts such as Kabala, Koran, Torah and Tao, sacred knowledge is shared. The great integrity, human consciousness at its best, determines traditions, rituals and ceremonies, and guidelines for individual and collective moral practice in families, businesses, and communities and in all relational realms. The living concept of the great integrity is a call to action for justice, generosity, wisdom and loving-kindness in all we are and all we do. It is a living pathway to our authentic presence leading us deeper to our virtuous humble self and our dance with destiny.

The path of great integrity, one of stillness, reflection and listening within, brings us closer to our center and to the attention and intention of the present moment, whatever we are doing. Listening to one another and nature's beings we locate ourselves within the larger realm of life. Authentic presence is a process and practice of individual discipline and collective learning that happens when we pause, reflect and deeply listen before responding. In this open collective space of present awareness we can access the deeper rhythms of our life and life around us. In calm and peaceful inner space, we can hear from within what authentically wants to be spoken. In the generative space of silence and alert stillness, the wisdom of the future emerges.

> *"At the center of your being*
> *you have the answer;*
> *you know who you are*
> *and you know what you want."*
> –Lao-tzu

My Journey Along the Eight Pathways

My personal journey into authentic presence comes into practice, play and horseplay in my daily life.

Creating positive, meaningful and joyful conditions in our daily life and in the lives of others we can co-create the possibility of the best possible future to emerge. Being authentically present we can do our part to repair the world and participate in creating a world worth living in.

These eight pathways guide my journey to the spirit of authentic presence by informing the direction of my life work, providing opportunities for collective creativity and inspiring joyful learning with people, horses and nature. Each path into authentic presence is an opportunity for life's grand adventure.

> *"No experience has been too unimportant, and the*
> *smallest event unfolds like a fate, and fate itself is*
> *like a wonderful, wide fabric in which every thread*
> *is guided by an infinitely tender hand and laid*
> *alongside another thread and is held and supported*
> *by a hundred others."*
> –Rilke

Section I — Pathways to Authentic Presence

Pause, Reflect and Respond

On your journey to your authentic presence identify three strengths you would like to build on and three challenges that you would like to explore to be the best you that you choose to be.

Reflect on a time when it took courage to be authentic and take action from your integrity. Have a conversation about that with someone in your life.

Take several index cards and write one word or phrase and/or image that came from your reflections and conversation on each individual card.

Save these cards as you will be reflecting back on them.

II

The Path of Collective Wisdom:
Learning from the Culture of Horse and Herd

Chapter 3
Meet the Herd

"Tell me, what is it you plan to do with your one wild and precious life?"
—Mary Oliver

Early morning, the sun is just coming up over the horizon as I arrive at my workplace and check in with my Spirit of Leadership team. This morning, as every morning, the members of my team welcome me by questioning my authority, challenging my every decision, demanding my complete attention and insisting on transparency, all in complete silence. They are unconditionally forgiving of my honest mistakes and genuinely curious about how I am going to be with them and with our work today. Through gesture, movement, heart connection and focused attention we greet one another. They are authentically comfortable being just who they are; their inner experience matches their outer actions. They expect the same from me.

My team can trace its lineage back 65 million years, thriving as a living system through collective wisdom—living cooperatively, collaboratively, and connected with each other and their environment. They are Equus ferus caballus, more commonly known as "horse."

The Spirit of Leadership team is a tight working herd of six intuitive draft horses, one lively pony and one courageous zebra. Their office is a field of both pasture grass and a field of dreams. The herd is a living system, a network of interconnected relationships sharing intuitive knowledge, resources and the oneness of love.

Horses as wisdom gatherers are remarkable teachers of relationship and facilitators of human development through embodied awareness, emotional resonance and mindfulness.

They have an amazing ability to tune into our true emotions and reflect back to us our authentic selves.

The horses work with people to help them discover their authentic presence, to explore what really matters to them and to inspire them to become the best of who they are in their workplaces as well as in their family and community lives.

In the emerging field of "experiential learning with horses," individuals, families, teams are guided through quiet reflection and action-oriented learning experiences that are immediately applicable to real life issues and work dilemmas.

The "horseplay" takes place on the ground. There is no riding the horse. The experiential learning opportunity is about making a commitment to authentic relationship, competent leadership and authentic presence. Within the quiet beauty of nature, in the presence of the horses and through empathy and mindfulness, we find a deeper more true relationship to ourselves, each other and the world around us.

Master teachers and mentors come in many forms; horses are one of nature's most honest and inspirational teachers, offering us valuable lessons about living responsibly, working productively and being more human. The power of the herd is its collective wisdom—the ability to connect and come together, to learn from one another, and to move forward toward a future that ensures the greatest good for all.

> *"Horses—and how they exist as a herd—have so much synergetic similarity to how teams in business work together to accomplish a common goal. It took us to a raw, real state of who we are—and who we want to be. We have new tools for teamwork that will help take us to new horizons together."*
> —Jodi Berg, CEO of Vitamix

It is with great pride that I introduce our Spirit of Leadership Pebble Ledge herd and the heart of collective wisdom to you: Bea, Raven, Sir Toby. Spirit, Bud, Chief Silver Cloud, Tess, and Holly

BEA

*"If you don't know what you are here to do
just do some good...
You know what's right...
Just do right...it will satisfy your soul"*

Maya Angelou, poet

Bea
Lead Mare, Gatekeeper, Inspiring Leader

I am the lead mare and I am wise, experienced, hard working, and strong willed. I am a proud black Clydesdale in my twenties. The first human I lived with was getting divorced and could not keep me. She wanted me to go to a good home. Many people wanted me, as I am quite beautiful and intelligent. She chose Pebble Ledge Ranch as my new home when she learned that I would be doing meaningful work guiding people in their important life decisions and helping them be better human beings. I quickly earned the respect of the herd and the right to be lead mare. I bring grounded stability to my herd and provide confidence in the midst of chaos. I teach that leadership belongs to all and is expected of everyone, horses and humans. I remind everyone to engage fully in life, to respect themselves and others, and to be who they are. I will let you know when you are welcome in the herd. Once you are a herd member, I expect you to follow the herd code of respectful and trustworthy behavior. As your leader, I will serve in your best interest within the herd and be forever honest with you and loyal to you.

Bea, the herd's lead mare, is a strong female presence that leads with passion and purpose, inspires confidence within the herd, and is decisive on behalf of her herd. When a new herd member enters her pasture, she is the gatekeeper, deciding when a horse can enter the herd and when they are ready to be accepted as a full herd member. She teaches us to stand proud for what matters, and to engage her authentically, being who we are. Horses are suspicious and uneasy when we are not honest with ourselves or with them. They sense when our inner experience is not in alignment with our outer actions.

They are aware of the incongruence when we are afraid but act unafraid or pretend to be calm when we are anxious. They sense when we are being dishonest or manipulative and generally will not engage with us. When we are honest with ourselves and with the world, we can stand confident and proud and the horses will respect and trust us and will stand with us.

Bea has earned the respect of the herd for her consistent behavior and trustworthy actions. From this stance of authenticity she has the ability, like we all do, to face challenge and manage conflict. In her willingness to take the lead and her ability to empower leadership in others, she teaches us that leadership belongs to all and is expected of everyone, horses and humans. Her steady, forward-moving hoof beats echo the earth's heartbeat and help people to discover what has heart and passion for them. Bea reminds us to engage in life fully with respect for each other, ourselves, and for all life.

Executive Team Coach

Bea is an outstanding executive coach, holding the executives she works with to a standard of excellence. A high-performing executive team from a global company whose headquarters is in Cleveland came out to the ranch as part of their annual retreat with the intention of strengthening their individual leadership talents and exploring new ways to optimize their team's potential. Through observation of the horses and herd dynamics and through active engagement with the horses, the team learned about intentional and authentic presence. Lead mare Bea sensed the strong leadership capacity of the corporation's lead mare and CEO Jane, and of her executive team. Bea willingly stepped up to play a key role in their learning experience.

Meet the Herd

The team, having had an opportunity to meet each of the horses and successfully earning the herd's respect and trust, were then ready to take on a challenge with the herd. The team's task was to work together to inspire all the horses in the herd to leave their lunch of green grass in the field and move the distance of about three football fields to the sand paddock, the goal line, where there was no lunch of green grass.

The horses were scattered across their twenty-acre pasture, some eating, others sleeping and some just hanging out enjoying the sunny day and cool breeze. The team was given a few minutes to plan their strategy and then to practice their leadership and teamwork skills by inspiring the horses to get moving in a coherent direction and by bringing the herd safely home into the paddock.

Having observed the herd, they noticed that Bea, the lead mare, had the influence and power to get things moving. Jane, the lead mare of the human team, had developed a good relationship with Bea. Based on these two factors the team decided that if they put their energy into moving Bea, the lead mare, all the horses would follow her home. Jane engaged Bea and the rest of the team supported Bea and Jane, encouraging them to move toward the gate with the expectation that all the horses would then follow. After several creative attempts and different techniques to get Bea moving, the executive team had not moved Bea, or any of the other horses a single step forward. The team regrouped and came up with a revised plan. They would circle back around to the other horses and see if they could inspire movement in the herd leading from Bea-hind without Bea's help. With a few whistles, determination and playful encouragement they got the horses moving. With collaboration, cooperation and focused purpose, the team was able to get the herd to move forward in a coherent direction toward their goal...all except Bea. Her ears forward and her attention alert, Bea watched the human team share leadership responsibility and work collaboratively under Jane's guidance to inspire the herd to get moving. After all the horses walked through the gate and into the fenced in paddock, Bea majestically began to move, her 12-inch hoofs creating a drum beat on the earth. The last horse in, she proudly walked through the gate to join the herd.

The team, having succeeded in bringing the herd safely home, circled up to discuss what they learned from the experience with the herd. They reflected on what worked for them, what did not work and what they learned that would have value for them back in their home pasture. They realized that while they were given the task to lead the herd, they gave their responsibility to Bea who politely said, "You are the leaders so lead." They realized that each of them has an important leadership role on the team and that it cannot always fall to the lead mare of the herd, Bea, or to the lead mare of their organization, Jane, to be out front. Bea, as lead mare, does not always have to lead from out front, but can also lead from behind or step back and inspire others to lead. She trusted Jane and her executive team to get things moving and lead the horse herd to their destination. Bea acknowledged and honored Jane and the team's leadership by becoming a willing follower. She demonstrated that a leader has the wisdom and confidence to know when to follow and when to encourage others to lead.

This real-time experience with the horses provided directly transferable learning about respect, trust, leading collaboratively, adapting as a team to changing conditions, being innovative to achieve results and seeing the potential of shared leadership. These essential qualities already existed in the high-performing team, but through the experiential learning with the horses, they were able to strengthen and better apply their talents to specific challenges and issues relevant to their workplace.

Bea's Journey to the Ranch

Bea is a draft horse, a very large breed of workhorse. I discovered the energy of draft horses in Montana, in a natural leadership group with a herd of horses, mostly wild, and two draft horses that had been rescued. One of them let me climb up on her back without a bridle, halter, or saddle. Her gentle presence, despite how big and full of energy, took my breath away. I was planning to add to the herd in Ohio, and when I got home I went searching for a draft horse.

Dream Horse is a website for people who want to sell their horses. I had an image of the beautiful Budweiser Clydesdales. When I narrowed my search to Ohio, I found one Clydesdale, a black horse, whom I drove to see downstate.

She was in a round pen, kind of a small enclosure. I walked up to her, and she seemed friendly. "Could I get on the horse's back," I asked the owner. She said she didn't have a saddle, but I climbed up anyway, and we walked around. The owner said, "There are many people who have called, and we really want her to have a good home. So would you write a letter about what her life is going to be like with you?" I wrote about the work we do and sent our website address so she could see about the coaching and leadership approaches in our program.

We were chosen as Bea's new owner and brought her to Cleveland in a trailer. Most people don't ride Clydesdales—

usually these horses pull a carriage—but I was too impatient to wait for a special saddle. I used a halter and rope and I got on her back to wander around the backyard. She was so quiet that I took her off the property and into a park where people were flying kites and picnicking. She was calm amidst all the excitement and we did just fine.

Three days later I went to get on her to ride again, but she wouldn't allow it. She kept moving away, pinning her ears back. I wondered, "What's going on here?"

The New Lead Mare Takes Over

I noticed that Bea was moving our other horses into the corner, leading them around and one at a time getting them where she wanted them to go. It did not seem to matter that they were not going anywhere in particular, but it did seem to matter that the horses went wherever Bea told them to go. In a matter of days, she took over the leadership of the herd from Rojo, an elderly horse that had been the lead mare for a long time. Within one week, Bea had four of the horses in the herd following her. The fifth horse in the herd, an older mare, did not follow her, but did not interrupt Bea's bid for the position of lead mare. Rojo stayed wisely and respectfully off to the side in a grandmotherly way.

It seemed that Bea's personality had changed. What happened? Why did she not let me ride with her? Why did she challenge my requests for her to walk with me or go in the direction that I requested? What happened to cooperation and the beginnings of a friendship? I took it all very personally. Did she just fake it until we took her home, I wondered? Have I offended her? I have no idea how to deal with this horse, I thought. What have I gotten myself into? I had never been around such a big horse. That afternoon a woman called and said, "You don't know me, I'm a natural horse trainer. I work with horses, and someone heard that you have a Clydesdale that is a very big horse, and you may need some help. I will come out and do three sessions with you and Bea, so you can get to know each other." Quickly, I accepted.

First, I had to learn how to get bigger and not smaller in Bea's presence, how to move slowly, and to set small, doable goals. As I did, I forgot about how big she was, and she softened toward me. We began to work out an understanding of patience and respect. Then, one day she just came over, put her head down, and breathed on my heart. We had moved from respect to trust to positive regard and maybe even love. I knew that we had made it and would be friends.

What I learned was that I needed to respect that Bea was now the herd leader. In her presence, I needed to be self-respectng, and safe, in order for her to trust me and be respectful. I decided we were more like co-leaders or colleagues than anything else. I found that there were times when I needed to ask her to move aside because I had some things I needed to do with the herd. Most of the time, 95% of the time, she was completely in charge of the herd, but when I needed to come forward to request the leadership of the herd, she respected my role.

The Give and Take of Relationship

One day, I was working the in the pasture, and, just feeling big hearted toward her, I put my arms around Bea's neck. She pushed me away. I had come into her space without asking her permission. I had barged in. Even though I had good intentions, it was all about me and my good feeling about her. I didn't stop to see whether or not she was interested. She backed away. I apologized to her and said, "You are right, you know I pushed into your space, I'm sorry. My interest was in letting you know how much I appreciate you." Later, she came over, put her head over my shoulder, and kind of wrapped her head around me. How often do we enter a person's space at work or at home without pausing and waiting for an invitation or asking if we are welcome even if our intention is good? Bea reminded me to be respectful of space, whether that is physical space or the space of an idea.

Bea loves community or group gatherings, so if we are circled up at workshops, she often walks over and stands in the circle. When we start a group workshop, or when we end a group, she often walks and stands with us. Sometimes she stands in the middle of the circle.

Sometimes she just joins the circle, but she has a presence that you can feel. She often joins in when we're doing something special. If you need some strong support, Bea will stand still and listen, letting you lean against her. She has beautiful eyes. When you look into them, you can find your own soul. You can hear her hoof beats as she runs, the strong connection to the earth. They shake the earth.

One day I was working with a woman who was doing some healing work from abuse. I asked her to tell her story from her heart to Bea's heart, with no words. This was a true and traumatic story that had happened to her and she had not yet been able to tell anybody, and some of the story didn't yet have words. I stepped back creating the opportunity for Bea to connect with her. Bea stood still while the woman told her story. Bea just stood there relaxed, being with her, and leaning in and resting her big warm body against the woman. Tears came down the woman's cheeks. Afterwards, she came over to me and said, "With Bea's help, I've finally been able to give words to my story and I feel like now maybe I can tell my story to some of the people who have been offering to support me. I found the words I need, and I've released the words that never need to be said."

I said, "Okay, do you feel complete with Bea or is there more?"

She said, "Well, maybe I'll just go over and see what else Bea has to say."

As she began to walk toward Bea, Bea walked toward her. Bea stretched her neck up and got even bigger, stomping her feet and marching around the paddock snorting. The woman said, "Wait, what's happening here? What happened to this horse that was so quiet and so interested in me? Why is she so angry?"

I asked, "What do you sense is happening?"

She said, "Well, there's part of me that is angry, too. I have never allowed myself to be as angry as I deserve to be, and maybe Bea is telling me that it's about time you got angry and stomped your feet and realized that what happened was not okay. You didn't deserve to have that happen to you."

"That's just as important as telling the story," she said.

Bea stopped stomping and quietly walked over to the woman and lowered her head. The woman wrapped her arms around Bea and with a big smile, gave Bea a big hug.

Bea Oversees Changes As the Herd Grows

Other horses in the herd respect Bea. They do not fear her, even though she is sometimes fierce. They follow her, I think, because they are inspired to follow her. She often is off by herself because she's got this job of needing to see what's going on and taking in the whole of the herd from a distance.

The other thing she's in charge of is schooling new members of the herd. When we brought in a thoroughbred horse that would be here only temporarily, Bea took him into a small paddock. He was running up and down the fence line, and as soon as he turned his back to her she would make him move again. She was basically like a cow pony, not letting him out of the corner, running him back and forth. As long as he showed his disrespect for her, she made him run over and over and over again. As soon as he stopped, and faced toward her with his head down in respect, she turned away and let him go. Bea works tirelessly on behalf of her herd schooling new horses into the culture of the herd and expected behavior of its horse members. As humans we sometimes don't give enough time and attention to bringing new people into our organizations and families, which often causes misunderstandings and confusion. Bea reminds us of the importance of sharing what is essential for all to belong.

A year after Bea moved in, I called to tell her previous owner what a wonderful horse Bea was and to thank her for choosing us as her family. "She has taken over all of us," I said. "She's in charge, the lead mare in charge."

The woman said, "Well I'm not surprised, I'm glad you called. Would you be interested in taking Bea's son? He's in need of a home." That is how Raven joined our herd.

Meet the Herd

I think the first thing that the lead horse does is teach new horses to follow, because if there is an emergency and the herd needs to run, all the horses must respect her leadership and move when she says move. The second thing she teaches new horses is to be authentically present in all their power.

When we brought Chief Silver Cloud to the ranch, Bea seemed to decide that she needed him to step up and be a strong horse. She would move him, and then she would walk around in front of him and stand there. As soon as he moved toward her, she moved off fast, squealing. She did this over and over again, until he realized he could move her. She was asking him to step up and be the strong presence in the herd, taking on his power and influence.

When she doesn't feel like moving, she won't. But when Silver Cloud asks her to move, she will in a way that she doesn't for anybody else because his role is as one of the defenders and protectors of the herd. He couldn't be cowardly. He had to take responsibility. I think she has been schooling him in that. Sometimes people look and ask why he is pushing her around? But if you look carefully, you will that she is getting him moving in the direction of her choice. It's part of the dance.

Of course, this is just my perspective. Somebody else might feel differently about it. But I trust Bea to know what she's doing. If she didn't like Chief Silver Cloud, didn't want to be around him, she would just stay away from him and ignore him. Instead, she's always with him, and when he's by himself she will stand next to his gate waiting for him to come out. When he first arrived, she wouldn't let him in the paddock. She chased him out every time he tried to come in. He stood in the heat, day after day. Finally, one day she let him in.

I don't know what changed but Chief Silver Cloud must have showed her that he understood what she was asking of him. Then, she let him into the herd. It was up to her, the gatekeeper. Bea is often the one to welcome people to her herd, sometimes by standing quietly in front of them and sometimes by asking them to move; both are lessons in self- respect and trust and respect and trust in others.

Bea invites people into her herd to learn a deeper way of being in leadership in our families and in the world. She challenges us to listen from within to our most important questions and to trust what we hear. Bea moves her herd, including us, with grace, power and spirit towards the most positive future.

> *"All that's required on your part is a willingness to make a difference. That is, after all, the beauty of service. Anyone can do it."*
> —President Barack Obama

RAVEN

"You belong among the wildflowers
You belong somewhere close to me
Far away from your trouble and worries
You belong somewhere you feel free"

Tom Petty, singer, songwriter

Raven

Leading With Honor, Confidence and Youthful Exuberance

I am a majestic black Friesian. I proudly carry my ancestry as companion to the Templar knights and my heritage as a proud warrior.

Courageous like my ancestors I face the unknown with curiosity and wonder rather than with fear. While I am the youthful, playful, fun-loving guy of the herd, I stand quietly while a military soldier weeps into my mane about the tragedies of war or a child touches my nose with unsure hands. A loyal friend to horses and humans I offer kindness and care. I am authentically horse and have never carried a human on my back, though I willingly carry people into courageous authentic places within themselves.

Bea is my mother. She has always been a loving, strong and courageous presence for me. I was taken from her side when I was only six months old, way too early to be separated from her. Caught in an angry divorce I was taken hundreds of miles away from my mom and horse herd. I was thrown hay and given water but was kept all alone in a field with no other horses to protect me or teach me to be a horse or humans to teach me how to relate to people. I was terrified, for living alone for a horse is life threatening. Fortunately I had the company of a cat to give me some comfort. When I was two years old a woman entered my pasture and walked gently toward me. She paused and waited for me to approach her. The cat walked over to her so I figured it was okay to come closer. She stood quietly for a long time and I could feel her encouragement to come closer to her. I approached slowly and reached out my neck to sniff her hand. She slowly reached back towards me and I felt her kind touch on my neck. She spoke softly and as she walked away I sensed my life was about to change. A few days later, I was not-so-kindly put into a horse trailer by a man that I did not like. Four hours later I was led off the trailer and saw not only the woman who had visited me but my mom Bea. Overjoyed I rushed towards my mom. But as I trotted towards her she galloped toward me with ears back and teeth bared. Terrified I turned and ran, almost crashing into the fence. My mom swerved away from me and ran fiercely toward the unkind men who had roughly loaded me into the trailer and had driven me there. The man jumped over the fence to get away from her crashing hoofs. I later learned that he had been abusive to my mom before I was born and she had not forgotten. She was not forgiving his cruel behavior to her and the other horses. There was more drama and I sighed with relief when the man was asked to leave. I was escorted to a small orchard with a kind grandmother horse named Rojo to watch over me. My mom Bea and I met over the fence for the next two weeks until I was less afraid of her and the rest of the horses. Rojo patiently taught me horse language and the ways of the herd. Jackie, the woman who came to invite me to my new home, helped me understand horse and human friendship. When I was ready, my mom Bea, the lead mare of the herd, brought me into the herd. It was an exciting reunion and for the whole next year I was afraid to leave her side for fear of being taken away again and abandoned to live alone. Many years later we still have a close mother- son relationship and if I sense danger I run to her for safety and also to make sure she is okay. If I get too rowdy she scolds me and if I seem lonely she nuzzles me. Toby, the stallion of the herd, has been a role model for me in how to be strongly gentle and gently strong. He has helped me mature into my "guy" self through the stallion play of rearing, jousting and running together.

Spirit has been my best friend from the very first moment I arrived. She stood by the fence watching over me while the grandmother mare Rojo helped me learn to be in good horse relationship. While I was learning human language and human herd manners from Jackie, Spirit would patiently wait for me while the rest of the herd was out in the field. When my lessons were over for the morning, Spirit and I would run gleefully into the field to join the herd.

We are still great friends and often hang out together in the pasture. I believe that one of my contributions is communicating to all the people and horses I meet the importance of authentic friendship, a relationship where you are appreciated and loved for being who you are.

Honoring Military Veterans

> *"Wake, soldier, wake...thy horse awaits."*
> —Thomas Kibble Hervey, British poet

A lone soldier looks across the field at the big black horse looking back at him. There is an instant recognition and connection. Raven stands tall, his eyes never leaving the man. He paws the ground impatiently and calls out to the man with a clear whinny as if to say, "Remember me." The soldier steps slowly back as Raven gallops toward him, coming to a prancing stop a few feet in front of the man. The mighty horse bows his head and the two warriors meet as kindred spirits. Raven looks into the soldier's eye and the soldier sees his own reflection in the eye of the horse. They stand quietly for a long time; then, Raven gently nudges the soldier and gently touches the soldier's heart with his nose. In the silence, the young man hears from the heart of the horse, "As my ancestors served their knights I am here to serve you for you have bravely served our country. It is now time for you to rest."

Mark has come to the ranch to be with the horses as have other US military veterans for the "Veterans and Horses, Uncommon Heroes for the Common Good: Bringing Leadership to Life" program. The intention of the experience for the soldiers with the horses is to strengthen the capacity of veterans to translate and incorporate their military leadership and team skills into their civilian personal and work lives. It is also an opportunity in the strong, compassionate and authentic presence of the horses to help them heal from the emotional wounds of war and to remember who they are as whole and holy human beings.

Mark had recently returned from Iraq after several traumatic deployments where most of the men in his platoon were killed and parts of his soul lost as well. Back in the States he is trying to make meaning of all that had happened to him in his service to our country and to adjust to the now very different world of family and civilian life.

Raven, as an impatient young horse, has a rebellious nature and a brave and lively spirit. He rarely is still and most often is running, play fighting and jousting with his horse buddy Toby. But when Raven met Mark, something different happened. He stopped his horseplay and stood quietly as Mark stroked him and began to quietly talk to him. For almost an hour the two stood together. Mark wrapped his arms around Raven and wept into his mane as the horse leaned toward the soldier giving him support and absorbing pain and tears with his big warm body.

After a long time of the two deeply connecting, Raven gave a soft snort, releasing breath and shudder as if to shake something no longer needed off. The soldier responded with a shudder and a big sigh. The two warriors turned, Mark had a big smile on his face and Raven seemed to be grinning. Horse and man walked side by side through the field, Raven stopping every so often to graze and Mark to simply calmly pause. They approached me, but Raven never left this soldier's side. Mark told me that this was the first time since he had been stateside that he has felt some sense of inner quiet and peace. He said he had believed that he had not deserved to ask for help. He had felt that there was nowhere to turn for support and nothing strong enough to lean against. Raven changed that for him. The horse's unconditional acceptance of him for who he is, willingness to stay with him and listen to horrific stories, offering of a strong physical presence to lean against and his gentle heart allowed the soldier to accept the support he so desperately needed. With Raven's honest, compassionate and unwavering presence the soldier was able to begin the healing process with the strong, solid, silent support of the horse. "I was able to reconnect with myself and those I love in a way I could not after returning from duty," Mark said.

Mark reflected on his time with Raven.

"I don't know why, but I feel more myself. I was able to get in touch with memories of war and I know Raven understood what I was feeling without words. In Raven I found a brother and we connected with unspoken understanding. He accepted me for who I was. I found acceptance and forgiveness of myself in Raven's acceptance of me. With Raven's trust and confidence in me, I trust that I can move forward.

"Maybe now I can learn to accept the help of my family and community to heal the invisible wounds I carry from war. Maybe now I can make peace with myself, balancing devastating memories with good memories. I have taken the first step with Raven's encouragement to find my way home. I am more confident that I can, with the courage, compassion and commitment Raven reminded me I have, help others heal and find their way home."

We at Spirit of Leadership and from the heart of the herd honor, respect and thank U.S. veterans for their past, present and future service to our country.

Raven, with his horse herd members, had the opportunity to partner with another group of soldiers, a small cadre of commanders from the Israeli Defense Force, the Israeli military.

They were visiting Cleveland to share their expertise in leadership with leaders in the Cleveland community, and to expand their own leadership skills.

These Israeli commanders were a group of special leaders who work with young Israeli adults at risk who would be serving in the Israeli military. They prepare the young adults who arrive in army boot camp with poor esteem and poor performance to be more confident and compassionate, to be better prepared to participate in military service to their country and better prepared to succeed in life. Typically, this at-risk population does not successfully get through military boot camp and they often struggle with basic life issues in their families and communities. These young people have had some tough experiences in life and with support and care and encouragement can heal and grow into their potential.

When the Israeli commanders arrived at the ranch we asked them what would make this day with the horses of value to them. They responded that they were interested in strengthening their ability to support these at-risk young people in building a sense of self- esteem and confidence and a sense of commitment to themselves and to their country. They were interested in learning from their horse experience how to better motivate the soldiers who were in their care.

The commanders began engaging with the horses by entering their pasture with friendly curiosity and engaging the horses with respectful interest. This created a foundation of trust between horse and soldier. Once they had a trustworthy relationship, the soldiers were challenged to inspire and motivate Raven to go with them through a set of obstacles that represented the challenges the commanders faced back in Israel. The commanders soon discovered that the only way that Raven would be inspired to go with them was if they were inspiring. Raven only was agreeable to follow them over the obstacles and toward the goal when they had a clear sense of where they were going.

What they learned, working with Raven and the herd, is that you have to start where horses and people are. You have to trust their honest tries, you have to discover what they value, what motivates them, and build on that. The leaders need to be motivated, so they can be excited about working with the young adults at risk. If the leaders are not excited, the young people will feel that. The same is true with horses. If you are really interested in them, and are excited about working with them, only then may you begin to build a trustworthy relationship. Meeting the challenges, everybody grows.

Think about how long it takes to build trust in human relationships and how quickly trust can be broken. The more credibility that you have in your relationships, the more small moments of trust can happen. Then, if you have one thing happen that is off-kilter, there's a good chance at some forgiveness.

I believe that horses expect each other to make mistakes, and they don't worry about honest mistakes. But if you make them over and over again, it's no longer an honest mistake; it's then being stupid or not listening to them, not caring, not valuing them, not pausing to pay attention.

What the Israeli leaders took with them on their journey back home was that building a relationship is a learning process for both parties. As the soldiers become more skilled, they will become more self-confident in what they do. Everybody's humanity increases with confidence.

Everyone learns from facing challenge with an open mind and heart. What happens with the horses is that the teams and people who give it an honest try earn respect, trust and positive regard and have more than the momentary gratification of instant success. They have a deep sense of personal mastery, team appreciation and spirited success. Optimism is not about everything always being good. In life, optimism is working from a place where everything has value.

Goodness is based on meaning. A good relationship has meaning. It may have pain, it may have moments of distrust, it may have challenge, and it may have anger in it. But there is a level of staying on the same field, a level of connectivity, and finding meaning in every step of how you deal with those mistakes or with those breaches in relationship that forges the strengths of each person, which ultimately builds self-esteem.

Near the end of the day, I noticed relationships building at the ranch. The Israelis, from a warm climate, were in Northern Ohio on a winter day that was very, very cold. When we finished our horse experience, I told the group, who were not accustomed to such cold weather, that everybody could go into the cottage to warm up. But three-quarters of the people did not leave the paddock. They stood, talking with the horses, saying "goodbye" to each, finishing conversations. They had their pictures taken with the horse with which they had created meaningful, intimate relationships in the space of a morning.

Our horses serve those who serve their countries with commitment, courage and compassion. They are uncommon heroes for the common good.

TOBY

*"Whatever you can do or dream,
You can, begin it.
Boldness has genius, power, and magic in it."*

Johann Wolfgang von Goethe, poet

Sir Toby

I am a free-spirited Gypsy horse who lived my first three years in the United Kingdom with a Romany family, pulling a cart, taking care of and protecting the children. I was a stud stallion in my younger years in UK, Arizona and then Montana. I travelled for six difficult days from Montana to Cleveland with my best friend and herd mate Lily. Together at Pebble Ledge Ranch we were warmly welcomed into the herd. I quickly established my herd position as resident stallion and took on the leadership role of keeping order when there was chaos and conflict. Lily and I had five loving years together, eating our meals out of the same hay pile, standing together keeping cool in the shade or providing each other warmth from cold wind. I affectionately and loyally looked after her before she peacefully died of old age. I mourned her for a year and then allowed myself to open my heart to the other horses in the herd by grooming them through gentle touch and allowing myself to be touched. Now at Pebble Ledge Ranch I help humans heal from loss and disappointments in life. I listen to their touching stories and through horse whispers help them discover their journey home to their hearts. I watch over those who are most vulnerable and help them recover their strength and confidence. Being a playful guy I help them find their sense of humor, childlike playfulness and ability to laugh. While playful and peaceable I have a fierce protective nature. I am committed to the leadership role of protecting the herd from dangerous aggression and making certain that no one gets left behind. If a horse or human threatens the safety and well-being of another horse or human or create chaos in the herd I will step in to restore peace. I have the most influence in the herd when it comes to resolving conflict and making important herd decisions. I work in partnership with Bea, the lead mare of our herd and I have her back, collaboratively leading from behind as she leads from out front. I teach people that a key responsibility of leadership is to stop injustice and to take action for justice and equality. I remind humans that we each have unique gifts of brilliance that no one else can offer, and that we all are essential in creating peace and success for the kingdom of life.

King of The Herd, Majestic, Authentic Presence

In the herd at Pebble Ledge Ranch, Toby takes the role of the stallion. He works with Bea, the lead mare, most of the time. Often, you see them standing together. They don't groom one another. To me, I don't see an intimate relationship. Toby does not tend to Bea the way he tended to his long-time best friend Lily. But there is a respectful relationship, one standing next to the other.

Bea's job is to set the tone of where the horses are going, if they are going somewhere. Toby's job is to bring up the rear and make sure that no one gets left behind. In the program at the ranch, we have an exercise that we do with human teams when all the horses are loose in the field. The human group is asked to bring the whole herd back home into their paddock, just using their relationship, their energy, their voices, and movement. Toby often hangs back, no matter what you do, until he sees that the rest of the herd is moving forward. Then he will move. Any amount of energy to try to move him or interest him, even though he's relational with people in the human herd, will not work. He never lets go of his responsibility to the horse herd.

Toby is tough, and he also is a gentleman. He is a Gypsy horse bred by the Romanichal people of Great Britain to pull their wagons. These horses are held in high regard and are part of the families, which take great pride in them and the traditional magic in the families' lives. They often are black and white, and they are bred to have long, flowing manes and tails. They are relational. These horses are prized for their good disposition and their beauty. Years ago, a U.S. horse breeder brought a stallion back to the United States to breed his own Gypsy horses, which are now an accepted breed.

Toby was brought across the Atlantic to breed. As a young horse, Toby pulled a Gypsy wagon, reported his former owner in England. "I loved him," she wrote in an email to me. "I bought him from a Gypsy family. He's a great horse, and it was really hard to part with him, but I needed the money so I sent him to Arizona."

I called his former owner in Arizona who had used Toby to breed. He also took Toby to county fairs and to horse shows. There weren't many Gypsy horses in the United States, and his owners wanted to show what a Gypsy looked like so they could begin to sell their horses. He was a stud and a star in Arizona until he was brought to live in Montana, where he had a similar life.

He was probably seven or eight years old when his Montana owners decided not to breed him any longer, and he was gelded. He lived in a field with shires, which are much bigger than he is. He became close with Lily, a horse that was twice his height. When Lily was sold because she could no longer have babies, we gave Lily a retirement home and bought Toby so she would not lose her closest friend. Toby and Lily remained constant companions until Lily died a peaceful death from old age. Toby mourned her passing and for more than a year he kept his distance from the other horses. One year to the day, I saw Toby grooming with one of the horses as if his period of mourning had come to an end and he could open his heart to the herd.

Becoming A Leader In the Herd

When Toby first arrived, he watched and waited and observed. Little by little, Toby began to establish his leadership in the herd at Pebble Ledge Ranch. The change was subtle. I could tell, because when any horse walked over to bother him or Lily he would put his ears back, and the intruding horse would simply move away. I could tell that the other horses respected his space and his leadership presence. He didn't make many decisions, but the decisions he made were valued.

Occasionally, Toby would ask one of the other horses to move, sometimes just by moving one ear, sometimes just by looking over at them. They would respond to his direction. I saw him as a quiet leader that did not need to use force, but instead used his subtle power. I don't know how he did it, whether something unfolded in the middle of the night, but he gained the allegiance and respect of all the other horses.

Raven, our male horse who grew up mostly with his mom and an older male horse, didn't know much about being a guy. I watched Toby occasionally separate Raven from the herd and chase him around, then let Raven chase him, and soon they were playing. It was stallion play, rearing, bucking, galloping as if Toby were teaching Raven how to be a guy in the herd.

Toby had not done this with any of the other horses in the herd. Not the older, grandfather horse that's male or any of the mares, but with Raven he still plays often, engaging in stallion play. You can hear their heavy breathing and their bodies clashing, but there's never a scratch on either of them. It is like tai chi or martial arts, preparation for strength and balance and battle, but it isn't a battle in itself. They have become very good friends.

Now, when a new male horse arrives, Toby establishes rules and guidelines for the horse coming in. He has not played with them in the same way; there's no stallion play. He doesn't have a training process, but he lets the new male horse know what the rules of the herd are, how to be polite, how not the barge into other horse's space. When Chief Silver Cloud arrived at the ranch and decided he wanted to take Lily for his mare, Toby let him know that wasn't going to happen. Chief Silver Cloud and Toby now get along, but occasionally, if Toby feels that Silver Cloud isn't being polite, Toby will physically move him away from the herd until he changes his approach.

We see a relational field and proper social manners around how horses behave in a herd. For instance, when Silver Cloud barged into a work session with a girl client, stepping up without asking for permission, Toby moved him away. When Silver Cloud waited, pausing to wait for an invitation, he was allowed to move in.

Toby's Role Among the Horse Teachers

Because learning about leadership from the horses is so important in the work at Pebble Ledge Ranch, we encourage them to engage in a spontaneous, authentic way with people.

Lessons tend to come out of that, rather than my saying, "I have a lesson that this horse can teach you." We humans step back, allowing the horse and the human relationship to develop and the experience to unfold. Then, my job is to help the clients make meaning of what has happened, to help them see what is relevant to them, and to help them translate that lesson back into their day-to-day lives, dilemmas, and the world in which they live.

Usually, we ask for several ideas, beyond their initial thoughts, because people often have assumptions. Once we start talking and thinking the conversation opens up, moving from our familiar or habitual patterns of thinking. We don't want to lose the good information we already know, so we aim for two or three possibilities, offering a broader, more aware perspective, so people may engage in a deeper inquiry.

So, the experience and the lessons evolve, and someone, horse or human, steps up to the issue. We might set up a plan, prepare the horses, and intend at the beginning of a day to work on leadership. We might ask, "Would you be interested in challenging yourself by exploring leadership with Toby."

Toby always has a lot of work to do. He is a great teacher. He is a quiet, kind and honest horse and I can depend on him to make good decisions. He isn't a horse that will bite or kick or step on anybody, but he is very persistent, and he makes everyone earn what he or she gets from him.

Toby, being a macho guy and the lead male horse, does not like to be told what to do, or be pushed around. But if you are being relational with him and having fun, if you engage his point of view, and you are determined, he will go with you.

Most any young child can get Toby to do almost anything; he will go anywhere they want because he has fun with them, and they don't try too hard. But many of our adult CEO clients can't get Toby to take one step. The lesson for some of the CEOs is to call on the wisdom of their youth, their innocence, their playfulness, their joy in what they are doing, and their ability to be surprised. When things are not working is when you might let go of being in control.

We developed a workshop for the Case Western Reserve University Weatherhead School of Management for some very high-powered CEOs from all over the world. Of the five teams, one team included a man from Scotland, one from Germany and a man from the United States. One of the tasks was to see whether you could inspire a horse to go with you around an obstacle course that represented the obstacles to their being good leaders in their organizations, and to see what they learned from that.

For a demonstration of their abilities, these three guys picked Toby because he is small and relational and seemed very agreeable. They decided that this was a great horse for succeeding. "We will win," they thought. "Our team will shine."

They had made a lot of assumptions. They watched other teams having some difficulties getting their horses to move. They smiled at Toby and patted his neck. Saying, "Let's show them what we can do, Toby." But when it was their turn, Toby didn't go anywhere. For ten minutes, Toby didn't move. They tried bribing him, they tried talking baby talk, they tried being direct with Toby, and they tried to threaten Toby. But Toby was not going anywhere.

I walked over and asked them how things were going. They were pretty red in the face, frustrated at this point, feeling angry. I said, "Well, you've got about three or four more minutes, and then everybody will report out on what they felt were the strengths of their team and what they accomplished, what their success was. So, I don't care what you come up with, but you will have to come up with a strength and success of your team. You have to pitch it, and see if it will fly."

Later, when I looked back, they were laughing and joking with Toby, and patting him on the shoulder. Their report to the group was, "Toby here, he has done this work so many times that he didn't need to do it again. When you are a leader, you have to step back to see the larger picture. So, we joined Toby in stepping back, watching how the other teams were doing. That's the sign of a true leader: Think for yourself, pause and reflect, work smart and dream big.

I think what they learned from Toby is that there always is meaning and value in every situation. When you let go of your expectations and assumptions to look at what is working, that opens up deeper understanding and possibilities for meaningful action.

As the two men walked to the front to report to the group, Toby began moving on his own. The men didn't notice as Toby walked over to them and was right behind them. Toby, with no rope or lead line, had joined their team, and went wherever they went. Toby seemed to say to his group, "progress does not go in a straight line, nor success in an expected way, and when things go right whatever the time… it is on time." Toby went with his team because they had earned his respect and allowed the outcome to include his ideas. Now, they had something of value, something exciting, an appreciation for each other and for him. Toby could go with that.

This lesson is shown over and over at the ranch, when people stop trying to make horses do something and take the time to respectfully invite the horses to join them, the horses are willing partners. Horses simply follow positive energy. It is one of the reasons that they are so amazing and offer essential feedback. Toby helps leaders be more aware of their use of power and to be better able to inspire their teammates to move together toward a common goal with trust and respect and positive relationship.

Toby often presents the lesson that we most need to learn and it is generally something that we don't know we need to learn until it presents itself. Then, either we step up to learn or not. At the ranch, our job is to create the most positive environment for people not to be embarrassed or threatened so that they can have profound learning experiences and make meaning out of whatever happens.

Sir Toby in his playful, royal way brings out the unique gifts of brilliance that each horse and human has to offer. He teaches us about the power of collaboration and cooperation rather than force and that the only way to move forward is to move together. He reminds us that we each belong, we are each essential and that we all matter in the kingdom of life.

SPIRIT

*"And Spirit grasped a handful of southerly
wind, blew breath over it
and created the horse....
Given the power of flight without wings."*

Bedouin prayer

Spirit

Leading with Purposeful Discernment

I am a beautiful black and white paint mare with spirit. In my dreams I see myself within a tribe carrying women and children across the prairie. My ancestral herd lived freely, choosing to live among people, following the buffalo, having our babies and learning from our elder horses. Though my generation of horses no longer lives in that way, the wisdom of my heritage is alive within my spirit.

I have a sensitive nature and feel life deeply. I was bred twice before I was six years old and hardly had time to grow up before I had babies. I was prepared to be a loving mother but my two babies, one a girl filly and one a boy colt, were sold and taken from me when they were three months old before I had a chance to prepare them for life or even say goodbye. I came to Pebble Ledge Ranch just days after my second baby was sold and abruptly taken from me. I was deeply sad about my loss and was too depressed to accept a new home. I was treated kindly but unable to open my heart to horse or human. After several months my pain dulled and I began to make friends with my horse and human herd members. My curious and spirited nature returned. I began to participate in the teamwork and leadership programs at the ranch, but I never fully trusted and I kept my heart guarded. From time to time, when a young child or sad mother came to see me, my heart softened. One day, many years after I came to live at the ranch, a big horse trailer appeared and instead of yet another giant horse stepping out of the trailer, out trotted a very small black and white Shetland pony. She seemed frightened and in great distress as she looked around at the strange surroundings and giant horses on the other side of the fence. The first night she was here she cried out her distress in loud pony calls and never settled down to rest or sleep. I watched over her, but from the other side of the fence there was little I could do to calm her. Jackie stayed the night with her but the human company was not what the pony needed. At daybreak the next morning, I came up to the gate and looked directly at Jackie letting her know that I could help the pony.

Jackie introduced me to the pony Tess and led her to my side of the fence keeping the other horses in a different area while Tess and I met each other. I walked over to her, my heart opened and I began licking her all over like I did my newborn babies. She calmed and nuzzled me back. She then gave a rebellious whinny and ran towards the far end of the pasture. I gave a firm, kind, motherly call and she galloped back to stand by my side. I watched over Tess for the next months while she made her way safely into the heart of the herd. Something healed in me, as I was able to do for her what I could not for my own horse babies, love them and prepare them to be in the world. Now, several years later, we are best girl friends, and you can often see us hanging out grazing together in the pasture.

In my horseplay and work at the ranch I now help humans, leaders with their teams, parents with their children, to open their hearts with courage and care. I challenge people to remember who they are at their best and to freely live their true spirit.

I have always been clear about my boundaries, honest about my changeable moods, sweet when I choose, and sensitive about my own space. I teach about "having a voice," being direct and speaking up for what you want and do not want and that "Yes" and "No" are both complete and valuable sentences. My body language speaks clearly. Ears pinned, flicking tail and scowling eyes, I say, "Back off, I need my space." Given time and respect for my request, I will often engage with sweet kindness and open heart. People learn from me the importance of honest authentic communication by aligning our inside emotions and thoughts with our outside actions.

Spirit and the Power of Inclusive Spirit

Spirit is a precocious mare with a "wild west" mustang spirit. Today, she lives up to her name in her liveliness and love of freedom.

A family that didn't know much about horses raised her. Raised a bit like a spoiled child, she was not a well-behaved horse. Spirit grew up without many rules or guidance, doing pretty much anything she wanted. She was pampered, and she was fed a lot of sweets.

We could see some results of her upbringing immediately when Spirit arrived at the ranch. One: When someone does everything for you, it's hard to develop self-confidence. Because no one gave Spirit the chance to make decisions on her own, or to take care of herself, she was not a confident horse. Second: Because she was not around other horses, she was not disciplined or well behaved as a member of a herd. She was like a willful wild child, which did not sit well with some of the other horses. Third: Because she was fed too many sweets and overly indulged, she developed a condition where she has chronic discomfort in her feet.

When I met Spirit on an Ohio farm where she lived, she was only six years old, yet had already had two very young foals.

She was young to be a mom, and she didn't have any experienced older horses around to help her. Worse, her babies were taken away from her, for sale, quite early in their lives. Mother horses and their young have a strong relationship, and it's not easy for them to be separated. So, here was this pampered and indulged horse that had everything done for her, and yet, what had mattered most to her, the chance to mother her young, was taken away from her.

For a while at the ranch, Spirit was either docile and sad or willful and wild. The other horses patiently and firmly helped teach her to be a herd member. Because she arrived with the least amount of confidence, she was the horse with the least amount of positional power within the herd. The lack of confidence and personal power is a challenge for horses or humans. As Spirit got older she grew into her confidence, but she has maintained the kind of relationship contradiction that we all at times experience. Sometimes, she wants to be affectionate, to be paid lots of attention or to be social, and other times, she wants to be completely left alone and might snap or threaten to bite you. Whatever her mood, what I admire about her is her absolute honesty and clarity. What is going on in the inside is what you see on the outside. She has become more emotionally intelligent by showing her feelings and taking appropriate action in a given situation.

When Spirit is with a person who doesn't have positional power or know how to use their personal power, she seems to step up to give them courage and confidence. She engages with them in ways that allows them to experience their most authentic and powerful selves. She is motivated to engage and cooperate with a team when it is inclusive of all its members and everyone has a place of belonging.

I remember a team of three people, two men and a woman, who came to the ranch and learned with Spirit. They were department managers from the University Hospitals, a highly regarded medical center. When I asked the team of three what they wanted from their experience with the horses, they did not identify a specific dilemma or stuck place they wanted to work on, but said that what they wanted from their horse experience was to work better as a team and to have some fun together.

I waited to see which horses might be interested in volunteering to work with this team, but most of the horses were kind of hanging back in the field. For some reason and much to my surprise, Spirit volunteered. Spirit is generally the last one to volunteer. When it's her idea to be with people, she is very engaging, but if she is not in the mood to engage and doesn't volunteer and you go get her, she may try to bite you or the client. She is clear about when she feels she has something to contribute and when it's her day off. This time, she just walked into the work area and directly up to the three participants who were waiting on the other side of the fence.

I asked the team members to step up to the fence and come over to Spirit, so I could introduce them. The woman, Monika, said that she was terrified of horses and did not want to come into the horse area. Our participants always have the choice about how and when to be with the horses. The only idea I had for her participation was to assign her the role of coach, which she could do from outside the horse fence. The two men, Jeff and Robert could more directly work with Spirit inside the fence to accomplish a series of physical initiatives and challenges. Monika, happy with her role, participated in the team experience from the perceived safety and comfort of her chair on the outside of the pasture fence.

Spirit seemed engaged in the project with ears forward and a willing attitude and did not try to bite anybody. The guys took their time getting to know Spirit, admiring her beauty and sweet nature. Spirit seemed to like Jeff and Robert a lot, and it looked as if they would have no trouble with their challenge. Their task was to identify a goal and then to lead Spirit across the entire arena to reach and cross a finish line of their identified goal. They explained their goal to Spirit, which was to have an inclusive team where everyone participated, spoke up and had influence. The two guys seemed to create a good working relationship with Spirit, were clear about their goals and were certain the task would be no problem. They began to move easily through the paddock and toward the goal line, with Spirit right with them. They went over the obstacle (a foot-high rail) of not listening, through (two barrels) the challenge of making time for important conversations, and around (a circle of cones) to taking in all perspectives. Spirit followed willingly—that is until they got within about fifteen feet of the goal line. Then, she abruptly stopped. I don't know why Spirit stopped. I didn't see anything happen that caused her to come to an abrupt halt. Soon, the men were pulling on her line, pushing and talking to her.

They made a series of efforts to move her to the finish line without success.

"How's it going, looking from the outside?" I asked Monika, the team's coach. "Not well," she said. I asked the guys, "Do you want help from your coach?" They said, "Absolutely." I said to the coach, "What would you suggest to them?" The woman stood up on her chair, put her hands on her hips, and said "Spirit, get moving." Spirit looked over at the woman and took off toward the goal, dragging the two guys behind her until they got about two feet from the finish line where she once again stopped. "We'll take it from here," one of the guys said to the coach. "We'll get her across."

They tried for five minutes to move Spirit the last two feet, without success. "Do you want to consult with your coach again?" I asked. "Okay, what should we do?" they asked their female teammate.

She stood up again. In a strong, clear, confident voice she said, "Spirit, two more feet. Go now!" Spirit looked toward Monika, looked at the guys and pranced across the finish line. Jeff and Robert looked astonished as Monika smiled and confidently sat back down.

The three team members and Spirit met at the fence to reflect on and to celebrate their success. Robert said to Monika, their teammate and coach, "This is what we need for you to do at work on the team. We've never heard you speak up and be that clear. That's what is missing from this team. Your voice, your 'let's get it done' attitude and your confident presence are missing from the team." Monika responded, "Well, if you guys would just make room for me, ask me what I think, give me a chance to be heard, I could contribute great things to our team." The men needed to actively make a place and space for the woman, and she needed to speak up, making room for herself. The team all agreed that they had learned something they could take back with them from the horseplay to their place of work and that is that all of them are better than any one of them. Spirit moved closer standing between Jeff and Robert, and reached her head over the fence toward the Monika. "We are all in," Spirit seemed to say, "and that is how it should be."

"I need to thank Spirit," said Monika, who jumped up out of her chair, opened the gate, and walked into the horse area.

She walked right up to Spirit and gave her a big hug around the neck. She asked me to take a picture with her and Spirit and said, "This is my new best friend." Monika talked about what she learned, about how courage comes from within, and that Spirit gave her confidence to speak up, use her power and take her place as a leader on the team. She said she realized that when she inspired Spirit that she could be inspiring and that gave her the confidence to be inspiring to her team. From a distance, she also realized something else. She is a powerful woman who is ready to face the barriers inside herself and out in the world. Monika realized that when she faced her fear with support, she could move beyond that fear and be more powerful. This was an awakening. Years later Monica still has the picture of Spirit and her on her desk at work.

Robert and Jeff spoke about what they could take from the horse pasture to their home pasture at work. "It's all about inclusion," Jeff reflected. "I want to make sure that all voices on our team are heard and ideas respected." Robert agreed and added, "There's so much more energy and possibility when we work together and make room for each other." Spirit seemed to agree as she softly nuzzled each member of the team.

I think Spirit recognizes that everyone has his or her own gift and purpose, and you just have to be patient and curious about what that is. You can't assume you know. If you don't assume that you know, you might discover there are many things that are possible. The team from the medical center exceeded their goals through horseplay and fun. They strengthened their team by having respect for differences, and practicing inclusion and collaborative forward movement.

They brought out the best in each individual and their team collectively through the spirit of inclusion that is only possible when everyone belongs, everyone is essential and everyone matters.

Spirit is a horse that recognizes when someone is having difficulty and will offer a helping hoof and an open heart in friendship. She notices when someone is left out and often finds a way to include them, bringing them into the herd in a valued place of belonging.

Now, as a more mature horse, she has confidence in herself and is clear about what matters to her, where she wants to be, and how she wants to engage, and she helps her human partners to do the same.

Another horse might be easier to get along with than Spirit. If she is not interested in engaging, she might ignore, scowl or walk away. If you put Spirit somewhere where she doesn't want to be with someone she does not want to be with, she will stand her ground, put her ears back in a threatening way as if to say, "What don't you understand about no?"

I think Spirit has learned from being in the herd and from her life experience with people an inner confidence to simply be who she is. She is discerning and takes action when something matters to her. Her advice is, *"Don't let people into your space if you don't want them in your space. Volunteer and show up when something matters to you. Be who you are."*

From that clear place of an authentic way of being, she can help teach people about being authentically themselves, clear about what they want and don't want, and comfortable in their own heart and hooves.

BUD

> *We see you, see ourselves and know*
> *That we must take the utmost care and*
> *kindness in all things*

Jo Harjo, Native American poet

Bud (Big Boy Tamarack)

> *"the stories buried in the mountains*
> *give out into the sea*
> *and the sea remembers and sings back*
> *from the depths*
> *where nothing is forgotten"*
> —David Whyte

I stand a proud and humble nineteen hands at my shoulder and am six-foot-three inches tall at my hindquarters. I am probably the biggest horse anybody will ever encounter. Named for the Tamarack tree, a tree that is known for its resilience and endurance and its ability to survive in challenging conditions I am sturdy even in the fiercest winds. In the Native American tradition the Tamarack is known for its many healing properties, as a pillar of strength and a reminder of lifelong connections. I was raised in Montana and in my early years was a logger, pulling logs out of the forest with my horse and human partners. We were a good team, working hard to together and being kind and considerate to one another. When I was too old to log, my horse partner and I learned to pull a buckboard wagon and worked on the Montana ranch. My life took an unexpected change when my horse partner of eighteen years died and my human companion of eighteen years took a job in the oil fields and was no longer able to keep me. He wanted me to have a good home in my retirement years and though it was a great distance away, chose Pebble Ledge Ranch in Ohio.

It was a long journey and I arrived in the middle of a dark and confusing night. I was unloaded from the horse trailer and was met by a woman less than half my size. She greeted me warmly and slowly led me through dark shadows down a long driveway, opened a gate and led me into an empty orchard. From a distance I heard thundering hoof beats and into sight came the shadow of a herd of horses. Several horses called out as if to say, "Who are you that arrives under cover of night?" Too exhausted to answer I found a tree to stand under. Too tired to eat the hay left for me and with the comfort of the woman next to me, I promptly fell asleep. When the sun came up the next morning I looked out into a landscape very different from my home in Montana. Where was the open space of the prairie, the vast big sky and mountains in the distance? What I saw was a meadow surrounded by trees and a small herd of large black, white and black-and-white horses. There was one small pony that did not even come up to my belly and there was a strange looking and smelling striped pony with a stand-up mane and funny tail, which I later learned was not pony at all but a zebra. All I wanted was to go back home. I missed the open space of my Montana pasture, my human companion and most of all I missed my horse partner.

Over the next few weeks I was introduced to the herd and wandered the borders of my new pasture that was not yet home. I spent most of the day and night standing in the middle of the field, just looking out beyond the fences, feeling lost, alone and terribly sad. The woman, I learned her name was Jackie, spent time each day talking to me in soothing tones and brushing my coat. She took my picture and sent it back to my human companion, as she knew he missed me as much as I missed him. She became my first friend. Her husband Herb also came to quietly reassure me that all would be well and to welcome me to my new home. He spoke of his love of the beauty and open spaces in Montana. It was good to hear a male voice that sounded much like my human partner back home.

Slowly over time, I began to meet the horses in the Pebble Ledge herd and made some human friends as well. They seemed like an okay bunch, but I still missed Montana and my life and friends there.

I have been here several years now and made the ranch home. I am still a cowboy at heart and like my open spaces. You will often find me a distance from the herd, though I feel like I am part of the family now. Not pushing my way in, I let the other horses discover me. I consider my herd mates my friends and have a good relationship with all of them as more and more I take my place in the heart of the herd. Tess, the little pony with the big attitude is my favorite and sort of my girlfriend. Because of her size she can literally walk underneath me, but she does not let me or any of the horses walk all over her. She's quite feisty and if she can't get my attention when she wants it, she will run up, rear up and bite me playfully on my neck. I kind of like that.

It's my style to be the pacifist of the herd. I don't seek conflict. I just stand calm and tall. I pause, reflect, watch and make sense of what is going on before I act. I enjoy being with people, sometimes even more than being with the other horses, and I engage easily and willingly with the people that enter our pasture. I like welcoming people, as I know what it feels like to be a stranger in the herd. I am the first to lift my head from grazing in a welcoming greeting. In my friendly and easygoing way, I help our guests feel safe in the herd.

I have found the work here at Pebble Ledge Ranch less demanding physically than pulling logs from the Montana forest, but challenging, demanding and rewarding in a different way. I am very engaged in the work here at the ranch, helping people heal from loss, find new meaning in life and be good team members and leaders.

If somebody in one of our programs is struggling with something, feeling stuck or trying to work with me on something, I don't give up. I stay with them until they work it out. I am a true friend, with unconditional loyalty and empathy. I have a heart as vast as the Montana sky. I offer my big heart and gently nudge people to be their big-hearted and lovable selves.

"Bud" Big Boy Tamarack is a giant of a horse with a generous spirit and great work ethic. You can count on Bud. For instance, when he is working with a client, he is loyal to that person. Once he connects with someone, he stays with them. Bud doesn't give up somebody who is having difficulty. He stays with them until they figure it out. He acts like a true friend.

He's been a true friend to me since he arrived at the ranch. I have asked him to step in and he has done it. He is quiet, calm, humble in spirit, and engages with a big heart.

Bud has become the herd ambassador of good will. He greets people and his herd members with friendly, outgoing and honest empathy and interest.

Bud and the ArcelorMittal Steel Management Team

Bud willingly partners with people to walk alongside of them as they walk towards their desired goals. I can count on Bud to help people who know nothing about leading a horse to successfully lead them in the direction of their destination, which might be represented by a barrel or a flag.

One morning, a management team from ArcelorMittal Steel Corporation was at the ranch learning from the horses about leadership and teamwork. Having met all the horses, each team of four ArcelorMittal steel managers selected a horse to join their team. One team unanimously chose Bud for his willingness to step forward and his friendly and cooperative nature.

Each team member identified a goal they had for themselves that they would like to move towards. One at a time, each person identified their goal, which the barrel or flag represented, and then had the task to motivate Bud to walk with them to their goal. The first team member identified his goal as "safety for all on the job." He was clear and committed to the goal and Bud allowed himself to be led, walking willingly to the identified goal. The second member had the goal of motivating his team to meet production goals and with confidence and a fast pace, he inspired Bud to move more quickly than his usual slow step to the goal. The third team member had the goal of providing for his family through upward advancement in the steel company and Bud responded to the heartfelt care for family and was inspired to walk with him to the goal.

The last team member to lead Bud was a woman who chose not to identify her goal.

Bud moved eagerly forward with her until they were halfway to the goal and then stopped. She attempted to get Bud to continue forward but Bud refused to take another step forward.

Instead, he dropped his head and simply looked her in the eye, then gently nuzzled her. The woman's fellow teammates began shouting their advice on how to get Bud moving, but none of their ideas made a difference to Bud. He was completely focused on the woman and seemed to be horse-whispering something important in her ear. She began to laugh and said, "This is so like my life at home and at work, everyone telling me what they think and what I should do and not asking me what I want to do. I need to take time to figure out what really matters to me—what is my purpose and what will make me happy? My goal is to not go anywhere till I am ready." As she said that, Bud lifted his head up and looked at her with a grin. She looked back, smiling at Bud and said, "I am ready now, Bud, let's get moving." Bud stretched himself up, looking even bigger, and began walking proudly with her to the goal line.

The team, including Bud, stood together reflecting on what they had learned from their leadership experience with Bud that would be useful to them in their positions of managers and team leaders at ArcelorMittal steel. They identified several key points that they felt were essential for leading their teams to the desired goal: know your goal, be clear, confident and committed, move forward safely, stop to listen, know what matters and has purpose, and work together with care. Bud responded to the authenticity of his team and when he sensed in each one the alignment of thought, emotion and action, he willing moved forward. When he felt confusion and was unsure of the truth of the direction or commitment to the goal, he stopped walking and would not take another step. Bud patiently waited for each of his human partners to discover their inner truth, direction and authentic self and only then would he move with them.

Bud, as do most horses, senses and responds to a person's emotions, inner intention and body language. Bud coached each person on the team by authentically interacting with them and giving them direct feedback in the moment with his unmistakable body language. He offered each person invaluable lessons about the importance of being authentically present in order to effectively reach their goals and desired destinations.

Our other horses have strong and assertive personalities, while Bud has a quiet power that requires no force. He is our gentle giant.

Bud has a presence that is honest, compassionate and kind. He calmly takes life in stride whatever the challenge. He has a loving way of being that has won the hearts of many.

He is the loyal friend that has your back, the team member you can always count on, and the family member you can turn to no matter what. He is the one that is unconditionally accepting of you even when you can't be accepting of yourself. Bud, in his authentic presence and boundless capacity for loving-kindness, truly makes the world a better place.

CHIEF SILVER CLOUD

"You do not have to be good.
You do not have to walk on your knees,
For 100 miles through the desert, repenting.
You only have to let the soft animal of your
body love what it loves."

Mary Oliver, poet

Chief Silver Cloud

> *"A horse perseveres with its loving heart and wins with its strong character."*
> —Fredrico Tesio

It's difficult to know who you are on the inside when all your life it has been your outer appearance that has been recognized. Though I had no mirror to look into, I learned who I was from how people saw me. I was told that that I was quite tall, a very white and beautiful nineteen-hand Percheron, a French draft horse with Arabian blood. Living in Philadelphia, I was a parade horse admired for my outer beauty and grace as I pranced down the street with silver harness trappings and a red plume feather atop my head.

From deep within I knew there was more to life and more to me than being a parade horse. Who am I? What is my purpose? How am I to contribute to the greater good? These are not typical questions a horse ponders or is asked, but I had time on my hooves. I lived in a barn and in between occasional rides with my human I was pretty much left alone in my twelve-foot by twelve-foot barn stall. I had a window and a pretty good view of the field. I would look out and imagine myself breaking free and jumping the fence to…well, I don't know where, but it seemed elsewhere was better than where I was. I felt so alone and longed to belong. Where was my herd?

Then one day as fate would have it, I overheard a conversation between my two human owners. It seemed that they were no longer interested in being in parades with me. They decided they wanted a horse that could compete in western horse contests like calf roping and barrel racing and that I was just way too big and slow for that. So, one day I had purpose and value and a home in Philadelphia and the next day I was on a trailer bound for Cleveland. For what purpose? I was both terrified and excited. Would I like my new home? Would I fit in and be accepted for who I am? And, who am I anyway?

A city horse, I arrived at Pebble Ledge Ranch in a rural area outside of Cleveland during a particularly hot summer day. I was relieved to get out of the stuffy hot trailer to stretch and breathe in the cool air. I looked around and there was no band to greet me, only the glares of six horses and a weird zebra. They were not impressed by my parade horse stance or my fancy silver harness with its special red plume feather that had arrived with me. They seemed not to care that I had been the lead horse in the Fourth of July parade. I had always lived among people and was uncertain how to get along with horses, and though I yearned to be in a herd I had no idea about how to live in a herd. I was accustomed to living in a barn and having everything done to me or for me. I would now be living outside, which at first was unfamiliar and overwhelming. I understood how to be a horse in a human world but did not know how to be horse in a horse world.

What I did enjoy was the freedom, but like a person who has just been released from jail or an animal from captivity, I was afraid to trust that the freedom would last. Jackie and Herb and their friends gave me a warm welcome with apples and kind words. The name I came with was Conan the Barbarian, but at my new home they changed my name to Chief Silver Cloud wanting to give me back my dignity along with my freedom to live a more natural horse life.

The beauty of my new name was more important to me than silver bridles and red feather plumes. I had also arrived with a plastic baseball bat with my name Conan on it, which my previous owners had said would keep me in line. I breathed a sigh of relief when the bat was retired to the manure pit along with the rest of the horseshit!

I was led to the orchard where new horses can rest from their journey to the ranch and settle into their new home. Waiting for me to keep me company was Lily, an elderly horse. Not having horse social graces, I approached her somewhat rudely and she immediately walked away. I followed her, but she made it clear that I was more than an elderly grandmother horse could handle. Jackie, my new person, took Lily from the orchard and brought in a good-looking little paint horse named Spirit as my bunkmate. Love at first sight for me, but not so with her.

This time I approached with more grace and a gleam in my eye. Spirit returned my loving gaze with a glare and proceeded to bite me on the shoulder followed by a swift kick to my rump.

Being a quick learner of body language, I backed off. For a week we lived in the same orchard, Spirit ignoring me from a distance and biting me if I got too close. We ate from separate hay piles and slept at opposite ends of the orchard. I was pretty stressed, but persistently hopeful that this relationship would turn around. Week two things went better.

Each horse in the herd had paid me a visit over the fence and Spirit was allowing me to get closer to her pile of hay. By week three, the herd seemed to have accepted my arrival at the ranch, so Jackie opened the orchard gate and Spirit and I walked out into the field to join the herd. My excitement turned to disappointment when Spirit ran off to join the herd and the herd chased me away to the far end of the field. This was not going as I had expected. I, who had never lived in a herd before coming to this ranch, was expected to learn the rules and values and behaviors of the herd's culture.

Observing the herd and watching the horses engage with each other, I began to see and sense what was expected of a herd member. I learned about respect for space and points of view, I learned about shared leadership and the responsibility of each horse to be a leader in its own way for the benefit of the herd. I realized that the code of the herd was "we all move forward together, with purpose, in a common direction, in the best interest of the whole of the herd". I began to remember how to sniff the air for danger, to stand with my butt to the wind and to run wild with joy, abandon and freedom. I was remembering how to be a horse. I began to understand who I was and what my purpose was, and how to belong in my herd. I began to grow into my name, Chief Silver Cloud, proud warrior. I developed character and a beauty that now came from the courage of my heart and the inner beauty of my soul. The herd began to see me as I saw myself, or maybe I began to see myself as they now knew and saw me. I was invited into the heart of the herd.

Surrounded by my herd of horses and humans, I am now valued and loved for being the authentic horse and natural beauty I am on the inside. In my parade days, I was expected to keep moving and I am still often on the move. But I move differently now; I have a destination, going to the next best place and motivating others to get moving along with me. I keep horses and people alert to danger and awake so as to be present to opportunity. I provide disruptive innovation, keeping my herd mates and human guests of the herd from getting stuck in the past by moving them forward toward a better future. My loving heart, strong character and positive presence inspires people to move in the direction of their greatness and for the greater good of others.

Parade Horse Joins the Parade

A white Percheron, Chief Silver Cloud is the tallest horse at Pebble Ledge Ranch. More than seven feet tall, he weighs more than two thousand pounds. He can be intimidating and assertive, but he understands and empathizes with those with a lack of self-confidence, as he has dealt with his own.

Chief Silver Cloud has a heart as big as his physical presence. He is unconditionally loyal and once you have his trust, he will be with you and for you one hundred percent.

Margie, A young woman who weighs less than a hundred pounds, was at the ranch as a client, working on confidence issues. Her purpose in coming to engage with the horses was to learn to take better control of her life, making meaning of her life and discovering what is of value to her. She wanted to work with Chief Silver Cloud, thinking that a horse that big could teach her about confidence and showing up big instead of playing small.

What's bigger than a parade? Chief had parade experience so we created an experience for Margie to lead the parade with Chief Silver Cloud along the parade route of confidence and courage.

Margie decorated Chief with ribbons and feathers and put a fancy halter and a lead line on him so that she could practice moving forward in taking the lead in her life with more courage and confidence and less indecision and fear. Chief seemed to enjoy the decorations and seemed to be "all in" with Margie. She chose her parade route and destination, which represented her goal to walk with more confidence in her personal and work life. Her intention was to no longer get knocked off balance by unexpected change in direction, and to be confidently persistent when the going got tough.

The beautifully adorned Chief Silver Cloud easily walked forward when Margie made the request, but was starting and stopping unexpectedly and crowding her space. She rightfully worried that he might step on her. Margie tried to take the lead to move in her desired direction without being dragged, but Chief Silver Cloud had other ideas and in pushing her around to his way of thinking, she was unable to reach her goal. Pulling and dragging Chief along by the lead line or getting pulled was not working. I asked her what else she might try that would feel safe to her and get her where she wanted to go with Chief. I suggested she consult Chief for his opinion since he was her horse coach in this learning opportunity. She said that she and Chief decided that she should take the lead line off Chief and trust that they could walk together more collaboratively and cooperatively without one dragging the other around.

Margie patted Chief, and smiling, walked forward toward her goal, and for the most part, he followed alongside of her. Sometimes he was distracted; sometimes he came right with her. It took him a while, but she got him to partner with her and go with her to her goal. When they successfully reached their final goal, Margie gave Chief a big hug in celebration, and wrapping his big neck around her, he hugged her back. I asked, "What are you learning and what might Chief represent? What is this really about?"

She said, "It's about being disappointed. When I stayed focused and kept moving, my disappointment moved. When I didn't trust and didn't have confidence, and got discouraged and frustrated, then he stopped and got distracted. I had to let go of my disappointment, get his attention, be patient, and believe that we could move together, and then we did. When I kept moving, he became unstuck. Maybe he also represents my stuckness."

She said, "Fear is really what my disappointment is about. I'm afraid that I will disappoint other people, and then I get disappointed and frustrated and feel stuck. I haven't admitted that fear to anybody. It's a little bit of relief to understand what I was really afraid of and to not pretend or keep it a secret." We talked about how horses never pretend, that they're always honest, and that what is going on inside is what we see on the outside. Margie realized that confidence and courage comes from the inside, and that if she felt disappointed or fearful she could look inside to learn what was really happening, what was underneath her disappointment and driving her fear.

We also talked about what she learned on her parade route with Chief. She said she learned that to succeed in your goals, you need to know what direction you want to go in, to get the support you need and to move forward with courage and confidence. You have to be resilient and if something does not work, you must try something else and remain optimistic that something good can happen by simply taking the next step.

Horses are persistent, resilient, optimistic and innovative; there's always a way out, always a solution to a problem. Chief Silver Cloud might want her to remember that when she hits one barrier, there's always a way around it, over it, or through it, if she stays authentically present and keeps moving forward with courage.

It was a good day. Some of the value was in our conversation. A lot of it was the horse. I could see in her face that a cloud had lifted, and some of the weight that she had been carrying became lighter. I don't think that would have happened if we just talked about it. I think that her physically moving, physically having that experience, learning by that experience, and her empathy for Silver Cloud and his for her is what allowed the change to happen. When we put ourselves in someone else's shoes and see the world from their eyes, we see our own world differently.

Sometimes a problem is huge. Yet, if we face our fear, some of it goes away. She couldn't really direct Silver Cloud all the time, or he her, but they had co-created a cooperative relationship. They achieved co-leadership in which each of them could take the lead, leading them to different information at different times toward a common goal.

Chief Silver Cloud Meets Chief of Surgery

When I think of someone who embodies greatness through authentic presence it is Dr. Thomas Marcus. I had the privilege to meet Thomas when he ventured out to the ranch as a participant in a Hospital Leadership Academy.

Thomas said that when he heard that the Leadership Academy (in which he was a participant) would be coming out to the ranch for a leadership day with horses, he was skeptical.

"When I arrived at this somewhat rustic ranch I said to myself, I know what this is about, it's likely to be touchy-feely. I had a healthy sense of reticence and did not think it would resonate but promised myself to keep open mind."

Having a positive outlook and being a good team player, Dr. Marcus decided to join the adventure and leave at least part of his skeptical attitude behind.

"The first horse that I saw with an equal amount of fear and awe was Chief Silver Cloud, the largest and whitest horse I had ever seen. It was fate that brought Chief and me together. He just stood in the distance looking me over. He seemed to reflect back to me my fears of being too different, too big, too standoffish, too strong and maybe even too black. I consciously chose to face my fears and took a step forward, getting close to all that strength and power in a giant white horse. I made the effort to connect with myself internally and from my heart to him. I realized how much Chief, a retired and hard-worked parade horse, and I had in common. We both felt different from others. We both were trained to be high performers in our professions and became used to being what others expected us to be. It seemed like both of us were asking the questions: Who am I? How do I fit in? Am I being who I am meant to be?

"In a dance of mutual understanding, vulnerability and trust, Chief stepped forward and began to follow my teammates and me. In that interaction, I realized the power of perception and intention, the power of body language and the power of spiritual connection. What mattered in that moment was that we were authentically who we each were, and we moved together in a common direction. As leaders and as family, as team and herd members, we can only be our best selves when we find the best in ourselves and the best in our herd."

Not only did Dr. Marcus's experience with the horses and with his colleagues that day at the ranch open new and important thinking, it opened to a deeper place—the wisdom of his heart.

I realized that I was in the presence of a man who had the courage to be his authentic, best self and who was committed to help others discover that in themselves.

About six months after the retreat, I braved a Cleveland blizzard to have a conversation with Thomas to learn if and how his experience at the ranch with the horses had impacted his presence and his relationship to his work.

Before going into his office he walked me around to each open door in his work area and introduced me to members of his "office family," now thought of also as his "herd." He told me why each person was essential to the success of the work of his department and thanked each of them for their service, much like Bea, the lead mare of our herd, introducing a guest to her valued herd members. Thomas acknowledged the importance of each person's contribution to the "office family" and the importance of their caring and collaborative relationships. The respect, trust and high regard that Thomas as team leader demonstrated is similar to the positive approach to leadership in the horse herd that is essential to its daily functioning and long term success.

The positive feeling of his office reminded me of being in the horse pasture. I felt a sense of peace and vitality. Dr. Marcus treated all people with positive regard. He operated from the belief that all members of his office were inherently good and that with a positive attitude anything is possible. Over Thomas's shoulder was a smiling picture of Nelson Mandela, and pictures of children. On the shelf was a model sailboat with an inspirational saying reminding us to catch the wind and move forward with full sails.

Thomas told me that if I were to understand who and how he is now and about his experience at the ranch, I would need to understand something about his background, people and culture. I learned that he grew up in a positive value system much like the herd. The collective love and wisdom of his family and community are the roots and foundation of the man he has become and is still becoming. His life purpose is an expression and culmination of the positive values and life experience of past generations of his family. His intention is to continue the family tradition of faith and to use his gifts and talents to serve the well-being of all. In his smiling and humble way he talked about his success as a medical student at Harvard, his passion for medicine, his love for the children and families he serves. He shared the challenges of leadership and his commitment to lead with compassion, collaboration and a positive and clear vision.

His connection and sense of belonging to a collective of people and cultivating collective wisdom is a similar dynamic to that of the herds that thrived for sixty-five million years. Like a true herd leader he promotes wisdom through the experience of what works best, supports connection and positive relationship and passes on the necessary learning for future generations.

"I still think of that day at the ranch and my meeting with Chief Silver Cloud," Dr. Marcus reflected. "How we treat each other matters. I shifted my attention from being an individual to being part of a group. Each of us, including Chief, treated each other with respect and trust. Individually we saw our situation differently, but together we were able to understand the whole of the system."

All participants appreciated Chief Silver Cloud's lessons from different perspectives; his new pal Thomas and the team created a wisdom that was collective and recommitted to care for the common good of the individuals, team and organization.

Chief Silver Cloud Meets Medicine Woman

An organization in urban Cleveland, the American Indian Education Center, provides opportunities for American Indians in our community to learn about their culture and traditions, many of which had been taken from and lost to them. In the 1950s, ten thousand American Indians from a variety of tribes and reservations were brought to Cleveland and plunked down in neighborhoods with the most poverty and social problems. Many of them did not speak English or each other's tribal language. Their spiritual practice was nature-based, and here they were surrounded by buildings and concrete with hardly a tree in sight. Unable to return to their home reservations, they did their best to create a community for themselves and their children. Russell Means, the well-known American Indian activist, grew up in Cleveland as part of this community. Russell was the exception. Though living with great courage, very few people brought to Cleveland had an understanding of what was happening and were not able to rise above the challenges of poverty and the loss of identity and culture. Now, two generations later, many of the people of that Indian community live in physical poverty. Thanks to the American Indian Education Center and wise elders in the community, they no longer live in spiritual poverty.

We had the privilege of partnering with the AIEC to offer a retreat for American Indian women of this community, affording them the opportunity to reconnect with nature, their nature-based spiritual culture and their inner nature. The horses were the primary guides for their experience at the ranch.

Sometimes when a group approaches the horse pasture, the herd hangs back, their grazing or grooming or other horse activities uninterrupted. While it's clear they notice the people approaching, they make no move to welcome them or engage. This time was different. The horses immediately stopped what they were doing, and ears forward, moving together as one, began trotting over to the fence where the women were standing, Chief Silver Cloud in the lead. I was kind of surprised to see Chief out front because he is often one of the last to make the effort to greet people, even though once he arrives he is very social.

Our plan was very simple. We would introduce the horses and women to each other and they could spend the warm sunny day simply being together in the field. In reconnecting with nature, engaging with the horses, and taking time to do nothing, something could happen. We provided journals and writing tools, rawhide string, beads and feathers, and paints and paper in case the women felt like playing with creative expression. The horses were very into it, connecting with the women by following them around, looking over the shoulders of the women drawing, and listening to their stories. Some of the horses were being brushed and some of the horses were gently brushing the women. On this lazy day, horses dropped to the ground curling up on the warm earth for a nap and a few women joined them. As a herd, women and horses, hearts and spirit they became one.

Chief Silver Cloud seemed very interested in River, a nurse in her community and one of the younger women at the retreat. Her beautiful long black hair and bronze skin stood out against Chief's shiny silver coat. He followed her around and seemed to nudge her along to the far end of the field where he had her to himself. I could see them together; sometimes their heads close as if telling secrets, sometimes walking alongside each other as dear friends do.

As the sun began to set, the women said their goodbyes to the horses for the day and we hiked through the woods to a clearing where a campfire was burning brightly. We sat in the dark around the fire seeing each other's faces in the glow of the flame and sharing the adventures of the day. River, Chief Silver Cloud's companion, spoke last. She spoke in a clear and confident voice, "Today I learned that I am a Medicine Woman and belong to a powerful tradition of Medicine Women that have come before me. In my chosen field as a nurse, I have been a healer in our community. What I discovered today with Chief Silver Cloud as my guide, were my indigenous roots and Medicine Woman heritage. In his presence I was able to understand the language of my people and begin to dream back our healing traditions and ceremonies. Chief Silver Cloud gave me my Medicine Woman name, Silver River, a name I will grow and flow into as I reclaim more of who I am."

The women walked in the moonlight along the path from the campfire to the cottage for dinner, a good night's sleep and deep dreams. As we walked, there, glowing in the moonlight of the field, standing tall and proud was Chief Silver Cloud, the Medicine Horse. As we watched him take a step forward and turn towards us, it looked as if he had a silver horn atop his head between his ears. Silver River trusted us and was courageous enough to be seen and acknowledged as a medicine woman, Chief Silver Cloud, with his strong character and loving heart, trusted us to see him as a unicorn!

Chief Silver Cloud is a great example of the everyday magic that becomes possible when we suspend certainty and admit that we don't know so that something new and unexpected can emerge. This magic of present reality can become our daily reality through the cultivation of collective wisdom, the everyday interactions of cooperative and compassionate relationship, and courageous, creative community spirit.

TESS

*"Let it grow, let it grow,
Let it blossom, let it flow
In the sun, the rain, the snow,
Love is lovely, let it grow"*

Eric Patrick Clapton, singer, songwriter

Tess

I am perfect for the Pebble Ledge herd, championing diversity and balance. I am a tiny pony with a giant attitude, energy, and presence that can hold her own in a herd of horses that are three times her height and five times her weight. Relational and friendly with a kind nature, I have definite points of view and freely express them. I love working with people, all kinds of people, even those I disagree with. Engaging with everybody, I can find the best of anybody and bring out what is special, no matter the extent of their importance. I remind my herd mates and human friends that a big heart, confidence and courage creates a mighty presence and that what is on the inside is more important and truthful than outer appearance.

Before coming to Pebble Ledge Ranch, I was a birthday party pony, equally important a calling as logging or leading parades or carrying Templar Knights. I was more than willing to take kids on a journey, but it made no sense to me to go round and round like so many grownups do, and not get anywhere. I was great at my job as I loved playing with kids, but like many horses and people, I worked for a boss who did not understand me or listen to me and treated me harshly. Often I was criticized and rarely appreciated for my talents. While I loved the kids, I began to hate my job and kicked up my heels in protest. My boss, not liking my rebellious attitude, decided to fire me and send me packing. Much to my good fortune I was rescued and taken into a great herd at Pebble Ledge Ranch.

It took me awhile to accept my new human family. They were patient and accepting of me when I arrived a high-strung and anxious pony. Maybe they saw the real me under all the stress I had been carrying and they made an effort to create a home for me to heal, become whole and be more of my big, lovable self.

My first day at the ranch I was met over the fence by a very cool paint horse named Spirit that had a spirited personality much like my own, and though much taller, looked a bit like me. I recognized her as a kindred spirit from the moment we sniffed noses across the fence and there was something warmly familiar about her. My first evening at the ranch, my new human Jackie slept with me in the orchard to help me feel at home and comfortable in my new surroundings. It did not work. I did not sleep all night and neither did Jackie because I paced and ran and called to the other horses throughout the night. All I wanted was to be with the other horses and especially with Spirit. Much to my relief, when morning came, Spirit was standing near me next to the fence while the other horses were busy at the far end of the paddock eating hay. Wisely, Jackie let me out of the orchard and into the field with Spirit. I held my breath and much to my delight Spirit slowly walked up to me, nickered softly to me and began to lick me from my head to my tail. I sighed and shivered with pleasure at her gentle, loving touch. Excited beyond belief I spun around, kicked up my heels and took off at a dead run across the twenty-acre field. Before I could reach the far end of the field, I heard Spirit give a commanding horse call that sounded something like, "You had better get back here and now!" She sounded an awful lot like the mother I had lost as a baby twelve years before. I turned right around, reared up in the air and galloped fast as I could, mane and tail flying in the wind, back to Spirit. All the horses had left their breakfast and were now staring over the fence to see what all the excitement was about.

Spirit gave me a quick scolding nip and then nuzzled me, welcoming me back to her side. Spirit became my herd mother until I felt safe in my new home. She brought me into the heart of the herd and watched over me until the other horses accepted me as a valued member. The other horses then "on boarded" me onto the Pebble Ledge Ranch horse team and helped me prepare for our work to help people be better human beings.

This job was better than giving rides at birthday parties. Rather than carrying kids on my back and walking aimlessly round and round in a circle not getting anywhere, I was helping kids and grownups find their own paths.

I love kids and they still are my favorite humans, but it is equally fun to inspire adults to be playful kids again. My special bonus was discovering Josh and having time to play with him. He is Jackie and Herb's special, very special-needs grandson who lives at the ranch on all his school breaks. Josh and I have a magical language and relationship between us; it's called pure love.

Tiny Pony That Believes In Everyone

Most of the herd at the Pebble Ledge Ranch is made up of two-thousand-pound draft horses. They are all big. We decided to find a smaller horse to bring into the herd, a horse perhaps smaller than a human. I searched for a Shetland pony, hoping to find one near our ranch in Northeastern Ohio. We found Tess, a twelve-year-old, black-and-white Shetland pony who had outgrown her love for being a birthday party pony.

Tess was the perfect pony for this herd because she had a plenty of attitude, which allowed her to manage well in our horse herd, and she was also friendly and good-natured.

She had been living around horses, but mostly in a stall. When I arrived home at the ranch with her, I put her in the orchard behind a fence, so she could meet the horses across the fence. She was agitated, just ran round and round. I brought my sleeping bag out to stay with her overnight, and she stopped running but continued pacing the whole night. The next morning, Spirit, who is sometimes a self-centered it's-all-about-me horse, was looking over the fence, so I brought the two together. Spirit began licking Tess. Spirit's two colts had been taken from her very early and she had never had a chance to mother them; she took Tess in as if she were her baby. They soon became good companions, though Holly the zebra is now Tess's best girlfriend.

She fit in, integrating more quickly than any of the other new horses because she has chutzpah, courage with audacity. Whatever she sets out to do, the other horses just look at her as if to say, "Okay, have it your way," so she has had little difficulty getting into the inner sanctum of the herd.

Tess never walks. She prances and runs or trots wherever she goes. She gets people moving, and is generally engaging and fun loving. She has added liveliness to the herd and a bit of a sense of humor. Her presence has lightened up the herd.

When we have a group of children, I can count on Tess. She will engage with them, watch out for them, and make them feel special, as she did with a Girl Scout troop that came to the ranch to do some learning about respectful relationship and how to stop bullying at their school. She has a big heart for everyone and makes sure all are included and treated kindly.

The Girl Scouts, under Tess's guidance, practiced appreciating each other's differences and accepting each other just as they were. In addition to being a Girl Scout troop, they became a herd with the responsibility of looking out for one another.

Tess quickly became an important member of the teaching team, especially in helping with people who operate out of their small selves, who are fearful and lacking confidence.

Sarah, a woman who was terrified of horses and other animals, came to the ranch for a coaching program. In her feedback to me following her experience with the horses, she said that the herd was the most important part of coaching training she has ever done. With Tess's help, she was able to confront her assumption that animals would not like her and her fear that animals would hurt her. In facing this fear she realized how many undiscovered fears she carried about being disliked, unwanted and in danger. These assumptions were like many other fears and assumptions in her life about being unsafe and not good enough. These had become Sarah's truth and reality and kept her from having meaningful relationships and from being fully present to what was really going on in her world. Tess provided her with an opportunity to challenge her assumptions and concerns about not being accepted and the danger of being vulnerable in her relationships. Sarah began to respect herself as good enough and began to see her world as a more safe and welcoming place.

I think that Tess helps people move from fearful to fearless because she is fierce in her optimism that things can always be better. Her nonthreatening size and resilient way inspires people to be their big and brave selves and see the positive even in difficult situations. People laugh because she never walks; she's always running. Laughter is healing and its energy opens space to engage in life with a lighter heart. While other horses may be plodding along quietly, Tess is almost skipping.

Tess's Contribution to Corporate America

Margo is a well-respected attorney, and Executive Vice President in a highly successful global company, but long before that, Margo was a girl in love with horses. As a young girl, Margo spent long hours playing and talking and hanging out with her pony. She intuitively knew her most precious secrets were safe with her pony and his with her.

Margo came to Pebble Ledge Ranch for executive coaching and to think through some important professional life choices. She came seeking some human guidance but knew that she was most clear thinking around horses so chose Tess the Shetland pony to help her through her dilemma. Margo, like Tess the pony, is small in size but big in her authentic presence and influence in the "herds" of her life.

In the presence of Tess and open space of the pasture, Margo was able to think more clearly, listen to her heart and tap into her intuition.

"I always trusted the wisdom of horses and I knew that Tess, in her persistence and ability to think for herself, was the perfect thought partner for me."

"Surprisingly," Margo reflected to me, "in the presence of Tess, the questions that emerged from within me were not the ones I came with. Initially, my question was, How can I do my job with more ease and less stress and how can I be a more effective and smart working boss in my law department? But looking into Tess's clear eyes and stroking her small but powerful body, I found myself asking deeper questions: What do I want my life to be about? What makes me happy? How can I contribute my best? What is my purpose in life and how can I bring my talent and passion for law to serve the people in organizations in which I work?

"Tess seemed to know when I was being authentic, being myself, even before I did. I sometimes forget who I am by working too many hours or moving too fast or by saying yes when maybe I should say no. Tess, in her horse sense way, reminded me that in my work, it is essential to stay present when there is conflict, listen with more patience and empathy and to move more slowly and gently in complex and sensitive situations.

"In the authentic presence of Tess, I realized that when I have a decision to ponder or need some peaceful downtime or just need to hear myself think, I know what I need to do. Okay Margo, I have to tell myself. It's time to head for the quiet of the pasture and the comfort and wise way of a horse."

While Tess is comfortable relating to powerful professionals like Margo, her first love is young children. When a baby or young child enters the pasture Tess is the first to run over and gently greet the young person. She will follow kids around having endless patience with their curiosity and tiny fingers that explore her face. One day when my year-old granddaughter Natalie was in the pasture in her stroller, Tess came up from behind and using her chest and nose helped me push her stroller through the field. She joyfully follows tiny toddler steps or exuberant little kid leaps, watching over them as she would her own young. She, like many horses, seems to have respect and care for that which is vulnerable, innocent and loving in spirit.

She is happier in her home her at Pebble Ledge Ranch where she has freedom of expression and she is happier in her job than working her previous gig. As a child's birthday party pony being told exactly what to do, no one was ever interested in her opinion, and she didn't have much choice about living in a way that was in rhythm with her nature.

Tess now has a family, herd and field where she belongs. She has a job where who she is and what she does is essential. She has a life that both matters to her and contributes to the well-being of others. Tess, as all horses naturally do, lives with authentic presence, being who she is and living the life she knows that she was meant to live. Tess believes in herself, and as important, with open heart, abundant generosity and indomitable spirit, she believes in everyone.

HOLLY

"Slow down you move too fast..
got to make the morning last
Looking for fun and feeling groovy...
Life, I love you, All is groovy"

Simon and Garfunkle, singers, songwriters

Holly

> *"I asked the Zebra,*
> *are you black with white stripes?*
> *Or white with black stripes?*
> *And the zebra asked me,*
> *Are you good with bad habits?*
> *Or are you bad with good habits?"*
> —Shel Silverstein

I am an energetic, fun-loving, sweet, curious and courageous zebra mare who turned six years old on my birthday in 2016. Living in a horse herd and human world in Cleveland, Ohio is very different from the African Savannah.

I am the first generation of my family born into captivity. My parents were brought to the United States against their will. I was conceived and born in Florida. Before my parents could raise me in the ways of the zebra herd I was cruelly taken from them at only three months of age. I was shipped in a large trailer with other frightened animals on an arduous journey to Ohio where I was to be bred and have babies to be raised by humans as exotic pets.

I knew in my zebra soul this was not my path. In great distress, I called out for help through what Jackie calls the "heart and hoof-wide web" to the Pebble Ledge horse ranch and herd, since there were no zebra herds nearby. Thankfully, my cry to be rescued was heard and the next morning two white women showed up at my stable. They didn't look African, but they approached slowly, spoke quietly and seemed kind enough, so things were looking up. I hoped that they were my ride to a herd and the next best place to home on the African Plains. They took me for a walk on my lead line and I was on my best behavior. It seemed to be going well.

They assured me all would be okay and they would be back to get me soon. I slept well that night and first thing the next morning, one of the women returned with a man who looked a bit skeptical. No problem, I thought. I looked him right in the eye, batted my long eyelashes at him and sent love from my heart. Soon I was out of the hands of the exotic animal broker and on my way to my new home and herd mates. I arrived at Pebble Ledge Ranch on a sunny, unseasonably warm day. Jackie, my new friend and foster mom, led me to a small but beautiful fenced orchard, a few apples still hanging on a tree, adjoining a large horse pasture. From the other side of the fence, six giant horses, bigger than any zebra I had ever seen, stared at me. I am doomed I thought. But much to my amazement and relief, they turned and ran away as if I might be the dangerous predator. They galloped to the far corner of the twenty- acre field and all turned at once, standing like statues in a line, and glared back at me. I began to zebra wail; this was all too much for me. The horses kept their distance, but Jackie and Herb, my human rescuers moved closer to me. Herb looked at Jackie and said with a grin, "She's yours."

Jackie disappeared, but quickly returned with some hay and water for me, and a sleeping bag and a few books for her. She gave me my space, staying at the far end of the orchard, but did not leave me all alone. I slowly approached her with curiosity when I noticed that she was asleep, sitting on the ground leaning against the fence. I walked cautiously over to her, gave her a sniff and lay down next to her, curling up with my head on her lap, using it as a pillow.

We both woke up to Herb standing outside the fence taking our pictures. Jackie stayed with me for a few days and I was okay with her leaving for short periods of time, but called to her if she was gone too long. Soon a few other women arrived to keep me company. I quickly adopted them, especially Lisa and Linda, as aunts, sisters and grandmothers.

I was building a herd but missing my equine herd of zebras. The horses were coming closer but with grave suspicion. One of the elder horses, Thunderheart, wandered closer with compassion in his eye and kindness in his heart. He was all white—seriously missing his black stripes—but he was half way there. I quickly figured out that if I loudly sounded my mournful zebra cry, he would stand next to the fence and I would feel safe and not so alone. Fortunately, Jackie noticed that Thunderheart had become my guardian and she brought him into my new home in the orchard. He looked down at me with curiosity, gave me a few questioning sniffs and seemed to decide though different I was okay. He nudged me gently, and in horse language similar to yet different from zebra language, he let me know he was here to watch over me. I was so relieved and grateful to have my first friend and protector in the herd. I relaxed and leaned my body against his warm furry flank and was soon fast asleep.

In the next few days, I was introduced to the other horse herd members who much to my surprise and delight greeted me warmly and protectively as the precious newly arrived baby of the herd. Jackie looked relieved that I had been welcomed so quickly and generously by the herd. I have come to know that sometimes it is not so easy for a newcomer to be accepted in the herd, as there are lots of rules you need to know to become a valued herd member.

I was not sure what Jackie meant when she turned to me and said, "Holly you are a zebra with a proud heritage. You are not a painted pony. You have a home here and all you need to do is be your authentic zebra self."

I felt a little sad; this was not my zebra family, nor my African savannah home, but I had the beginning stirrings of happiness. I had a welcoming horse and human herd, a safe new place to live and an invitation to be authentically me, Holly the zebra.

Now, many years later, I know that I am more than a pony with stripes; I am a proud zebra who has earned her stripes. When I had my first birthday, complete with horse treats, I began taking to take care of Thunderheart like he was my grandfather, watching over him and out for him as he was aging. At my second birthday, I found myself grieving and guarding over him, thanking him and honoring him as he died.

Learning about love from Thunderheart, compassion from the herd, and remembering the healing wisdom of Africa, I have become the Medicine Mare Zebra in the herd. I tend to sick horses in the herd and stay with them till they feel better. I bring healing to the humans who are lost and help them find their way safely home. I offer humor and playfulness as healing medicine; people laugh with me and their heavy hearts lighten and their spirit becomes whole again.

Celebrating individual uniqueness and collective tribal wisdom, I bring the essential values of difference and inclusiveness to the horse and human herd. I am always watching out for the herd, and I really enjoy stirring things up with my lively and mischievous nature. Most important to me, I remind people that when we are able to adapt to unexpected change and find a herd to help us be who we are, we can thrive in unexpected places. More than we think is possible can become our new reality."

Holly the Courageous Zebra (Much More Than A Pony With Stripes)

Holly, a zebra, arrived at Pebble Ledge Ranch in the fall of 2009. Only four months old, she was seriously in need of a home and a herd. In the time she has been with us, she has found her place in the hearts of all of us. She is of the wild and is sensitively in tune with the environment and life around her. While zebras are of the horse family, their instincts and personalities are quite different.

Holly listens to her ancestral wisdom and knows that her survival and well-being are dependent upon belonging and being accepted as a member of the wise collective called "the herd."

She is a first-generation American. Her parents were captured and brought over from the wild of Africa, and though Holly has adjusted to her more tame life, she still answers to the call of the wild. Before we decided to take Holly in as a baby zebra rescue, I contacted the Cleveland Zoo to learn about the requirements and responsibilities of caring for a baby zebra. We at Spirit of Leadership had the previous week facilitated at the ranch a leadership-with-the- horses retreat for the zoo, so I called them to ask who could tell me something about the care of zebras. I was referred to Adam who was responsible for the care of the animals in the Savannah area of the Cleveland Zoo. He told me that in Ohio, zebras were considered equines, so no special permit was required; if we had a friendly herd of horses to take her in, she would be okay. Believing that Holly belonged in the wild—free, naturally alive and being her authentic zebra self—I asked how much it would cost to return her home to Africa. I was willing to raise the money to return her home to the wild. Adam recommended that I just do my best to give her a home on our ranch, as she probably would not survive the journey back; and if she did, she would probably not be prepared to survive in the wild.

Pebble Ledge Ranch has become her home. She has learned from the horses that in this place, humans are safe and can be trusted to do her no harm; and, in fact, are honest with her and loving toward her.

I think she learned to be comfortable with humans in part from the horses because zebras have the reputation as one of the most dangerous animals in a zoo, at least for zookeepers. Zebras have a reputation for being mean and unable to be socialized. They will kick or bite, and they will attack you. That is not our experience with Holly.

When Holly came to the ranch, we told her, "All you have to be is a zebra. You are not a striped pony. We will not train you, halter you or lead you around. You can freely live here. We will care for you as best we can in accordance with your zebra nature. You will have a place to live." What a gift it would be for all of us humans to be free to live according to our nature and be confident and feel safe enough to show our true stripes.

In the beginning, I thought that we would never see Holly roaming our twenty-acre pasture. I expected that she would be hanging out at the far end of the field or hiding in the trees. Much to our delight, Holly chose to be visible and not hide her stripes. She generally can be found right in the center of what is happening, both in the horse herd and human herd.

Slowly, Holly has reached a point where she is very social with people. The higher the number people in a group that arrives at Pebble Ledge Ranch, the more comfortable Holly seems to be. It may be because a large group of humans seems more like a herd. Zebras are used to hanging out with a lot of other zebras. They roam and they rest together. They are not accustomed to being alone. A zebra alone in the wild is in great danger. Holly seems to assume that big groups are natural. She sometimes gets suspicious when only one or two humans are around.

Holly is a great example of the best of diversity and inclusion. She is recognized by the horses as different, and her difference is of great value to the herd. They have taken her into the herd not only for what they have to offer her, but also for what she has to offer them.

It might be evident what a herd of seven horses can offer her—protection, companionship, and a place in the herd. I have been more interested in understanding what Holly brings to the herd.

Holly, as the minority member, offers unique perspectives and added value to the majority. It seems that she awakens more of their primitive instincts and life skills, offering the herd opportunities to be more of the wild than they could be without her. Holly's ability to be herself—with courage, determination and playful persistence—strengthened the herd's capacity to be resilient, adaptable, empathetic and generous. How might our world be a better place for us all if we all could learn to be more inclusive like Holly and the herd?

Holly Arrives At the Ranch

The story begins on Halloween in 2010. A group of people was gathered at the ranch for a workshop on making horse masks. Animal masks are a Native American tradition, as well as a tradition in Mongolia. People design an animal mask as a way to step into their power, to find their qualities, or to honor something about themselves. Often, Native American tribes would create a mask inspired by their horses, or for the horses that were going to carry them into a hunt or into a new place that would require strength and character. Usually, the masks represent a person's best qualities, though sometimes they would represent the horse's best qualities, which would also help the person find their own.

On that rainy, cold Halloween evening, we had gathered to spend time with the horses for inspiration, and then planned to go back into the house to make our masks. We all were sitting in an enclosed horse area. Bea, our lead mare, was the first to walk in and join us, and minutes later all the other horses followed her. The horses circled around Bea; then, one at a time, five horses lay down in a circle around her. One horse, Thunderheart, remained standing at the door, like a guard. Bea, in the middle of the circle, seemed as if she were meditating or dreaming. This lasted for about an hour. When all the horses stood up, except Bea, who was still lying down snoring, we left for the cottage to make masks.

Later that night, I was doing research on the Internet, looking for explanations about what horses mean in dreams in preparation for a workshop with the horses to help people understand their dreams and see more clearly their visions. One link I found said, *"A zebra is a dream of a horse."* I followed that link to one that said, *"Laid-back baby zebra needs a home."* I clicked on that link knowing a homeless zebra could be anywhere in the world. To my amazement, the baby zebra was in a small town, Canfield, about forty-five minutes from our ranch.

My good friend Lisa and I went to meet Holly the homeless baby zebra. She was alone in a huge barn that looked more like a cathedral than a barn with its stained glass windows and gas lamps. Wearing a lavender halter and tied to the wall of her stall with a lavender rope she stood quietly. She seemed calm and gentle despite being a zebra of the wild. She was about the size of a Great Dane dog. I walked her up and down the barn aisle and, though frightened, she willing walked with me. I think even a human walking with her was better than being alone and tied to a wall. She touched my heart and I knew we had to rescue her from her current circumstance and bring her home to the ranch to be cared for by the Pebble Ledge horse and human herd. We returned her to her stall and told the man who owned her that we would pay her way out and would be back for her the next day.

On our way back to the ranch, we stopped in a small town called Chagrin Falls to consult with our friend Cynthia, the local psychic and wise woman. We walked into her art gallery and she looked at us; and, before we could speak she said, "The answer is yes." We told Cynthia the name: Holly. "Perfect," she said, "It's the name of a holy plant, don't change it."

We then told Cynthia of our morning adventure and she laughed. "The answer is still yes," she said, "and her name needs to remain Holly."

Our next stop was my husband's office at the ranch. I walked into his office and without looking up he said, "No more horses."

"It's not a horse," I replied, "it's a zebra." "Right," he said.

"Just come meet her," I suggested.

"Tomorrow I'll go with you to meet the zebra, but just so you know, I think this is a bad idea. We're not a petting zoo, and besides, zebras are wild animals and they're dangerous."

The next morning I discovered several articles on the breakfast table about killer zebras in zoos and circuses.

I had tried to borrow a trailer, but all my friends who had trailers were busy. I called the zebra's owner and told him my husband was coming out to meet the zebra but we had no trailer to bring her home that morning.

"How likely is it that you will take the zebra?" he asked.

"90% yes from me and 10% yes from my husband," I answered.

"I'll take those odds," he said, "and I'll have a trailer waiting."

We arrived at the cathedral barn and walked down the long aisle to Holly's stall. There she stood quietly, tied by her lavender rope. She turned around and batted her extra long eyelashes at Herb; it was love at first sight for both of them.

An hour later Holly walked off the trailer and our zebra adventure began.

We all believe that Bea and our herd, hearing Holly's frightened zebra cry for help, was responsible for her coming to the ranch. We think it all began on that cold Halloween evening when Bea and the horses formed a circle, and communicating through the heart and hoof-wide web, dreamed her here to the ranch and into the herd. A week after the Halloween ceremony, Holly was happily living at the ranch.

Zebras typically stay with their mother until they are about two years old. Holly was about three months old, just a baby, when she was transported from Florida to Ohio. She had probably been away from her mom for about a month when she arrived at Pebble Ledge Ranch.

When we got her home, we put Holly into a small orchard surrounded by a fence. The horses, on the other side of the fence, got their first look at the tiny zebra and all ran to the far end of the twenty-acre pasture, where they stood in a line, just watching. Clearly, they sensed that even though she was small, she could be dangerous. She looked different. She made a funny noise. Her smell was different. They all stood there watching her, and she started to cry, a high-pitched cry that did not stop until I went into orchard with her.

I moved into her paddock with a sleeping bag and some books for two days. I cleared my work schedule. About half way through the first day, I was reading, lying on the ground, and I fell asleep. When I awoke, Holly was curled up next to me, sleeping. After that, she followed me everywhere. I was the closest thing to mom.

Whenever I would leave, Holly would cry, so I would go back in, then leave for a few minutes, and go back in for a couple of hours. Little by little, the horses would walk closer to us. I watched over Holly and waited for the herd to act. One day, Thunderheart, our grandfather horse, walked to the fence between Holly and the herd. He stood quietly next to the fence. She stood nearby. He seemed to be watching over her, so I left, and she began to cry. He moved even closer to Holly, and seemed to take the watch until I came back. When she settled down, he walked away.

Later, when I left Holly, Thunderheart would return. This went on for several days. Then I introduced Rojo and brought her into the paddock. Rojo, our oldest horse and mare, was the closest thing to a mom. Rojo started to teach Holly about being a herd member, kind of moving her around as a mother mare will do, but Holly was terrified, as Rojo was not warm and cuddly.

I led Rojo out and brought Thunderheart back in. Mostly, he stood quietly, not asking anything of Holly. I put some food out. He ate; she ate with some distance between them.

Soon, she moved closer to him, then closer still. He stood, not paying any attention to her. They seemed safe, so I left for a while to give them a chance to bond. When I returned, Holly was sleeping, leaning against Thunderheart's side. From then on, he was her caretaker. He would watch over her. He stayed with her, fenced off from the other horses for about a week, as the others began walking over to the fence to see what was going on. I brought them into the paddock one at a time, starting with the horses that seemed the least assertive, until Holly had met them all. Then, I put Holly out with the herd, and they all seemed to take care of her.

Holly did not receive the kind of testing that horses get when they come into a herd, such as being chased away or being required to learn the language of the herd. The horses seemed to accept her for who she was. When they started running or were playing rough in a way that Thunderheart thought might be dangerous for Holly, he would separate her from them. Thunderheart would move her to the side, let the horses run through the gate, and then go back to bring Holly in after everybody else was inside. Or, when the horses were heading out to the pasture, Thunderheart would wait until everybody left before he took her out, making sure that she wasn't in any of the typical horse chaos.

When Holly was about eighteen months old, the relationship began to change, as Thunderheart was nearing the end of his life. Zebras need their moms until they are two, so I told Thunderheart, "You need to stay around until she is at least two."

In the final months of Thunderheart's life, the roles had reversed and Holly would guide him out of the way when the herd would get active. She always knew where he was, even when she would go out into the field with the horses, as she was becoming buddies with others. I believe that when Thunderheart realized that Holly was fully integrated into the herd, that she had other protectors, and that none of the horses were overly aggressive toward her, he passed on.

One evening while out in the field, Thunderheart lay weakly on the ground preparing to die as the other horses circled around him. When it got dark, the other horses headed back to the barn, but Holly stayed with us in the field, out there in the dark, keeping him company as he died. Holly called for Thunderheart all through the night. For the next two or three weeks, she would walk out into the pasture to where she last saw him alive, and she would look for him and call him. She stood, ears forward, listening for him, and when she heard the horse whisper of his spirit, only then would she join the rest of the herd.

Holly and The Gang

Holly soon began to test her power and influence in the herd. She first developed a relationship with Spirit, and they are still like sisters—playing a bit, arguing some. They have their conflicts. Sometimes Holly chases Spirit around, or she won't let her into the paddock, like a human child not letting her sister into their shared room. It doesn't matter that Holly is the younger one; she thinks she has the power and Spirit humors her. Sometimes, she is affectionate toward Spirit, but other times, if Spirit doesn't do what she wants, Holly chases her.

The other horse in a relationship with Holly is Raven, the big Friesian. He was Holly's first love. In an adolescent way, Holly would initiate a kind of amorous horseplay. She would nip at him, tease him, and get him to follow her, and then see if she could persuade him to groom her. Then, if he didn't do it just like she wanted, she would kick at him or bite him. He would walk away, not sure what to do. She would go after him, and let him try it again until he got it right. Now, Raven will do pretty much anything she asks him to. They are good friends. Sometimes she will kiss him on the nose. Many nights, she will walk to stand next to him as darkness is setting in, looking to him for protection. Raven is now one of Holly's best playmates.

Holly's relationship with Bea, the lead mare, is respectful. If Bea looks over and tells her to move, Holly will move. Every once in awhile, I see Holly challenge Bea, and Bea will lean her shoulder into Holly, and give her a big bump. Holly will run, and the communication of "Now you know who is in charge here" will last for quite awhile.

Toby, the stallion of the herd, has the most power and influence. Holly won't cross him; she knows she has to listen to him and behave. When he looks at her, she will move away or will stop doing whatever she is doing. If she is being respectful, Toby will let Holly eat with him. If she's not, he will chase her away.

Holly likes Chief Silver Cloud and will follow him around. When she tries to get his food, he looks at her as if he is saying, "Really? You know, I'm 2,300 pounds, and you are 300 pounds, don't you?" He tolerates her antics, so she is more playful with him than with Toby or Bea, who won't put up with it. Chief Silver Cloud is more like an uncle or a big brother who tolerates the youngsters.

When Tess the tiny pony arrived at the ranch, Holly, no longer being the smallest in the herd, was more than a little excited. She was the first to run up, but she didn't run up in a friendly way. She bared her teeth and pinned her ears, as if she was protecting the herd against a predator. I separated them, and this went on, her charging the fence with her ears back, for probably a day. Then, I noticed Holly standing quietly, so something had changed. I took Holly to join the pony and they became fast friends. Holly kicked up her heels and ran round and round Tess while Tess just stood her ground, watching Holly with a kind of amusement.

Holly and Tess often get into mischief together, maybe because they are about the same size, small with big attitudes. Holly was the one to show Tess around and to bring her into the herd. They are the best of friends and can often be seen playing in the pasture in what looks like a lively game of tag.

The newest horse to the herd, Big Boy Tamarack, better known as Bud, is one of our biggest and strongest horses having recently retired to the ranch from a logging career in Montana. When we introduced Bud to the herd, Holly was the first in the herd to engage with him, staying with him when none of the other horses were interested.

Bud tends to like his space and Holly generally gives it to him. One day when the horses were standing sleeping in the pasture, Holly decided to take a shortcut to where she was going and ran right under Bud's belly to get there. Bud opened one eye and looked at her, seeming to say, "What were you thinking?" But in his quiet gentle way, he let her get away with it.

Holly is now clearly in the heart of the herd, one of the family at the ranch: in her striped uniform, she's an active member of the Spirit of Leadership team, and she loves children. If we have a group of kids at the ranch, Holly thinks they are her herd to play with. She will go into herd behavior, trying to take over and get them herded up to go where she wants them to go.

She is also the watchdog of the herd. Whenever she senses danger in the pasture, such as a deer or coyote, Holly is the first to run out with her ears up, moving toward trouble and warning it off. She doesn't watch and run the other way; she watches and steps out to greet it. Here's this little 300-pound zebra that is protecting a herd of big draft horses.

She is perceptive. When a group of Israeli army officers was at the ranch one January, Holly walked over to where they were standing. This was a pretty tough group of women commanders. They talked about themselves as being like big cacti, prickly on the outside but sweet on the inside. They said they have to be tough in their jobs, but that they have warm hearts toward the soldiers under their command.

One of the commanders approached Holly, who gave her a kiss on the nose. The commander started to cry, and Holly gave her another kiss. "I'm really not sure why I'm crying," said the commander. "It's just that I am so touched by her seeing past my tough exterior. I feel like she sees into the sweet and gentle woman I am on the inside."

Adaptability and Resiliency

Holly's adaptability and resiliency is amazing; she's always making the best of every situation. She has come into a herd of horses, into the human world, and into a physical world that is quite different from the one of her zebra family. She reached out, with curiosity, for new relationships, challenges and opportunities.

Holly adapted physically to a new climate. In winter, she grows a thicker coat and, as zebras can, grows an extra layer of fat and muscle under her black stripes. Her skin absorbs whatever heat is in the air. The white of her coat reflects it back, which works thermodynamically like a layer of heat above her coat. She grows a long, oily coat to keep her dry, and a kind of a down underneath that. On particularly cold and windy winter days she strategically positions herself between two of the larger furry horses and stays cozy and warm.

In summer she sheds her winter coat and her body absorbs the fat of the black, so that the white stands out. The white reflects the heat, working as a cooler. The stripes also keep insects off her, as flies think that she is moving. Most flies and insects prefer to land on a plain surface rather than a striped surface, which protected the zebra from the tzitzi fly in Africa.

Zebras with the most stripes survived, and it works for Holly now. Sometimes, when the horses are out in the pasture covered in flies, Holly is standing without any flies at all. This is part of her physical adaptability.

The ability to adapt to changing conditions relatively quickly is a huge plus for animals in the wild. We might call this in our human world causal analysis, the ability to accurately understand the causes of a dilemma and respond accurately. Humans can sometimes adapt to changing conditions, but for us the question is often how fast can we adapt? We might be able to adapt to cold, or perhaps even an ice age, over several generations. But if we can't figure out how to do that relatively quickly, our solution may be too late. True adaptability is very quick, very much in the present moment and comprehensively to present conditions in order to be prepared when the future arrives.

Another resiliency factor that Holly demonstrates is empathy, the ability to read cues to emotional and physical states. Holly helps humans see that people who are different—who feel lost or ashamed or alienated by their difference from their family, for instance, or from their organization—can begin to see the value in their uniqueness.

Holly's confidence in her ability to belong by owning her difference inspires people to celebrate their difference rather than hiding from it. In Holly's presence they realize that they can still belong while continuing to "own" their own stripes. They can own their uniqueness. They can own their individuality, and yet belong. People do not have to blend in with everybody else in order to be authentic; in fact, they often can't blend in and still be themselves.

How do we adapt while maintaining the authentic essence of who we are?

Holly is different from the rest of the herd because she is not a horse. She is not a pony with stripes, and she never will be. But that doesn't keep her from finding a way to belong. She belongs by living with authentic presence.

We have a slogan at the ranch, "Herds are inclusive; everyone belongs, everyone is essential, everyone matters." Everyone needs a place to call home, where they feel safe, accepted, and welcomed, they can grow, they can make mistakes, and they can learn about who they are. Everyone is essential. Everyone has his own unique contribution that no one else has.

Holly brings to the herd what no one else ever will bring. What she brings has become essential to the well-being of the herd.

Everyone matters. Everyone needs to know that someone is watching out for them, that their absence would be noticed, that their presence is recognized, that in some way, the herd is no longer who they are without them.

Inclusiveness is not just acceptance. It is about advancing to be more than we were without the difference, being impacted by that difference. Inclusiveness is core to authentic presence as we offer our best true self when we are open to the gift of relationship with the best true selves of others.

A gift is not a gift unless it keeps giving; otherwise, it becomes a possession. Holly teaches us the difference between being a possession and being a gift. A gift is given freely; we give something without strings attached. Holly can sense when a human has an expectation from her. If she feels that you have an agenda for her, she will not come over to you. She will go the other way. On the other hand, if you are openly curious and are offering an invitation in which she has the freedom to make the choice of whether to come to you or not, and you will be unconditionally accepting of her choice, whatever it is, she often comes toward you. She will freely offer the gift of authentic connection.

Holly is very sensitive and particular about her personal space. Someone might be waiting for Holly to walk over, trying to attract her. They might click at her, call her name. They may be smiling, trying to get her to move. It generally does not work.

For Holly, it's the sort of thing that people sometimes experience in a handshake when someone crosses the centerline into your personal space. Maybe the person calling to Holly is friendly and honest, but still, it's all about that person's desires, not Holly's. Holly senses the person's desire through body language or in their eyes. They may be in her space. They often have not taken into consideration what Holly wants.

If the person's greeting shifts to, "Well, I only want you to come over if you want to come over. I am here. I am available, and if you don't come over, it's absolutely fine." This approach leaves an opening to receive Holly's advance, rather than moving toward Holly. It's about moving back, not forward. Sometimes, you can step back without moving back. This dance is about your intention. Your body language and your intention have to match. If you step back to give her space in your intention and in your physical space, she usually will walk toward you.

She may not come all the way to you, but she may; she may even let you scratch her and have a zebra kiss.

Holly offers great biofeedback on your authentic presence because you can't fool her.

You can't pretend. You can't fake it. You really have to be who you are and let go of attachment in order to get her come to you.

I think that sometimes in life we find it difficult to let go of the fear that we won't get something that we want and find it challenging to come to peace with accepting the outcome if something we want to happen doesn't.

This is similar to what I was talking to a client about: You have to be willing to celebrate when things come to you as equally as when they don't come to you. When you reach that moment of celebrating that Holly didn't come to you, she will then often come.

When Holly chooses to join you, the experience is that you earned the relationship. She is there because she wants to be there, not just because you want her to be there. It's a gift of non-attachment that implies, as Holly would say, "I am here for you because I want to be here, no one made me be here. I am a wild creature who has chosen to be with you of my own free will."

This is a privilege. Once you have experienced that privilege, it changes you because you know what it feels like. It's a touchstone for other parts of our lives when things are out of control or not going the way we want them to. We can remember that there is a place inside us where we can simply let go and release. Resiliency and realistic optimism is the belief that things can change for the better and that while we might not be able to control life, we can control the direction of our lives. The zebra factor—if we can have one moment of that experience, it opens us in a new way to our own humanness.

Holly played a very important role is helping Dawn, the championship ice skater, develop more resiliency by helping her be better able to bounce back from adversity. Dawn arrived at the ranch that day feeling hopeless because she had not met her goal of performing at her best and scoring high in her most recent competition. The horses and Holly were at the far end of the field as Dawn shared with me her frustrations and fear of failing. Dawn had another goal, seemingly unrelated to skating, but important to her, and that was to get close to Holly. Just like her highest skating goal, the goal to achieve closeness to Holly was just out of reach. As Dawn compared her discouragement to connecting with Holly to her discouragement with her skating performance Holly began to make her way across the field at a brisk trot in Dawn's direction. She walked right up to Dawn, gave her a nudge with her nose, offered a quick zebra kiss and leaned against Dawn's side asking for a zebra scratch.

Dawn's face brightened as she smiled. "Giving up is not an option," she said. "That is Holly's message to me."

Holly helped Dawn find the true meaning of success with zebra courage and common sense. Holly gave Dawn valuable zebra coaching: stay calm under pressure, shut out distractions, own your competency and confidence, and although things are out of your control, you can always discover something of the best from the worst. Holly reawakened Dawn's heart to her passion for skating. She reminded Dawn that there is nothing more resilient, powerful and inspiring than the human spirit when you reach toward what you love.

We prepare people for their experience with the herd as if they are coming into a different culture.

When we prepare them to meet the horses and zebra, we tell people about what we have observed in being around them, about their language, their culture, and their dynamic, We explain how they manage new herd members coming in, and what they expect of us as new herd members entering their world.

A zebra has a set of cultural norms and body language similar to that of horses, yet it is also quite different. We learned the differences by listening to Holly and letting her teach us about herself. Some of what we had been told about zebras were assumptions that may be true about some zebras, but aren't true about all zebras and were not true about Holly.

One expectation was that zebras are nasty and that you can't train them. We found that Holly is quite capable of learning. She can be very social and friendly to people. We were told that zebras don't jump, they crawl under fences; but twice Holly has jumped the fence because she wanted to join the herd on the other side of the paddock. She showed us that she could jump when she's motivated to do so.

We all have assumptions that we consider "truth," but Holly reminds us to pay attention and be open to challenging our assumptions because they may get in the way of seeing what's really happening and the more essential meaning.

We tell clients about Holly's unique language. For instance, if you approach her like you might approach a horse with your hand outstretched, she might see that hand as a spear or a tiger's eyes. She will run. But if you are quiet, and you offer a non-threatening presence in your body language and your thoughts, and you don't invade her space, she will approach you. If she is approaching you, and because you are afraid, you back away from her (people sometimes are afraid of her), she will will often come toward you with gentle curiosity because you have given her space. The result is that she may walk away from people who love animals, but may go right over the person who is a bit reticent and backs away.

We say, "If Holly is coming too close to you, simply raise your hands towards her. This is what a horse might do—stick its neck out as if to say, "Back off," and she will respond to that. If you put your hands out slowly, as if you are moving toward her, she will move back. If you start flailing around, she will take off running.

This example helps people realize how much of our energy is involved in communication.

Holly has a variety of ways to help us learn to be more resilient. She helps us learn to regulate our emotions and energy and to manage our impulses. It's a lesson about being confident and in charge of your own space in a way that doesn't disrupt the relationship between you and others. Telling Holly that you don't want her to go away forever, but you are just asking her to back off a bit, is a learning experience. She's good at teaching us about the necessity of space and emotional regulation in relationship.

Holly also teaches us to slow down, manage our reactions and be calm even when excited. Like the horses, Holly teaches us about resilience in times of challenge and about mindfulness in her peaceful silence, in her quiet authentic nature This silence is not just the absence of sound—a quieting outside—but also a quieting inside. If you move slowly, you are more aware of what's going on in the moment. In the calm, you can communicate with Holly, you can read her communication. If you're moving quickly and you're noisy, you will miss all the cues that she is giving you.

When we are mindful, when we slow down, when we listen to the quiet and not the chatter, we tend to open our hearts and become present in the moment. Then, we are able to receive information that ordinarily is not accessible to us. Often, this is the most pertinent information. In relationships with Holly and with the horses, the more quiet and subtle we are on the inside, the more we are able to be in relationship them and with ourselves.

When the farrier-blacksmith arrives at the ranch, we bring the horses into a shed one at a time to get their hooves trimmed. The other horses remain free to wander around to do whatever they want wherever they choose.

That is all except for Holly who watches over each horse's blacksmith appointment, keeping them company and making sure they are safe. She walks in where the blacksmith is working as he gets out his tools; he makes lots of noise but Holly just stands quietly, unafraid. I know when she is afraid because her tail swishes. After the blacksmith is finished, Holly walks out with the horse and then comes back in with the next horse. She never leaves any horse by itself. She is the member of the herd that makes certain that no one is ever left alone. I can't compare Holly's behavior to zebra behavior in general. She is the only zebra I know. But this may illustrate the zebra factor of inclusion, resiliency and optimism.

Tending to the Herd

Holly took on the role of caretaker for Lily, an elder horse, just before Lily died. Her role was remarkable.

In Lily's last days, she would lie down to rest, and then have difficulty getting up because of her arthritis. She would lose feeling in her legs and then be unable to stand. Holly would walk over to Lily and use her mouth and her teeth on each of Lily's legs individually, moving them around to get blood circulation going again. She would use her body to rock Lily to get her moving, and then she would give one big shove to try to get Lily up.

Usually, the first time that Lily tried to stand up she couldn't, so she would lie back down. Holly would wait about five minutes, and then start the process all over again. She would use her teeth to work from Lily's ears all the way down her spine to her tail, moving like a chiropractor would, and then she would rock Lily again to get her circulation going. By the second time Holly gave her another big shove, Lily could get to her feet.

I started to film this the second time I saw it happen. Then, part way through the filming, I felt disrespectful, and so I stopped. But I do have pictures of it in my heart.

Once Lily was standing up, Holly would nip at her until she walked forward herding Lily to the water trough for a drink of water; she would wait for her, and then guide her back out into the field with the rest of the herd. Sometimes later in the day, the same thing would happen. Holly stayed with Lily for a whole week tending to her like a hospice nurse.

One evening, as I left Lily in the paddock with the other horses and walked into the house, I had the sense that it was going to be Lily's last night. So, I went back out to say "goodbye," to tell her that I cared, that I appreciated what she had offered of herself, and to let her know that it okay for her to go.

When I came back out in early the morning, Lily was lying on the ground, having passed away during the night under a full moon. There were no signs of struggle. When I got there, Holly was standing over her, and stayed with her until we moved the body. Holly trumpeted sharp zebra calls, almost like someone playing "Taps" over the body, before she joined the rest of the herd.

Bea may be the leader of the herd, but Holly has become the busiest. She takes on the most herd work responsibilities and a variety of roles that help we humans be better people.

One day, we had two groups at the ranch. One was a positive psychology group. These are people who work with organizations to reach their potential by using a positive approach.

The other group was working in non-violent communication.

We used the same exercise with each group that I have used with schoolchildren. Their task was to be a good zebra herd. If they could learn to be a good zebra herd, Holly would join them. To be a zebra herd, people needed to stand relatively close together and walk in rhythm with one another, keeping a peaceful positive attitude among themselves.

The positive psychology folks and the non-violent communications people had the challenge of walking three or four people across in a tight line across the horse pasture, about twenty people total. We asked each of them to find something that they appreciated about the person in front of them, the person behind them, and anyone next to them in order to create zebra herd harmony.

They had to continue that appreciation, whatever it was. It might be that they liked a person's smile or that the person was walking with purpose, or that they had a good work ethic. They were instructed not to focus on what they didn't like. The key was for everyone to have a positive vibe, a resonance of positivity. They each needed to value the people around them for who they were so they could work together, all moving harmoniously in the same direction. If the group was successful, Holly would join them.

Once they got moving collectively and coherently together, much to their delight Holly joined their herd, following closely behind the last person in line. She moved with them every time they moved, wherever they went, following them through gates and around the field.

Holly showed them that attitude is everything. Groups of people often do not realize the power they have when everyone is moving in the same direction with positive appreciation for one another, and for each other's well being. Other people often want to join this kind of group because it actually gets somewhere in a meaningful and heartfelt way.

Teaching Humans About Group Behavior

We never pair Holly with a client as we might one of the horses. She gets to go wherever she wants to go. She is predictably unpredictable, and with her we have learned to expect the unexpected such as chasing bubbles or our barn cat for fun, or chasing coyotes to protect the herd. She might cheer people up when they're down, or help an elderly horse get up when it's been struggling to get off the ground.

Holly is often the catalyst for group focus. She senses when there is disharmony. She tends to turn her attention to a group where members seem to be out of sync with one another. They might be arguing or simply not paying attention; perhaps they are texting. Holly will walk over to the group, and as soon as she does, all the attention, all the focus, turns to her. Now, the group is more of a team. At the very least, the group now has one common focus. Once they have that focus, the conversation changes, and they can focus as a team on other things.

As a group leader, you never know what is going to catalyze a team, but you have to find something of interest to the whole group, even if it's not the task at hand. Once you have the interest, the awareness, and the cooperation of the whole group about something they have passion or curiosity about, you then have a team that can focus on a task in a different way. You've shifted the way they are together. Holly often shifts the way people are together. When there is disharmony, she comes in and creates a distraction so people pay attention; then, the group is in harmony again.

I think that Holly's senses of harmony and disharmony are associated with how zebras survive in nature. They need to be focused, coherent and clear, working in the same direction as a herd. That is how they survive. They can't go wandering off from the herd. The one that wanders off, focused on texting for instance, will be eaten by the lion. Better that the lion grabs one of the old or the sick because the herd needs the strong ones to survive, and they all need to pay attention.

Zebras can live longer than horses, typically more than thirty years. Holly is still maturing and has not yet reached her full potential, whatever that may be. I never underestimate the fact that she is a wild animal. She is not a cute stuffed toy. She is not a domesticated dog or striped pony. She is of the wild. I am always watching for when she might make a decision that could endanger people because they have made a decision that she feels is threatening. We make sure that she is never cornered, that she always has a way out. She has always chosen to move away to a better place for herself rather than confront, and for that we are grateful.

Sometimes, when the horses are circled up, Holly will join the circle. She might even walk into the circle. But she is always aware of the way out, and we leave open a space so she can get out if she prefers.

Drumming Circle

Sometimes we do a drumming circle with the horses. We invite the horses to participate from outside the circle, but Holly is allowed inside the circle with the people drumming. She loves the drumming. She will come straight in and stand in the middle, not disturbing anyone, sometimes taking a nap in the grass, sometimes dreaming.

Clearly, she likes the feeling of whatever the drum creates, as it brings the community together. You might think that the drum would scare her, but it attracts her.

One day a mother and teenage daughter were at the ranch learning to manage their differences, to be more authentically present with one another and to have a more peaceful home. Their challenge was to have honest conversations with each other without getting into major fights, tears and hurt feelings. We began the session with each of them spending time with the horses reflecting on what they each thought were the most important things to talk about. The daughter was hanging out with Bud, her favorite horse, getting clearer about what she wanted to say to her mother. Bud was giving the girl lots of attention and seemed to be really listening to her without getting distracted by what was going on around him.

The mother was deciding what horse she wanted to approach when Holly the zebra walked right up to her. The woman was really surprised because she had on many occasions attempted to get close to Holly and Holly always backed away. The woman stood quietly waiting to see what would happen next. As she patiently waited for Holly to decide what she wanted, Holly rubbed softly against the mother inviting her touch. The woman responded to the invitation and slowly and respectful reached toward Holly and began to stroke her neck. Holly moved in even closer and the two connected through mutual trust.

I asked the mother what she learned from Holly that would be helpful to her in her relationship and communication with her daughter. She told me that Holly gave her invaluable parenting advice. She said what she learned from Holly was the importance of using fewer words and more messages of the heart. "I need to look for opportunities to simply be together with my daughter without a plan or agenda. I should listen for what she wants before offering what I think she needs. I have to practice giving her the space to come to me. I need to listen to her without preconceived ideas and without judgment. I learned the importance of teaching my daughter the qualities I want to offer her by example, by being myself, and to love her for just who she is." The mother thanked Holly for her "motherly wisdom," and Holly, her job done, went out into the field to join the rest of the herd.

When we pause to look closely at another person, seeing who that person truly is, not whom we hope or think they should be, we discover the beauty and value of that person and an appreciation for why they are in our lives.

This process of being fully present with ourselves and learn-ing to be more present with those we care about is what happens when people come out to the ranch and spend some time with the horses and Holly. One reason to engage with horses and a zebra is that while humans often have chal-lenges managing complex relationships, horses and zebras are good at it because they think and act from their hearts. In the presence of the horses, people see themselves and each other differently and with more care and kindness because that is the way horses relate to them.

In the quiet of nature and with the grounded presence of the horses and the unique talents of Holly the zebra, people can reflect on what really matters to them, address matters of their hearts, and make decisions that are in resonance with their deeper values. In this field of possibility, we can discover what is best in ourselves, and what is best for the collective. My deepest gratitude goes to Holly, our lively zebra, for her honest and en-gaging presence, and for her authentic willful spirit of the wild.

4
Honoring the Horses That Have Passed Away

We remember with gratitude and honor the members of our horse herd that have passed on within the last several years. They opened their hearts and shared their spirit with many people and with their horse herd mates.

We often look outside ourselves for answers to our essential life questions. These horse spirits now guide us from the other side reminding us to look within to discover our true spirit. We sometimes see their images in the clouds or the mist that rolls across the field. We sometimes feel their breath or sense their presence. They remind us of the timelessness of wisdom, friendship and love.

Lily

Lily passed over peacefully at the age of over thirty years old in 2016 under a full moon and beautiful night sky surrounded by her beloved herd.

I am a long-legged black shire mare. I offer a gentle open-hearted welcome. In my quiet way, I live with dignity and strength.

Her gentle, motherly nature was extended to horse and human alike. In her quiet, graceful and warm-hearted way, she mothered us all. Lily was a willing team member and put her heart and soul into helping a team or family learn about working together, moving in a common direction, and looking out for one another. She offered us the expertise and confidence that she learned by leading a six-horse carriage team. Lily taught that when we all pull together, no burden is too heavy, and that forward progress is possible. Most of all, Lily showed us that non-violent communication is possible, and that goodness and kindness is a leadership capacity that engages and inspires the best in ourselves and others.

Thunderheart and Rojo

We are best of friends. Both of us passed over in the field at 44 years of age. You will see us or feel our presence in the spirit of the morning mist, the presence of butterflies, rain-bows, wind and magic. We watch over the horse and human herd from the other side inspiring love.

Thunderheart

Thunderheart was a big white magical horse with a generous presence, empathetic heart and sweet nature. He was easy to fall in love with and he had many best friends.

Thunder pulled a wagon to Cleveland from the commune called "The Farm" in Tennessee many years ago. He was featured in magazines for his talent as a horse that could paint and had several "signed" works displayed in art galleries. Thunder loved storytelling and enjoyed listening to stories of courage, healing and even leadership and organizational dilemmas.

Thunder, as a "hippie" horse given his birthplace, was a storyteller and artist who viewed the world with curiosity, optimism, innocence and appreciation. He reminded us that the world is a beautiful place if we look through the lens of amazement, gratitude and beauty.

Rojo

Rojo was a chestnut mare elder, the feisty "grandmother" of the herd, and she commanded respect in her quiet but determined way. She was a good teacher of going after what you want with style and grace. Once the lead mare of the herd, Rojo followed an essential succession plan and graciously transferred the lead mare position and responsibility to the mare best suited to take on the leadership role for the herd. She then functioned as "chairman of the board and respected elder of the herd." Rojo was a brilliant reminder of the beauty, wisdom and power of aging and life's transitions. Though Rojo could no longer see or hear very well in later years, her keen intuitive senses guided her through her world. She was the guardian angel of the young and vulnerable in the herd. In her presence, we remembered to use all of who we are in our actions.

Jet Set

I am the first horse Jackie partnered with. Together we began this journey of bringing people and horses together for healing and well-being. I helped her raise her three boys to be respectful loving beings. I believe in the goodness of everyone and the spirit of unconditional love. My mission has always been to inspire people to find love in their hearts and goodness in their lives.

5
Jackie's Story: The Human in the Herd

"A person can learn a lot from a horse if they are that kind of person. For most people, getting help from someone who has more knowledge, maybe the horse itself, is real beneficial. There are just some things a horse needs a person to understand."
—Bill Dorance, author, *True Horsemanship Through Feel*

I am the human member of the herd at Pebble Ledge Ranch. Over time I have earned the privilege of being accepted into the horse herd. I know that I am not the lead horse. That would be Bea. Being the lead human in the herd, I am the bridge between the human and horse community. I honor the horses as horses and respect the integrity of herd culture. I trust in their intuitive capacity to know what is best for them. I appreciate their ability to be authentically present in each moment and in every situation informed by their horse sense- ability. I am in awe of their collective intelligence, collective wisdom and collective consciousness. I love the majesty, mystery, magic and magnificence they embody in the life form of horse.

Jackie's Journey Into A Herd and Into Living Authentically

For much of my life, I never considered a horse's view or a herd's world. Then, more than two decades ago, I had an experience that transformed my understanding of horses with people and my place in their horse world.

I traveled for a personal retreat guided by a woman and her herd of eighteen horses. She lived in a small Colorado town, Westcliff, surrounded by the San Christo mountain range. I spent about a week with the horses, which were just getting used to people hanging around with them in their forty-acre pasture.

Each day when I entered their pasture, I watched them intently. I followed the horses from a distance, observing, reflecting, listening and tuning in to them. While they grazed, I sat in their field, paying attention to how they communicated, noticing their individual relationships. The lead horse, Roxy, was a feisty buckskin mustang, butterscotch-colored with a black tail and mane. Roxy, though one of the smaller horses, clearly was in charge of the herd.

I tried to get close to Roxy, and she would walk away. Day after day, the dance continued. When I walked toward her, she walked away. A couple of the other horses would come close to me as I sat in the field for a curious sniff or to ask for a scratch. Attracted to challenge, it was Roxy that I wanted to win over. I knew Roxy was watching, maybe thirty feet away, always walking parallel to me, never closer.

Then, one day as I sat against a rock warmed by the sun, I fell asleep. When I awoke, the whole herd of eighteen horses was gathered around my rock. They were silently listening, reflecting and observing me. The horses watched as Roxy walked up to me and gave me a gentle nudge in a quiet, clear welcome-to-the-herd way. My heart opened. In simply being present without wanting, asking or doing, the relationship I had been trying so hard to create became possible. By simply doing nothing, something happened.

Jackie's Story

The First Time I Really Saw A Horse

This was the moment I began to gain an understanding of the thinking and being of horses. For days, I had been trying to get Roxy and her herd to join me. That didn't work. But when I was completely at rest, and not exerting any want from her or agenda for her, Roxy seemed to feel that she had the space to come over to me, and to invite me into the herd. That was when I began to sense horses and to gain a feel for what it meant to be in their world, as opposed to bringing the horse into my human world.

Following Roxy's touching gesture, each horse came over to me and nudged me or blew a soft breath over me, as if to initiate me into their herd. I felt welcomed. But the welcome was not over.

The herd turned and casually walked away, while I sat quietly. After a while, I stood and began my walk back from the pasture to the ranch house. As I moved, I heard hoof steps behind me. I turned to see the whole herd following me, led by Roxy, who fell into step next to me.

The herd escorted me across the entire pasture to the gate leading out to the rest of the ranch. When I stopped, Roxy nudged me toward the gate. I looked at her. She looked me over, offered me a feeling of acceptance and then turned and took off at a dead run, followed by all the other horses, to the far side of the field where grazing was the best.

I never saw horses the same way after that, as I began a journey, moving from observer of a way of life to becoming a participant in their way of life. I was changed forever, opening my mind and heart to understand the unique intelligence of horses and the living system and collective wisdom of their herd.

Sometimes, one has to leave home and what is familiar to discover the journey of living one's own life fully. Horses and the collective wisdom of the herd can open the pathway to this journey.

Early Adventure with Horses

I always loved horses and believed in my heart I was part horse. As a child, my imaginary friend was a horse who carried me everywhere, especially into places I was afraid to go by myself. Growing up in a modest suburban neighborhood, owning an actual horse was out of the question. Instead I dreamed of horses running free and coming home with me. I also dreamed of being a cowgirl. My heroes were the independent and fiery horsewomen Annie Oakley and Calamity Jane.

I carried my dreams into adulthood, and one morning I woke up and knew it was time to do more than dream about horses, it was time to live my dream with horses. At the age of twenty-five with two young children and a mostly willing husband, we moved to the country to give my first real horse a home with our family. El Nejar Rudan was an Arabian thoroughbred mix the red-gold color of sunset. We found each other at a boarding stable close to my house where his previous owner had abandoned him six months prior without paying his board. I agreed to pay his back boarding fees and a few hundred dollars for the privilege of bringing him home.

I had never saddled a horse before and it had been many years since I had ridden a horse but was determined to ride my new horse home. I put the saddle on his back, tightened the girth that holds the saddle in place, grabbed a fistful of mane and launched myself onto his back. He stood completely still as the saddle, not quite tight enough, slipped to the side. I found myself looking precariously up from practically underneath Rudan's round belly. He looked patiently down at me and stayed quiet while I disentangled myself and less than gracefully returned to the ground. I took the saddle off and placed my money into the hand of the stable owner and my trust into my new horse. Already in love with this good-hearted horse, I walked him to the fence, and climbed up and onto his bare back. Together we walked alongside the road to his new home and to the beginning of our many adventures.

El Nejar Rudan moved into a small barn I had created out of a shed, and into a modest pasture less than fifty yards from my back door. I could see him from my kitchen, living room and bedroom windows.

Before long, another horse and a pony arrived, and we had a lively herd of three equines and three children. My children and I rode the horses, brushed them, and cleaned their stalls. The horses became part of our daily lives, in a routine that included feeding and caring for them the first thing in the morning and last thing at night in sunshine, rain, sleet and snow. The horses and pony soon were playmates of the kids, joining in pirate adventures and all sorts of make-believe games. The horses depended on me for food, shelter and mobility. I depended on them for a wonderful ride through the forest. I cared deeply for them in many ways, saw their beauty, and appreciated their companionship. I understood them as being horses and different from humans. What I did not yet appreciate was their remarkable horse sense and amazing culture as a herd. I had not considered that our experience together was one-sided, dominated by human perspective and a human position of power and control. All that began to change as big upheavals in my life began to take place.

While my home life was nature based, my professional life as Director of a Jewish Community Center was office based. I decided that what I really wanted was to integrate my work life with nature and to design my workspace within the natural world where I could best support people on their life journeys. I created an outdoor office in the forest behind the barn and horse pasture. A yurt, a Mongolian tent, served as my workplace when the weather was too cold or wet to work directly outside. This temporary shelter had a tribal feel and was within nature, rather than defended from nature.

The wandering creek, hundred-year-old oaks and steep hills were great partners in providing a natural context for people who chose to come and work with me. The rich diversity and authentic relationships in nature inspired the discovery of answers to life's most important questions and for healing from life's challenges for many. As their coach or therapist within the expansiveness and collective wisdom of nature and the wild, I held a space for them to build capacity to manage the complexities of their life journey.

It was also a time to find the courage to make changes in my personal life. My then husband and I decided to part and while continuing to support the well being of our children, we left our marriage to find our separate life paths. A single mom for the next almost ten years, the horses stepped up to help me in parenting the kids. The herd's steady, grounded presence provided stability in times of uncertainty, compassion in times of heartbreak, wisdom in times of challenge, and humor when laughter was the best medicine.

I did not always make the wisest decisions and made many mistakes, but I learned by living them. I brushed off the dust when I hit the ground and became more humble. Facing challenge with good spirit offered a clearer sense of integrity. Being willing to live with life's uncertainty helped me to develop trust in myself and in the world. In the care of horses, children and the wild, I learned about unconditional love.

Happily single, loving being a mom, excited about my work, I felt life was complete; that is, until I met Herb. On a spring morning in the parking lot of a Spirit of Nature workshop, I almost tripped over a long pair of legs in tight blue jeans and the rest of this cowboy, which looked just as good. As the mischievous nature spirits would have it, six months later Herb and I were living together. The cowboy began to transform, and as Herb reclaimed his Native American heritage, he allowed his beautiful black hair to grow into a braid representing the change within him. The kids were off to college and creating their own lives. And Herb and I were creating ours with nature being central for both of us, and the herd part of the family.

With the kids no longer at home, the horses, being empty nesters, began looking for jobs. When I walked with clients to my outside office, we passed the horse pasture and passed it again when I walked them back to their cars. One day when the horses sensed us coming, they were waiting for us at the fence and began flirting with my clients as we came by. This became their daily routine and soon my clients began to say things like, "You know, when I stopped to chat with Thunderheart, I was better able to make sense of my relationship with my father," or "Jetset had an excellent insight in helping me make my decision about what job to take," or "Rojo's compassion allowed me be more forgiving of myself."

My work took on another dimension as I added the horse pasture to my office space and horses as my co-workers. The horses loved their new work and I decided to bring on more staff; soon our herd had expanded to five.

As often happens when a business expands, you outgrow your space, and so it was with us. Our current pasture was not sufficient to comfortably support the work and life of the herd, and, Herb and I were ready for a change in environment. We began the search for a new home for our animal family and us. Before we knew it, all of us, Herb and I, a wolf dog, a scrappy mutt, a scruffy tomcat and five horses were creating a new home together on eighty acres of land, which included a twenty-acre pasture. When we first turned the horses out into the pasture, they ventured out into about two of the acres, as that was what they were used to in their past home pasture. It only took a few minutes before they were off at an excited gallop exploring their new digs. They rolled, they kicked, they played, making the space their own, and then they settled down to graze in the plentiful green pasture grass. Every once in a while they looked up and nodded their approval. "We dreamed us all here," the herd seemed to say. "When you collectively believe in dreams, they have a great chance of coming true."

My childhood horse dreams followed me, and led to my adult dreams coming true.

As a kid I had imagined that I was a horse running free and living with other horses; now a woman, I have the spirit of horse within me, running free and living within a herd.

I have had many dreams, but I never had the dream to start my own business, though I did inherit a strong entrepreneurial spirit from my parents and pioneer spirit from my ancestry.

My grown-up dream was to be outside in nature as much of the day as possible, to be with horses, to have a flexible schedule that I was in charge of and to be self-supporting. I dreamed of many loves and children and family. These dreams became reality without a strategic plan or any plan for that matter. I just followed my interest and what I loved to do and when windows of opportunity opened I jumped right through. Miraculously, I most often landed on my feet and then figured out what to do in the place in which I had arrived. When I didn't land on my feet, I dusted myself off, healed the bruises and smiled at the adventure of it all.

One window I leaped through offered the opportunity to incorporate my love of horses and desire to be in nature with my professional goal of guiding people on their journey of discovery, healing and growth. When the dust cleared, I realized that I had unknowingly started a business. The dream of owning my own business emerged from following and trusting my heart, staying focused on and committing to what I authentically loved. It also required being willing to show up, jump the hurdles and do the hard work. The reality is more than I ever imagined or dreamed could be possible.

With encouragement from the horses, my family, especially Herb, and with my unconditionally positive spirit, I dug in my hooves. I took ownership of what luck, fate, perseverance and effort had brought me. I consulted the horses and my inner voice for a name for my business and what I heard back was Spirit of Leadership Services.

In indigenous tribal cultures, names matter. A name tells who you are or who you are becoming, and so the name of my business needed to reflect the authentic meaning and service of the enterprise. The name, Spirit of Leadership Services, captured the concept I was reaching for and I knew it was a name I would have to grow into. I included the word Spirit as it defines the spark of aliveness inherent within us, and the connection to that beyond us from which we flourish. The meaning I bring to the word Leadership is that leadership belongs to everyone, whether a leader of a global company, a seller at a street-corner lemonade stand, or someone with the responsibility of leading her own life. The word Service reflects a particular leadership style. It is one of mutual benefit for all the people that my business touches, the horses, clients, employees, and stakeholders. Nature and the wild are essential stakeholders in my business decisions and their voice is always at the table.

After discovering the name of my business I designed a business card, web site and brochure. With a hearty nudge from the horses, I began to market my business by sharing my excitement for our new venture with whoever would listen.

The name Spirit of Leadership Service speaks to the values we hold as we guide people in their journeys of authentic presence. Within this enterprise, my human colleagues and I are able to integrate love and respect for horses and nature with the opportunity to work with people by offering personal and professional discovery, coaching and retreat experiences.

Energized by the pioneer spirit of this work, I enjoy walking where I make the first footsteps. There may be some footsteps next to me, but I'm not walking in anybody else's. I am an explorer, which is why learning with the horses and bringing people and horses together to learn is work that I love.

Being Authentic, Living Joyfully

My life is a blessing to me. I am married to my soul mate. I have raised children, and more important, have been raised by my children who are now each one a uniquely outstanding human being. They have families of their own, and we all remain close to each other. I am blessed to a grandmother with several amazing grandchildren. My developmentally different grandchild Joshua is not able to speak with words, but speaks through his courageous heart, honest gestures and a beautiful mind. His lively conversations of the heart with the horses and me are brilliant. Jaren is unconditionally optimistic and caring, always lively and often wise beyond his young years. Ethan is an amazing source of endless curiosity and imagination. Natalie is the brightest of lights and exudes joyful exuberance for all of life's adventures. Aria has a sweet nature and indomitable spirit that is always on the move toward her goals. I have learned deeper love, humility and a second youthfulness from each and all of them.

Part of being authentic is to follow your curiosity and your lifelong love.

Bringing dreams to life required commitment, passion, focused work and faith. Engaging in work that has passion, meaning and purpose and that is great fun has helped me understand living with authentic presence. Part of being authentic is to follow your curiosity and your lifelong love. Following my curiosity and joyfully engaging is a priority and holds high value in my life. It is a natural course for me, in my work, to support other people by asking about their values and what matters to them. People are being their authentic selves when they are living comfortably, purposefully and joyfully according to the values that matter to them.

I have lived long enough to have had many highly rewarding experiences, some on purpose, some not. The totality of life experiences is a resource to draw upon. I love to dance and the freeing movement of dancing. I notice the dance of people, how they move through space, "own" their space and give space to others. Learning from the martial art form of Tai Quan Do and Aikido has helped me understand balance, resistance, mindfulness, and embodied spiritual practice.

The approach of positive psychology, emotional intelligence, appreciative inquiry, systems thinking and emergent process informs my work as a coach, therapist and educator and my worldview. I value learning by doing, being aware of the experience and then applying the meaning it has to everyday life. Volunteering in an AIDS clinic, doing hands-on massage and energy work with people in the HIV spectrum, I learned to listen for the health and wholeness of the person and trust the body's capacity for healing.

One of my favorite work adventures was working with youth in Israel. Our journey was in nature, tromping through the desert, and hillsides and ancient villages learning about inner wisdom, about being a community and being part of something larger than you. Part of my work in Israel was within a project to bringing Palestinians and Israeli local leaders together in a more peaceful understanding. These work experiences touched on culture, inclusiveness, and collective values, and stretched my understanding of what it means to be human.

Believing in the power of creativity as a healing art and being at home with the idea that we all have the capacity to create, I encourage my clients to express themselves and communicate their thoughts and feelings through poetry, visual arts and movement. I really enjoy the communication of drumming. The drum is a way to communicate across distance. In our twenty-acre pasture, sounding the drum to gather people scattered about the field is more efficient than trying to gather them by shouting.

Jackie's Story

The hoof beats of the horses are a form of drumming on the earth, a drum song connecting them to each other and the wisdom of the earth. Tess, our pony, loves to drum my drum with her tiny front hoof when I place a drum on the ground. Our horses Bea and Bud stomp their massive feet in rhythm, drumming their message on the earth. Toby the gypsy horse likes to drum by using his rear hoof to drum on the fencing as a call to attention and intention. Raven and Spirit like to softly drum using their noses on my drum. Chief Silver Cloud, the former parade horse, follows the sound of the drum wherever it goes. Holly the zebra ears forward and at attention, loves to listen to the call of drum; maybe it reminds her of her home and lineage in Africa.

I learned to listen and speak beyond words from the drum, one of the oldest forms of communication between families, communities, and the ancestors and the Earth. The drum can locate a lost member of the clan or send a warning to aggressors. Drums invite the earth to open to seeds in the fields and welcome the fruits of the harvest. Babies are coaxed into the world and elders accompanied into their death by the song of the drum. Drums open the gateway for healing, celebration and ceremony. The heartbeat of the drum calls us to awareness. The silent spaces between the drumbeat and our heartbeat is the connection to the deep silence within ourselves, the place our soul calls home.

Within the sacred language of rhythm, movement, dance, and resonance we create a conscious power of grace. We can create a spirit dance from the inevitable falls, spins and leaps of life. We awaken our hearts and discover purpose through creativity and spontaneous expression. As we follow our own drum song, we can join others in a single heartbeat.

Awakening our hearts through creative expression, we can each discover the beauty of our authentic self and our purpose in life.

Each of us has important stories to tell and important stories to which we are to listen. We each have a dream to share and a dream to discover in someone else. I believe the most important story is our own story, and the most important dream our own dream; the one we are meant to live. Our stories and dreams become much greater, more real and have deeper meaning when they are held within the heart of the collective, be that herd or community. As we tell our authentic story from our unique perspective and life experience, it becomes part of the larger story of all of us. Patterns and connections in our life stories create a web of collective wisdom that opens new energy, insights and possibilities for each of us. Our stories become intertwined and a shared wisdom that we did not have individually becomes available to us.

The story of collaboration and cooperation for the greater good and the natural instinct to create community as a gathering place can be found everywhere in all life. Authentic presence is found in the heart of family, herd, and nature's communities, and is best learned by living and loving.

6
Horses, Humans and Magic Moments

*"Magic is believing in yourself, if you can do that,
you can make anything happen."*
—Johann Wolfgang von Goethe

People often say to me, "Oh, the horses are so magical." For me, it's not that the horses are magical; it is that being with the horses is magical.

Horses can inspire people to believe in themselves and to believe in each other. What I see is the magic of reality. Horses bring out magic in people. It's not the kind of magic you see in Cinderella, where all of a sudden there's a pumpkin and poof, outside-of-yourself miracles happen. No, it's the everyday miracles of good will, kindness, challenge, courage, accomplishment, and the transformation of people. Horses can inspire people to believe in themselves and to believe in each other. It happens over and over again.

Often when people are engaging with the horses, something out of the ordinary happens, and sometimes I hear people say, "Oh, that's a quirk," or "That was just one of those things."

But when magical happenings and amazing connections happen between horses and people and between people in the presence of horses, day after day after day, one begins to believe differently. These instances are not the exception; it's more unusual when moments of extraordinary connection don't happen. In the good company of horses, the everyday magic of hope, faith and trust that lives within us can emerge to inspire all that happens around us.

A group of eight people were here at the ranch participating in one of our programs, "Five Coaching Competencies You Can Learn from Horses," to expand their coaching skills with business folks. We were ending the last day of the program in the horse pasture, gathering the collective wisdom of the day in a closing circle. We bring all our programs to a close with the participants reflecting on their experience and making individual statements about what they learned from the involvement with the horses, what meaning they were taking away from the retreat, and what they might take back and incorporate into their work and daily lives. The people were sitting in one circle and the horses were standing in another circle of their own, seemingly done with their work of the day. The horses looked over at us with some interest while this was happening, and slowly the horse herd joined the human herd, becoming an outer circle around us.

> **Listen to the whisperings of the horse...clarity of purpose and compassion.**

Holly the zebra moved from the outer circle into our circle. We were sitting in chairs and she took an important herd leadership position with the responsibility of sentry. When one member of the herd lies down to rest, one herd member always stands. The little zebra was standing guard while all the humans were sitting.

Bea, our take-charge lead mare, walked between the chairs to the center of the circle and stood. Then Toby, the resident herd stallion and Bea's loyal companion, moved into the middle of the circle standing next to Bea. The two horses began to groom one another, nibbling on each other's necks in a gentle caring manner. This mutual affection between the horses is where our human concept of "necking" came from. Spirit, Raven, Tess, Chief Silver Cloud and Bud held the outer circle in place.

Horses joined our human herd in a circle around us, a zebra was standing guard, two giant draft horses cared for one another in the center of our group; what might they be communicating to us with their actions? We turned the question to the coaching group participants to see how they made meaning of the horse's behavior. One perception was that the horses were reminding them that in their coaching practice, their responsibility is to stand guard for their clients as they faced difficult situations. A second view was that the horses were telling them that when we face challenges, we might look for support and find it all around us. Another person thought the horses were reminding us about the importance of self-care and care for others. Individual perceptions, multiple realities and diverse possibilities emerged and became the collective wisdom of the group. Sharing information about what we learned, and listening to one another, we created collective intelligence that was more than what we learned individually. This lived experience of learning from their individual perceptions and from the collective perception was something each person felt was of great value and had immediate application in their work and lives.

I have noticed that the horses feel our energy of engagement, camaraderie and generosity. Horses are attracted to that. But there's more, I believe. The horses had an impact on us. We were sharing things that mattered and honest emotion with each other. When the horses joined us, our perceptions and hearts opened wider and more deeply. Part of the impact of the experience is recognizing the privilege of being with each other and with these horses, and how precious life can be in such simple ways.

As the program ended and people began to leave the pasture, one man in the group hung back, walking alone. Holly the zebra became his personal guide. With her high-pitched zebra sound, Holly called to him, running back and forth to try to get the reluctant walker to go back and join the horse herd or to go forward to join the rest of the human herd. She finally succeeded; the man rejoined the other people. All walked towards their cars, preparing to leave the ranch to go home.

Holly ran to the gate of the pasture, and in her unforgettable zebra language, loudly called with great passion to her new herd members to come back. Sensing the human herd and the horse herd as one herd, Holly was distressed when the human half of the herd left. In a zebra herd, if you leave, you might not survive. Safety is in staying together, so in her leadership role of protector she was trying to gather the herd back together.

People come and go all the time from Pebble Ledge Ranch. Even during most retreats, people leave to go home at the end of each day. I think what Holly tuned into this particular day was the deep connection this group had with each other and with the horses. People had been sharing things with each other of importance and personal meaning to them; they had connected with each other at a deep level, and had become one herd with the horses. I guess it made no zebra sense to Holly to walk away from that field of good feeling.

I went out to the pasture to try and calm Holly and to keep her company. After a few minutes, Holly turned and galloped back to the horses scattered about the field. Not giving up on her herding idea, she ran back and forth across the field rounding them by running around them till they got closer together. Her mission accomplished she came to a stop, gave a big shake to release the stress she was carrying, breathed a loud sigh, and standing close to her best buddy Tess, she began to peacefully munch grass with the herd. All had changed. Her plan did not go exactly as she had wanted, so she came up with a revised plan without giving up her intention of gathering the herd. She did the best she could with optimism, and with resilience shook off what could not be without regret.

The little zebra with a courageous heart looked at what she had of value in this present situation and moment. She had her herd close together and all was once again right and at peace in her world.

One more Holly the zebra story: On a beautiful sunny fall day, a team of hard working people from a variety of organizations was at the ranch for a leadership and team-building experience with the horses. Most of them arrived at the ranch feeling tired, stressed and discouraged about some of the issues they were trying to manage in their work lives and the negative impact these issues were having on their personal lives. We were out in the pasture and each person was asked to speak about the dilemma they were facing. The horses were at one end of the field and we were at the other end. The horses had looked up when we came through the gate to their pasture but did not come to welcome us to the herd. This is unusual because generally the horses are eager to welcome the new guests. I wondered if it had anything to do with the discouraged and stressed energy of the group of people.

I called to my horse team to come and join the people who had come to learn with them; they again looked up but chose to stay at the far end of the field.

I reached into my pack where I had a container of bubbles that my grandson and I had been playing with the day before. I held up the bubble wand and the wind carried the bubbles into the air and across the field. The horses looked up and slowly began to walk towards us, all except Holly the zebra; she came running towards us at a full gallop. She slowed as she approached and began chasing the bubbles and popping them with her nose. One bubble landed on her backside and suddenly she was running away from the bubbles as if they were chasing her. She came to a stop, gathered her courage and then ran around to get behind the bubbles so she could chase them instead of the bubbles chasing her. All stress disappeared from the faces of the people as they began to cheer Holly on and laugh. The group members agreed that if a courageous zebra could chase away bubbles, maybe they could pop the bubbles of their problems and chase them into possibilities. They began to work together, excited to help each other find the magic in their work and unexpected solutions to their dilemmas. Magical moments like zebras chasing bubbles to chase people's troubles away and people turning to one another rather than from each other are examples of the everyday miracles that happen within the herd at Pebble Ledge Ranch.

Our programs at the ranch begin with two separate groups, humans in one area, and horses in another. At first, people casually stroll around the pasture, and at first, the horses just stand around. Then, something always happens. Maybe a horse is welcoming, or a human walks toward the horses. Suddenly, you can't tell where the horse herd starts and the human herd ends. We magically become one herd. This usually happens when I'm not looking. If I watch for it, I don't see it. If I turn my back for a minute, it has happened. I believe that when we get to know people, when we slow down and take the time to see people and interact with them, when we go to a deeper place in ourselves and with others, the magic moments become part of our lives. This is happening all of the time. The miracle of magic moments is not the exception to daily life. Daily life is the miracle.

The herd tells me how things are going. I don't know how fast they figure it out, but it's clear to me, in attitude and work, that when they've got more work than they can handle, they are not as motivated, and there is much more conflict within the herd. When they volunteer to participate of their own free will and are sharing responsibility for the workload, they are much more engaging and generous with their attention. This is something horses have in common with people.

We promise visitors to the ranch three things, and we deliver every time; you will be safe physically and emotionally, you will discover and take with you something of value, and you will have fun.

This is the way horses live. They are looking out for safety all of the time. They thrive because they are able to adapt to change faster than almost any other mammal. They respond only to what has value, and they do it together, which is safer, more resourceful and more fun.

Our horses work as an interconnected and self-organizing team. The older ones have probably worked with more than two thousand clients, including businesses and organizations such as Lubrizol, Cleveland Clinic, University Hospitals, Case-Western Reserve University, Weatherhead School of Management, Humana, Mars, Banfield, AcerlorMittal Steel, Ohio Insurance, Ericson Manufacturing, Catholic Charities, Jewish Federation, Rape Crisis Center, and the Cleveland School System.

We have worked with officers of the Israeli army, men from transitional housing, people living beyond cancer, courageous individuals reclaiming their lives from trauma, CEOs inspiring social change, teams regrouping after a merger, and kids who are our real leaders, present and future.

Often people ask me about what I think the horse is doing or trying to tell them. The first thing I say is that I know what's happening between me and the horse, and I have a pretty good guess about what horse behavior is. What I don't know is what is happening between you and the horse. You're the only one who would know that, so can you tell me what you think is happening?

Usually, we ask for several ideas, beyond their initial thoughts, because people often have habitual assumptions. Once we start talking and thinking the conversation opens up, moving from our familiar patterns of thinking to new perceptions and ways to approach the same situation. We don't want to lose the good information we already know, so we aim for two or three different possibilities, offering a broader, more aware perspective, so people may engage in a deeper inquiry.

There are several common patterns that we often observe when one or more of the horses move on by a person or walks in an opposite direction. People usually have an interpretation of what the walking means and it often reflects old and not very useful patterns, such as, "The horse doesn't like me or is afraid of me. "I am too big" or "too small," or "The horse doesn't even see me." Limiting patterns often from childhood become the lens through which we see the world. Engaging with the horses often allows those old patterns to become visible.

My responsibility in co-facilitating with my horse partner is to bring to light what may be self-limiting patterns when they come to the attention of the person. I am looking to see if those patterns seem to create a downward spiral of poor self-image or identity, or lack of regard for oneself. Bringing these limiting and often old behaviors to the person's attention allows them to open up their awareness to a more upward spiral of self-care and positive regard for self. We move toward the confusion and old fears or future uncertainty, not away from it, and with the support of the horses, more options become visible. We learn by a balance between being challenged and being supported. The horses seem to inherently know how much challenge and how much support will be most useful to each person to learn what it is that person is meant to learn from them on any given day. Engaging their dilemmas in the presence of the horse's nudges, people can explore their self-limiting perceptions and patterns with curiosity, compassion and courage. With a gentle nudge of a horse to help them, people can learn to reframe their negative thoughts and ask, "What else could it be?" We often ask people, "Can you find three other possible stories or interpretations of what you see?" or we might ask, "If you don't like the story, how do you want to change it to one of possibility, learning and positive direction?"

So, the experience and the lessons evolve, and someone, horse or human, steps up to the issue. We could set up a plan, prepare the horses, and say at the beginning of a day to work on leadership. "Your challenge today is to explore leadership and teamwork with these three horses," for example. But what happens next is the difference between an exercise and an experiment.

In an experiment—or an experience—we plan a direction, and we might even have a framework, a series of action steps; but, we have no attachment to the outcome, and we never know what the outcome will be. When we do an exercise in this work with the horses, generally we have an expectation about the focus of the learning. The only outcome that is essential, however, is that the exercise needs to have been fun, to have increased their ability to move forward, and to have gained knowledge; in other words, to have been of a valuable positive experience.

To know what is going on with horses and with people, or have an idea about it, takes time, commitment, and respect for different points of view. It risks a willingness to be in a place of not knowing, and an interest to know more.

I am fortunate to be with horses so much. We have many opportunities to chat. When you are with them a lot, you hear their stories. A lot of what goes on at the ranch is storytelling. Yet, there are certain stories that are not mine to hear. When I bring a person out to the ranch, part of my responsibility, in my work, is to create the opportunity for the client to have a relationship with the horse. My job is to match the right horse, at the right time, with the right person. That includes making sure that the horse is willing, that the horse says "yes" and the person says "yes." Then, after I help create that connection, I step back and let the most important conversation be between the person and the horse.

"What do you think the horse is trying to tell me?" people often say to me, and I respond, "I can tell you what the story is from my point of view, but the story that's most important is your story, what's happening between you and the horse, and the meaning that you are making of your experience. Tell me what you think is going on, and the story behind that." Possible questions begin to emerge. "What's the surface story? What's the deeper story? What in your life connects with that story? What does it make you think of? What's the deeper connection to that? Why this story, now?"

I say to clients, "In the presence of a horse, what comes up for you? I don't want to make the horse into a therapist, or a consultant, or a human. I don't know exactly what the horse is saying, nor will you. You can guess, but we don't speak horse language. We can read a little bit of the body language, but we're only scratching the surface. You are the expert when it comes to your experience and your thoughts. You can say that in the presence of this horse, these are the thoughts, feelings, ideas, and realizations that are coming up for me. I will help you with that."

Anybody can have the opportunity to learn from horses, if they are curious, interested, and non-judgmental of themselves and the horse. They find a good moment when the horse is available, and they meet at the common place of "yes." They trust an experience, and are aware of the multiple realities to any situation. Several people might see the same thing and explain it differently, or make different meanings of it. All could be true, based on who you are and how you experience life.

People tell stories about horse whisperers, but the horse whisperer is not a human. The horse is whispering. We all have the ability to hear that by slowing down inside, paying silent attention and being curious about what is being spoken. Listen to the whisperings from the heart of the horse to your heart for compassion and clarity of purpose. In the silent, grounded bigness of the horse we can more easily give voice to our heart, to our inner sense of truth and let this voice guide us. We can bring greater wisdom to solving dilemmas and making our decisions.

Sometimes I will say, "I wonder what horse would like to help out?" and a horse that I thought was sleeping will appear, ready. Or, we will talk about what are we going to do next, and all of a sudden one or two horses are out there standing, waiting for us.

One weekend, in horse program, I was about to demonstrate how to facilitate a respectful and trustworthy meeting of human and horse. I said, "We will work in the round pen with only one horse." I asked for a volunteer, and when I looked over at the round pen, Raven was standing in the pen, in the middle, waiting for the demonstration. "That's our volunteer," I said.

Often, humans have layered their emotions with rational common sense. A client may come to the ranch and say, "I'm here to work on this or that." Then, they stand with the horses and they begin to feel the deeper core issues. What is coming up in the client is emotion that the horses have picked up. The horses don't know what the memory is, but they've picked up the feeling, and reflected the feel of it back. A coach who was working with an administrator in a school system suggested that Tom, who was his client, come to work with the horses to help in his decision as to when to retire and what was next for him. In the presence of the horses Tom became very quiet and I noticed his eyes tearing. I asked him if he wanted to say something about what was unfolding for him.

He replied that though he came to better understand a professional decision, what came up for him was the struggle his son had had with drugs and his inability to help his son through the many challenges. Tom stayed longer with the horses and discovered that he had been holding in great sadness and guilt. As his tears fell he was able to feel the compassion of the horses and be more compassionate towards himself realizing that he and his son had done the best they could in a difficult situation. Adding horse sense to common sense, we can experience, explore and resolve some of our more hidden dilemmas. One of the gifts of working with horses is that our authentic selves and heartfelt emotions are more available, allowing us to move gracefully through challenges and developing our character with grace.

The relationship between horse and human can be mutually beneficial. As we interact with horses we develop our own character. As we develop our own character, the horse's character further develops. In Greek culture, young men were given a very young horse. As they grew up together, the boy's job was to help the stallion to be a horse that he could ride and be capable of a relationship with the rider. If the boy developed the horse, the process helped develop the young man's character because the boy would have to learn patience, perseverance, and insight. As they developed together, there was a relational field. One of the ways in which horses can serve today is in developing our character. The love of a horse is often the first love of a young girl. The power, honesty, and faithful loyalty in the relationship between horse and girl strengthens her ability to respect honesty and loyalty and to be more powerful in her relationships. It's happened within our herd between horses and humans. Our horses have grown in character, intelligence, and consciousness, learning from us; and we have grown in character and consciousness in our human development. It is either a partnership of learning, or they already knew it all, have grown to trust us, and then revealed it to us.

When cognitive learning and emotional learning happen, kinesthetic learning may happen, too. This learning is a direct transmission. If we knew it was being directly transmitted, our cognitive brain would interrupt the process to try to make sense of it, and it no longer would happen. I think that this is embodied knowledge, a language of the body that never gets translated into words. Yet, somehow, a week after leaving a program at the ranch, or maybe three months later, people feel more grounded, more confident and at home in themselves. They find themselves saying more about what is true, what is authentically true. They are more generous in their relationships. They think more about the collective and a 360-degree perspective; all the things that horses prepare them for that they might not have prepared themselves for begin to show up in their lives. The change may be subtle, but I know it's true for me, and I trust it has been true for others. If they cognitively knew it was happening, their reasoning would likely stop it from happening.

Teams and families visit, seeing how horses live and work together. They realize that collaboration and cooperation, more than competition, improves possibilities. They begin to understand that if they have a relationship that is respectful and trustworthy, their horse and human partners may accomplish great tasks. If, on the other hand, humans try to force or bully a 2,000-pound horse—or a resistant human partner—neither horse nor human will go anywhere with them. The horses teach us through honest responses, physical challenges and a call for heartiness and hardiness. They mentor us with care, gentle nudges forward and compassionate challenge.

The real learning for me has been in my relationship with them—what they have learned from me, and what I have learned from them within the context of our connection and interactions. Mine is not just learning about horses; it's me learning from them and with them. The more I am willing to listen, the deeper I am willing to explore, the more my actions reflect a humble way of being, the more they offer to me. There seems to be a natural intuitive connection and possibility of shared collective wisdom when I am coming from the heart.

In the presence of the horses, I am learning to be a better human being and to understand what it means to be authentically present. I have evolved simply as a woman and they have evolved simply as horses. We have evolved together and that is the real magic between horses and humans.

Human Guests in a Herd of Horses

"Ponies, ponies, now don't you worry, we have not come to steal your fire away. We want to fly with you across the sunrise, discover what begins each shining day."
—John Denver

At Pebble Ledge Ranch we are human guests in a herd of horses. Entering the culture of horse and herd rather than bringing horses into our human culture offers us a chance to see our own culture from a different point of view. Our way of relating to and being with horses at Pebble Ledge Ranch changes the way many people relate to horses. It also gives us the opportunity to relate to our human herd mates with more awareness and choice. We strive to create with horses and with each other relational alliances—positive relationship that come together in value, creating mutual benefit for a common purpose.

Here humans are the horses' guests in the horses' home playing field and horses have the home court advantage. We enter an ancient culture of amazing intuitive knowledge; to find shelter and food and care for the elders and young ones. It is a world of mutually beneficial relationship between herd members, a world of horseplay, herd work and shared leadership. There we find respect for their natural resources and the forces of nature. It is a species that listens to the call of the wild and responds with a freedom of spirit.

At the ranch, humans do not have authority or priority over the horses; they are not in charge, nor are they the horses' leaders. We are not controlling or dominating the horses but instead participating with them as equal partners. It is a relationship not of power over but power among. We don't do anything for them that they can do for themselves and we are responsible stewards of their care. In this way, people become respected, trusted and honored guests of the herd. The horses know that we are people and not horses who have come to visit their field. As people enter their field, the herd begins a process of observing them first and then integrating the people into their herd. They have curiosity about us, and compassion for humans, and so go easier on us than they would a new horse entering their pasture. We are similar to "visiting family" who come for a while and leave at the end of the day. The visitors need to follow basic "home pasture" rules and cultural guidelines but are not held to the standard of a resident member of the horse herd.

We can learn by engaging with the horses how to more respectfully engage with cultures different from our own so as not to steal the fire that sheds light on the beauty and inherent value of that culture. We can learn from the culture of horse and herd to live in a present that is connected to a future, which is already there and waiting to taking us to a higher level of humanity. Listening to horse whispering we can hear whispered from within our authentic purpose and why we are meant to be here. Entering the world and collective wisdom of the herd, we encounter different perspectives, participate in new ways of being in relationship and awaken the innate human capacity for goodness. I have found that when we can move between different worlds, we can be more tolerant of differences in others; more creative in our thinking; more innovative in economic, social and ecological challenges; and more available to our humanness.

Horses at Pebble Ledge Ranch are not working for us; they are working with us. That concept can be confusing to people who never have considered its value. In our day-to-day lives, most people are not asking, "What can I learn from you today?" Instead, they are asking, "What can you do for me today?" In organizations and businesses, leaders are too often asking their employees, "What can you do for me today?"

Humans can learn about shared leadership from horses as good leadership focuses on the question, "What can I learn from you, for you and with you?"

We listen to horses so that we can understand what is going on within us and around us. Learning to listen from another's perspective is a major part of our horse work and essential in our people work. It is one of the contributions the people of this ranch, and the horses of this ranch, will leave for others. The real horse whisperers are the horses themselves. They teach us to listen deeply within ourselves to hear from the heart, and to listen compassionately and effectively to others.

We are only scratching the surface of horses' intelligence and our own intelligence, which goes beyond cognitive intelligence and incorporates diverse and expansive ways of knowing. This intelligence is in the horses and in our intuitive consciousness. We learn about deeply resonant herd intelligence, a collective wisdom gathered from body, mind, heart and soul. When we listen to the whisper of the horses, when we deeply listen from within, when we listen from the heart to each other, what we hear is collective wisdom.

In my professional work with individuals, families or corporations, I am a guide, partnering with horses to invite people into the interconnected culture and worldview of horse and herd. Within this experience of the herd is the possibility for clients to expand their perspective regarding their organizations, their families, and themselves. They can then energize the quality of their relationships, the impact of their strategies, and the outcome of their decisions and actions.

Venturing Into the Herd

Margaret Mead, a respected anthropologist, approached entering an indigenous culture by respecting its inherent integrity. She waited patiently at the boundary of the culture for an invitation to enter from someone in the culture. Once the invitation was offered and received, there would be an exchange of gifts.

Our process at the ranch each time we enter the herd is much the same. We wait for the invitation from a horse or the herd. We pause. observe and wait for a readiness, a "yes" from the horses and from inside ourselves, before we enter their field. The invitation from them might be a glance in our direction, or movement towards us. Perhaps we just sense from within us a gesture of welcome from them.

Venturing into the herd in a respectful and trustworthy way, we patiently pause, sensing our way in by paying attention. We then join the horses first as guests, and then as visiting members, and then maybe we will be invited into the herd as extended family. We wait for a common place of "yes" within each of us for a collaborative meeting of mutual acceptance and interest in one another. Our goal is to create a relational alliance as we co-create a human-horse partnership where we offer and accept each other's authentic presence; we begin to matter to one another and we share common ground and common good.

We bring the possibility of a relational alliance by approaching with a mind open to respecting their ways, a heart open to engaging with compassion and a purpose open to creating responsible relationships and actions. This embodied, real-time experience of creating the best conditions for a positive meeting with another being and that being's culture is directly transferable from the horse field to the home field—in our families and in our places of business—as we engage within our human herds.

The horses communicate with us through their embodied presence and the body language of movement. They respond to us with compassionate hearts for our honest mistakes and a generous and willing curiosity to engage. In response, people engage with the horses and their human herd with expanded sensitivity, compassion, and curiosity and an awareness of the impact of their body language and authentic presence.

The Spirit of Leadership Approach: Un-training for Leader-ship and Life

Most people don't know much about horses, but our horses know a lot about people and enjoy connecting with them.

The Spirit of Leadership approach at Pebble Ledge Ranch is to prepare horses and people for life and their work, not to train them. If anything we are un-training them so that they and we can be more authentically present, resourceful, emotionally agile and resilient. We create the conditions for horses and humans alike to discover their own true purpose, not a purpose someone else has imposed upon them. Like horses shedding a furry coat that was once needed in a snowy winter but no longer needed on a warm spring day, people can shed what they have outgrown, what they no longer need, or what no longer serves them.

We use the same approach with people and horses. We prepare the horses to expect kindness and fairness from people. We do not bring any human artifacts into their horseplay when they engage with people that they have not already had a chance to investigate and get familiar with. We prepare the herd to confidently and comfortably engage with the people who enter their field. Horses are then willing and eager to be with people who have come to explore life choices in leadership, teamwork, and all matters of the heart.

You can train for a task, which is important but not sufficient in times of rapid or unpredictable change. If what is needed is not what you trained for, what is more essential is being prepared. When you train people, they are prepared for what is expected of them. When you prepare people, they can think for themselves. They can adapt their knowledge and skill to meet the current need if they are prepared for both the expected and the unexpected.

Our intention, again, is not to train people, but to engage them and help them prepare to engage with greater resourcefulness in times of change. This ability to be agile in the face of change is one of the most important capacities for surviving and thriving for humans, horses and all nature in conditions of anticipated or unanticipated change.

Engaging with the horses with right use of influence and power prepares people to be more aware of their leadership presence, more inclusive in their leadership practices, and to expand their range of choice in how they lead. Partnering with horses to work through relational dilemmas and moving together with them to overcome physical obstacles, we help people build on their strengths and face the challenges in their leadership roles and in life. Our approach is about cooperative teamwork, about how to lead a team as a collaborative leader toward a common, actionable vision. It's about being innovative in our work and being able to turn challenges into possibilities. It's about learning to operate from our inner knowing and from what has the most meaning for us. It prepares us to be optimistic by finding value in any situation and to be resilient by being agile as we face the challenges of our lives, in the world, and in the places we work. It's about trusting the collective wisdom of interconnected relationships and interdependent actions.

At the core, this approach is about creating the best possible conditions for people to discover how to be their real, authentic, best selves. It is also about helping with the process of change, whether people are grieving a loss, merging a company, or transitioning as part of a succession plan. It's an approach that creates highly engaged families, teams and leaders who will do well by doing good.

A lot of people don't know how to create an engaged family or team or what it means to experience being connected. We are a culture of individuals, not a herd. A team is a collective. A herd is a collective that is relationally connected. Working within the herd helps us find a way to belong, to be more of who we can be together rather than alone, to be able to participate in creating common good for all. While interacting with the horses, highly engaged leaders, followers and teams experience meeting the goals of the individual while moving toward a common vision that benefits each one and everyone. People can learn what it means to experience a relational alliance from the horses; we learn "we are stronger together" and "all of us is better than any one of us" when we help each other reach our goals and achieve our purposes.

I have been inspired by the people who come to Pebble Ledge Ranch and their capacity to step out, to be fully engaged, collaborative, and compassionate with themselves and each other. A lot of this happens with clients at the ranch because of their experiences with the horses and the natural world. My work is to create a design and context that offers inspiration and opportunities for people to get to places within themselves and with others that they might not have found their way to in their daily lives.

Preparing for a Day at the Ranch

In my morning team meetings, the horses challenge my authority, question my decisions, and appreciate that I am willing to listen. The members of my team are horses, but the challenges they offer are probably similar to the challenges faced by everyone who works with teams or supervises employees. Horses and people need herds, families, communities and work places that are interested in what matters to them, are willing to champion their purpose and offer them the opportunity to belong to something greater than just themselves.

When we feel we have a purpose and we have value in our herds, we are likely to be more engaged and interested in participating, more motivated to contribute and more inspired to offer our best. When horses and people feel cared about, including an appreciation for who they are, they can better achieve their personal purpose and contribute to the larger purpose of the whole.

We take great care to prepare people before they enter the culture of the horse herd, so that they and the horses can take something of value from their experience; they can be safe physically and emotionally and can have fun, meaningful horseplay and learning. The first step is to create the best possible field conditions for developing respect in preparation for a mutually beneficial relationship between horse and human, and human-to-human relationship.

We warmly welcome each person as they arrive at the ranch and see to their comfort as they get acquainted with an environment that for some is beyond their comfort zone. Once greeted, the participants attending the program are asked to write on a sticky note one or two strengths they want to build on and a "stretch" or challenge they want to explore during their experience at the ranch. We ask them to put their notes (for their eyes only) in their pockets for reference during their day with us.

We gather the human herd and circle up just outside the horse pasture for our first of many "wisdom gatherings." This is an opportunity to meet one another, get to know what is important to each other, to build common ground as a herd, and to share what we are learning. This process begins to build a resource of collective wisdom, which can benefit everyone. We trust that each individual in the group has something important to contribute—a unique point of view, a difference of opinion, an amazing insight, or words of goodwill and kindness. In sharing with others, our individual thoughts and experiences co-create a collective intelligence and wisdom that is more inclusive of ideas and more expansive of heart than what we can create individually. As we connect and listen deeply to one another, our inner selves and the outer world is enriched and the whole of the horse and human herd benefits.

We begin the process by asking each participant to introduce themselves with their names and to answer two questions, "What would make today a success for you?" and "What will your horse name to be for today?" Asking what would make today a success and how they might contribute to that success begins to create a field of appreciation for the collective process of the day and a positive regard for relationship with one another. We ask them to choose a horse name for the day to playfully disrupt their preconceived or habitual identity in a respectful and non-threatening way. We suggest that they choose a horse name that represents a quality that they feel would be of benefit to them and would contribute in a positive way to the group. We then invite them to tell the group their horse name and why they chose that name.

One of the men visiting the ranch chose the name Silver, the horse of his childhood hero the Lone Ranger, who carried his rider on adventures to help those in distress. One woman chose the name Buttercup, her first pony, best friend and a source of support growing up in a family that was too busy for her. She said she was bringing support to the group and attention to her team members in a way that did not happen at work when they got too busy doing their job in the workplace to notice who might need help. Another person chose the name Lightning hoping to reignite his passion for his work. Another person chose the name Black, a name taken from the movie "The Black Stallion" about a horse that broke free and discovered his strength. He said he chose that name to honor the journey of people of color to be free and strong. He said that what would make the day a success for him would be to build on his strength of courage, to break free of self-limiting ways of being, and to stretch himself by asking others to join him in that challenge as a team.

Learning what was of value to each person and hearing each other's horse names began to create a sense of curiosity and interest in the members within the group to build group compassion, empathy and collective wisdom. We can be more respectful of others, especially those different from us, when we are curious and interested in who they are and how they see the world, rather than being judgmental and critical of their way of thinking or being. Respect is less mysterious and confusing when we have a common language to communicate our good intentions and to get a sense of what is going on inside each person and between people.

Understanding one other builds trust so that the actions we take and the actions of others represent the spirit of the intention.

We prepare people to listen and to respond to the horses by teaching a basic "horse language" that helps them understand what the horses are trying to tell them and to help them be clearer about what they are trying to tell the horse. This gives people the opportunity to directly communicate with the horses (without an interpreter) and it makes the horses' job of being with people and bringing them into the herd easier.

Beyond verbal communication, body language and embodied presence are keys to authentic presence. Horses are the ultimate teachers of this. When asked, "What is your first language?" most people reply with the first spoken language they learned such as French, Spanish, English or Chinese. I remind them that before they had their preferred spoken language, they all had and still have body language. My infant grandchildren made their needs and emotions clearly known through gesture—like reaching toward or moving away—and through the sound and volume of laughing, crying, and babbling, things we learn to understand through context.

Bringing attention and intention to knowing through embodied language and presence gives us essential information about our authentic selves, our relationship with others, and the systems in which we participate. Our embodied presence is our unique human signature. It holds our history and contains everything about us. Horses are brilliant at communicating through embodied presence and by reading horse and human body language. What they look for is congruency: Does the intention and energy match the actions, movement and subtle energy?

Embodied Communication, Horse Whispering and Essential Listening

The real horse whisperers are the horses, and we are the listeners. The first skill of "embodied communication" means to listen with more than our ears to what is going on within us and to be aware of what you sense is going on with the horse and human herd. Listening with all our senses and by way of our minds, hearts and guts, we can hear what most wants to be spoken, honestly and with integrity.

The second skill in communicating is to align what is happening within us, with our intentions and choice of actions. We can think of this as "mindfulness in action."

The third skill is practicing compassion and loving kindness by listening through our hearts to ourselves, our human herd mates and our horse herd mates awaiting our arrival into their field.

The fourth skill that is useful when communicating with horses is "horse vocabulary." Horses communicate with each other and with humans through body movement and energy, sometimes subtly and sometimes not so subtly. The horses' communication and engagement with each other and with us is beyond verbal; it takes place through movement, location and relational alliances. Learning horse language and communication can awaken our capacity to listen from our bodies and hear from more places within us when communicating with people.

- Embodied Communication: Listen with all your senses
- Align Intentions and Actions: Mindfulness in action
- Practice Compassion, Empathy and Loving Kindness: Toward yourself, your human herd and horse herd
- Learn Horse Sense-ability and Vocabulary: Movement, location and relational alliances

Horse Vocabulary

Horses communicate through movement, location and relationship. We offer people who visit the ranch the following information. Movement of the horse's ears will tell you what the horse is paying attention to and how interested it is in engaging.

Two ears focusing forward say, "I am very interested in what is in front of me." One ear pointing one way and one ear pointing another way or moving around tells you the horse is paying attention to something from two or more different directions. Two ears slightly back might tell you the horse is listening to something behind them. Two ears flat back with its head out and a scowl can mean a number of things:

"No," "Maybe," "Not so fast," or perhaps "No, don't approach from my right side, try the left side." It can also mean, "No, I am not interested in engaging right now, but don't go away because that might change in the next moment," or simply, "What don't you understand about no?" It would be handy if we humans had ears that moved so we could communicate more clearly with one another.

Movement of the tail is another way horses communicate. A tail that is gently waving indicates, "I am paying attention to what is around me and behind me with interest." A brisk tail movement is negotiating space, and probably saying "give me space," or "get out of my space," whether to a pesky fly, a fellow herd mate or a human that is too close in proximity or energetic field. How great it would be to have a tail to say, "Bug off" when being bothered or "Back away" when feeling closed in?

Breath is a more subtle but powerful form of communicating through pace and intensity of breath. When horses are calm or at rest they breathe deeply and slowly. When on alert or ready to run, they breathe more rapidly. When releasing stress, they exhale with a long sigh or snuffle. Excited, they might sound a snorting breath as an alert to the herd of danger or a warning to intruders, or as an invitation to another horse to join in vigorous play. I have never seen a horse hold its breath like humans do. If we are holding our breath (not breathing) while engaging with them it might be confusing to them. If we are breathing rapidly, they might think we are communicating danger. If we are relaxed and breathing slowly, it communicates calm and peacefulness. Our breathing affects our inner state of being in a similar way. Horses can provide great feedback to us about communication with them, ourselves and with the world through our breathing patterns, of which we may not be aware.

Human Guests

Body movement can offer both subtle and obvious cues. What I believe, after watching many horse-with-human and horse-with-horse greeting rituals, is that the moving toward is an invitation to join the herd and to begin to communicate the culture and code of herd behavior. They may be trying to teach us common horse sense and self-respect.

Movement is a way for horses to welcome us to the herd, preparing us to be good herd members. A horse moving toward us is an honor as it means the horse notices us and we matter enough for them to go out of their way to engage with us. A horse walking toward us and stopping could mean, "I am coming to welcome you," or to simply say hello or check us out. If a horse approaches us and stops about a handshake-distance away and gives a small bow, it is probably an invitation to meet. If you extend your arm slowly and softly, palm down in the shape of a horse nose, the horse might sniff your hand as a way to take you in. Polite protocol then is to slowly bring your hand away and step back, giving the horse the choice to make the next move toward you or away from you. A horse walking toward you and not stopping might mean, "Get out of my way," or "Just letting you know who is in charge here," or "Do you have the horse sense to move, so I don't bump you or step on your foot?" The horse may be saying, "If you don't have the common horse sense to move when I ask and you allow me to push you or step on you, then you have little self-respect and common sense and you might be a danger to yourself and other herd members." A horse walking toward us and by us might be inviting us to join him on his journey and to keep us company as we walk forward on ours.

The horses are compassionate and forgive honest mistakes but even a horse has a limit to its patience with us. Bringing attention and intention to these sacred meetings with the horses awakens us to how we might be more conscious about how we greet people and how we meet the world.

> *"All living things emit a subtle energy field. The earth, our environment is full of interacting subtle energy fields"*
> —James Kepner

Movement of energy is clearly sensed by the horses but often not sensed by people. Often people sense or feel the energy but don't know what they are feeling or what to do with what they are sensing and feeling. We all have unseen but felt bubbles of open space and boundaries, the felt place of where I begin and the felt place of where I meet another or the environment. This is the meeting place of contact or connection between what is me and what is not me, what is me and what is you. The shared space is "us."

If you extend your arm out in front of you and turn in a 360° circle with your arm extended, the distance between your torso and extended fingertips is your personal or intimate space. For some of us it extends out farther and for others, in closer. For horses familiar with people, their personal intimate space extends about twenty feet out around them; for wild horses, one hundred times that. We can begin to sense our energy field and that of the horses with our hearts, hands, and our intuitive senses.

> *"I love you in a place that has no space and time, I love you for my life, you are a friend of mine."*
> —Leon Russell, "A Song for You"

The horses can sense when we enter the outer edge of their energy bubble and through each layer as we move our attention and intention physically and energetically closer to their intimate space. Within this space, invisible to the eye but visible through other senses, we can communicate with the horses far beyond verbal communication. In this shared energy field, we become more aware of a deeper inner self—the authentic and essential "me." We can, within this invisible bubble of time and space, access emotion and feel the grounded support of the herd as we feel our emotions ever more deeply. In the silent, honest presence of the horses, we become more honest and compassionate with ourselves and with others and we can access personal inner wisdom and collective wisdom.

According to Arawana Hayashi, we can look at space in relationship to our three bodies: a physical body, our earth body and our social body. The physical body includes all our senses. The earth body includes our relationship to earth and gravity, air and breath and all the forces of nature. Our social body is our ever-changing relationship with the outside world.

Movement of the social body is easy to notice if you are mindful and know to look for it. The social body is the dynamic and ever-changing relationship between the horse herd members, the horse and human herd members and the environment. The physical body registers its experience from the earth and social bodies and offers its own unique movement to interact with them. It sounds complicated, but it is actually a beautiful dance that reveals the ongoing story of the horses, humans and all surrounding life. You begin to notice the relationships between the horses, who buddies up with whom, where there is conflict and how it gets resolved, how power and leadership are shared, how friendship and loyalty are expressed.

Last, as we look at movement we hold it in context, watching the congruence of all aspects of body movement, individual characteristics and style of movement, and movement at the level of the collective. Engaging with horses helps us relate to the world with a 360° perspective. In the business world, we talk about "360° awareness," seeing a more complete picture of a person or situation. It is agreed upon as an important idea but often forgotten when there is a pressing problem to solve. We sometimes narrow our focus and move faster in these situations when what would benefit us is pausing and reflecting from a wider perspective before acting.

Fear can prompt us to look from a more and more narrow and closed-in perspective when what we might need most is to be more expansive, looking up and out to discover the needed resource of information or choice of action. In the presence of the horses, we can slow and reflect and expand our vision. As humans we are capable of seeing about 180°, although much of the time, especially in front of computers or reading from our smart phones, we narrow our vision to about 20°. While a narrow focus is sometimes beneficial, we also need to be able to see the big picture for important decisions. Horses can see 340° without moving their heads.

They cannot see the 10° behind them or the 10° right in front of their eyes. Has anyone ever asked you, "Can't you see what's right in front of your eyes?" That phrase likely comes from cowboys and their experience with horses. With a slight shift in position, horses can change their perspective to 360°. We can learn from horses to shift our perception to have a 360° perspective. We also can have a memorable experience in holding a 360° perspective by simply wandering around the field with a herd of six horses, each a thousand pounds of movement, a fun-loving pony and zebra engaging with each other and with you. This hard-wired human capacity, to pay attention to the larger field, will awaken primal instincts to pay 360° attention. With a full range perspective we perceive with all our senses, and we begin to know what is whole and holy all around us and within us.

Paying attention to the different levels of system offers another lens for exploring and understanding what is going on between the horses and between the horses and us in a relational field. This ability to notice levels of system also helps us understand each other when there is a "miss" in communication.

- The first developmental level of system is, "It's all about me...how do I move in my world?"
- The second level of development is, "It's all about you and me...how do you and I move together?"
- The third developmental level is, "It's all about us...how does my family, team, culture move?"
- The fourth level is the larger system of the environment we are presently in, "How is the world of life creating movement?"

Spirit, our highly sensitive horse, offers a great example of applying the lens of levels of system. Spirit often pins her ears back and glares at you in a clear "No." Is she saying, "No, I don't feel in the mood to engage today"? Is she saying, "No, I don't want to hang out with you today"? Is she saying no to the other horses so they do not interfere in her conversation with you? Or is it something in the environment causing her to say, "No, I don't care to chat. Can't you see that it's windy and I am trying to keep warm?"

There is communication and information we can begin to notice and appreciate in the dynamic nature of the herd, which is a living system and interconnected field of interrelated social relationships. We can pay attention to social space through distance and proximity, and social order through influence, decision-making, purposeful movement and action.

Connection Between Horse and Human

The horses begin to relate differently to each other as they welcome new members into the herd. The people participating begin to relate differently with each other as they are invited into the herd by the horses and experience a culture based on interdependence and interrelationship.

Paying attention to how we enter each other's space can be an expression of respect.

We invite the participants into a process that requires entering the herd with respect for themselves, each other and the horses. We ask them to bring to mind the strengths and challenges they wrote down when they arrived, and to incorporate them in some way when entering the herd. We suggest that they extend their interest or intention in some way to the horses before approaching them. They can do this through their eyes or heart or through the spoken word. We ask that they wait for an invitation from the horses and also get a "yes" from within themselves so they can meet at a common place of "Yes, we are ready to meet." We invite the guests of the herd to be aware of what is happening within them and around them and to listen for the relationship to unfold. We encourage people to be clear about their intentions, align their intentions with their actions, and let go of attachment to outcome, This mindful and heartfelt attention and intention creates respectful relationship, clearer communication and more meaningful and trustworthy relationships.

Learning to be guests in a herd of horses, we learn about respect, trust, and care. We learn in the presence of the herd about deepening the connection to our purpose, enhancing the quality of relationships, being more of an embodied presence and experiencing ourselves interconnected with the world. The power of the herd comes from their culture of collective wisdom. As we join the herd, we become part of that larger culture of collective wisdom and can bring that wisdom into our human herds, creating a world in which we are all proud to live.

Section II—The Path of Collective Wisdom

Pause, Reflect and Respond

On your journey to your authentic presence bring to heart and mind one of the horses you have just met or a horse who has made a difference in your life and have a silent conversation from your heart to the horse's heart about something of great importance to you.

Reflecting on that conversation, give yourself a horse name that captures the essence of your best self or the self to which you aspire.

Identify and create your ideal herd from some of the people whose values you respect who and value you.

Take several index cards and write a word or phrase and an image that came from your reflections on each individual card.

Save these cards as you will be reflecting back on them.

III

The Path of the Natural World and the Call of the Wild

Chapter 8
Nature and Human Nature

"Look deep into nature and there you will understand everything."
—*Albert Einstein*

My work coaching and guiding people in their personal discovery and professional development through learning by experience with horses and nature was born from my love of horses, a draw to the wild and a need to be outside for more of my life. My family, as I was growing up, encouraged our love and respect of the natural world through camping trips, hiking through forests and the rigor of adapting to living outside.

The intention to make nature more central to my professional life began one Monday morning about thirty years ago. I was sitting at my desk, as director of a large community center, looking out the window at the American and Israeli flags blowing in the wind. I longed to be out in the wind with my feet on the earth. I yearned to be where I could be more directly engaged with nature's beauty and wisdom. I compared the straight black letters on flat white paper stacked on my desk to the vibrant colors of the flowers out my window. The linear walls of my office were stifling compared to the movement and flow of the landscape outside my door. I began to realize that I was working in a setting and living in a way that no longer fit my authentic nature, and as a result my creative spirit and life force was suffering. I was doing my job, but my passion for the work and excitement to be at work each day was diminishing. I had always loved my work, but was now finding that I was caught up in mindless distractions. I had somehow lost the sense of meaning and purpose that I had always valued in my work. My senses were dulled, my creativity dwindling and my connection to my instincts confused. I knew something had to change in me or in my job. I needed to either find work that I loved, or find a way to love the work I was currently doing.

That night as I prepared for sleep I heard a whisper from the night calling me to come outside. I took my blanket and pillow and made my bed on the ground. Stretching out, heart and belly against the comforting earth with the awesome expanse of the stars above me, the soothing night lulled me into a deep, healing sleep. I awoke the next morning my face washed clean by the dew, my skin a more comfortable fit, senses awake, my body and spirit renewed. Responding to the need for movement I went to the pasture, and inviting my horse Jetset to come with me, I headed for the forest path across from my home. Jetset, as always, was up for the adventure and pranced eagerly by my side. Guided by nature and with the exuberant and good company of the horse something began to awake in me. As we wandered down the path, our senses alert, my awareness expanded, my thoughts began to clear, and my heart opened. With each breath and footstep I began to know from the inside out that I was in the midst of an important life change and new rhythm of being. My intimate relationship with the powerful forces of the natural world began to speak to me of change. Jetset's silent horse whisper seemed to say pause, listen and follow your heart home. On many wild rides through the forest, this feisty mare always showed me the way home when I was helplessly lost.

I realized that now I was hopelessly lost in life direction. Leaning against her warm body, I gave her a hug and on we walked. Jetset was once again guiding me to find my way back home; this time, to me. I realized that my life passions needed to be more in an integral rhythm with my work and how I lived my life. I began to know that my inner nature needed a more direct relationship with outer nature and engagement with the natural world.

My footsteps and Jetset's hoof beats through the woods led me back to memories of my childhood, much of which was lived outside. The apple tree was my home; its limbs filled with my important kid stuff. I spent hours and lifetimes in that apple tree thinking, dreaming and honing my survival skills.

As we followed the trail along the river, the outdoor kid opened her eyes, and began to see through the adult woman reminding me of how to play, be passionate and purposeful.

So, at the age of almost forty, Mother Earth under my feet, a family of trees watching over me and in the company of a good horse, a new vision for my life began to emerge.

I envisioned bringing my love of nature more directly into my life and taking my work into a setting in the natural world. The vision began to take form. I would create a place to work surrounded by nature. I would be in partnership with nature and invite her wise voice to be heard. It would be called The Hearth, a place where the heart and earth could come together in support of the wholeness of being—my wholeness and the wholeness of those who would come to work with me.

My dream, born that morning as I followed the path homeward, became reality. Now, many years later, I have continued to live the reality and have created a business based on this vision. My workspace has no walls. I work close to the earth, alongside a stream, within a family of trees, and in the company of horses and other wild beings. I have developed an intimate and respectful working relationship with the forces, elements, and creations of nature and most especially the horses. All of nature's beings, the wild turkeys that strut across the field, the hawks that circle above, the butterflies and dragonflies with their magic wings, the crickets and tree toads with their songs are teachers, guides, mentors and co-facilitators in my work. Nature as a partner provides endless lessons with a balance of enough challenge and enough solid ground of support from which to grow, heal and learn and change.

I no longer drive to my workplace; instead, I walk to the places that best support the work of the moment. I follow the path outside my back door, stopping by the pasture to give the horses a good morning greeting, listening to their welcoming nicker and running my fingers through their silky fur.

Preparing for the day, I open myself to the natural world through my senses. Slowing down, observing, noticing and reflecting, I become aware of what's going on around me and inside of me. Sometimes I wander alongside the stream entering the forest greeted by the chatter of birds and the vibrant wildflowers of blue and purple growing from the green of the forest floor. Tall hills gently descend to a quiet clearing, creating a sense of welcome and well-being.

I smell the forest scent, the pungent earth, the mysteries of rotting leaves, the tanginess of onion ramps and sweetness of wildflowers. I listen to the bubbling of the stream and the competing styles of bird whistles, chirps, and cries. The shrill call of the hawk seems to still the sky. I see the variation in the brown colors of tree trunks and countless greens of leaves and plants. I look for the wide, double umbrella of the female mayflower hiding her fruit alongside the single leafed male. I feel the rolling contour of the earth under my feet and the textured back of the bark I touch as I walk by. A hundred-year-old oak gives shelter to this sacred space. I check in with the horses; they respond with honesty to my behavior and to what's going on within me. They react with displeasure and unease to any incongruence between my inner emotions and outer behavior. They approach me willingly and engage me with interest when I am authentically present and in alignment with myself and them and my world. I appreciate this honest feedback and trust that my day will go better for their rigorous, honest and empathetic coaching.

Showing up, being aware and present to the moment, my senses alert, my heart more open and receptive—this is the preparation to partner with nature in guiding people to solve their life dilemmas. I have to live each day according to life's principle of "life creates conditions conducive to life." As a respectful and trustworthy partner with nature and practitioner with people, I have to come from an inner place of authenticity and can only guide people to where I have been or am willing to go with them.

People begin their personal development or professional discovery as we enter the horse pasture together, or on a rainy or snowy morning walk down the dirt path along the river to my Mongolian tent. An enclosed but open-to-nature work space called a yurt or gur is a circular space twenty foot across with windows open to the four directions and an opening in the center to the sky high above. Its nomadic presence suggests a dwelling in harmony with the natural world. On cold or rainy days we can work next to a warm fire burning in the wood stove, hearing the rain above our heads or watching the snow swirling outside. On temperate days we have the option of working completely outside. The graceful arms of tree boughs shelter the workspace with shade and magical serenity. Purple wildflowers surround our two wicker chairs offering breathtaking beauty, or they border a blanket in vibrant color as we work directly on the earth. The stream nearby reflects the sunlight and provides a gurgling chant as calming background music. The gentle hills rising up on either side of the stream create a sense of protection, welcome, and reassurance that all will be okay.

> *"Nature's peace will flow into us like sunshine flows into trees. The winds will blow their own freshness into you, and the storms their energy, while cares will drop off like autumn leaves"*
> —John Muir

How It Works In Real Time

Working with nature as my partner, I collaborate with my client. The client brings something of interest to explore and I help them shape it and focus it into a question. We then decide where and how in this expansive "office without walls" we are to begin the exploration and journey of discovery. Sometimes we are drawn to the soothing rhythm of the stream, other times we climb to the top of the ridge to discover the overall view or larger vision. Some people choose to do their coaching or therapy session in the pasture with the family of horses offering lessons of leadership and teamwork and personal competency. The heart of the horse listens in a way people can better hear themselves and others. The grounded strong trunk of a tree can support a person's backbone to be straightforward in a way a chair cannot. Sometimes movement directs the work. We walk, creating our own path, climbing the hill, stepping on stones to cross the creek, moving over logs and under limbs, sliding, slipping, falling, losing and finding our balance. The physical exertion causes our hearts to beat faster, our blood to flow, our breath to be fuller, and our perceptions to be clearer. Our bodies' sensation and awareness is heightened revealing wisdom only our bodies know to be true. We can explore with all our senses and be more aware of our feelings and our primitive instincts.

My outside office is a playground for the inner child and a platform for the wise elder. Nature's workspace is a quiet island from the chaos of life, a safe refuge for physical and emotional exploration, a place to hear inner thoughts, a space to rediscover direction and wisdom in order to grow and transform. The resources of the natural world are an abundant source of creativity and healing energies. They provide us with reflections of ourselves, the awaking of our senses, and awareness of our strengths as we face challenges. The art of working with people in nature is first to dwell within the power of the landscape, the contours of the earth, the diversity of the trees, the movement of the streams. We can offer a safe place in the sacred space of the natural world to open the way for experience and dialogue and then stand aside and allow the process to happen. The encounter between the person and nature and in relationship with the horses in particular can be deeply meaningful and holds the possibility of understanding life dilemmas differently, expanding life skills and for transformational change.

One of my more lively outdoor sessions occurred when I was working with an anxious 65-year-old woman named Judy who was fearful to engage in life. We had agreed to cautiously climb the hill to experiment with looking out and over the valley to experience a more expansive and far-reaching perspective of the dilemma she was facing, which was how to better "take the lead of her life". I began by leading her carefully up the challenging hill. Part way up I turned to her and said, "Would you like to lead? I will follow closely behind you." "Yes, I would like to lead," she said quietly. She turned toward the hill and before I knew it she bounded off, scurrying quickly up the steep tree-covered slope, holding roots and trees for balance along the way. Startled, I struggled to keep up with her. When she got to the top she laughed and shouted, "I'll bet you didn't think I could do that. Neither did I!" She sat down to catch her breath between laughter and tears. The climb up the hill allowed her to re-experience early developmental patterns of yielding, pushing, reaching, grasping and pulling. Physically moving through these developmental tasks, her body began to release fixed patterns of helplessness and create patterns of agility and strength for better self-confidence. In this natural setting, she was able to experience herself in a bolder, more sure-footed and competent way. She discovered that instead of being fearful and unsure and letting life lead her, she could trust herself to lead her life. One simple experience like this can lead to many more.

Being in nature can interrupt our familiar and habitual patterns so that we can live more fully in the present. There is a practical wisdom in nature that enhances self-awareness. Spending time in nature teaches us the skill of observation, paying attention to what is actually happening in the present, and also teaches us to be receptive to whatever success is emerging in the future. We all have blind spots and simply cannot see what we cannot see even when it is right in front of our eyes. Nature improves our vision.

The workings of the natural world have the potential to promote transformational change and support meaningful life. Sharpening and expanding our ability to sense our awareness, the "what is" becomes clearer and more defined. The power of nature cannot be accessed through books or guided imagery in the same way it can through the direct experience of our senses. Standing on the earth we can experience physical and emotional support, being grounded, feeling a place of belonging, and feeling held and safe. Sitting by the stream we can see, hear and feel movement and can also feel our own watery flow of internal movement. Looking down from the top of a high ridge, the larger view from above supports us right-sizing life's dilemmas from a larger perspective. How can we live closer to our individual natures, our own natural rhythms? We might have to leave the flatness of the sidewalk for a dirt path and the linear walls of our house (and thinking) for the random wilderness of the forest. In our homes we strive for predictability, neatness, and order. Nature is messy. Leaves are scattered, branches are broken, trees live where they fall, rocks are scattered about. Nature is freedom of expression, a dance of movement and dynamic change.

One day I worked with a woman who chose to have her coaching session along the stream to address issues she was having at work with her father, who was also her boss. As she quietly gazed into the water, she began thinking about her conflicts with her father and of what remained unspoken between them. We created an experiment whereby she listened to the water for what she wanted to say to her father and had not been able to say, and what she could say that would bring them closer together. With the gentle encouragement of the stream, she listened to the words from within; she found her voice as well as the courage to now have some important conversations with her father. On the way back through the pasture, she paused with Bea the lead mare to practice speaking what was important to her. Bea seemed to look her in the eye, and gave her a nudge forward as if to say go for it.

> *"If we surrender to earth's intelligence we could rise up rooted like trees."*
> —Marie Rainer Rilke

Moving with consciousness through the natural world, we are able to expand our awareness, mobilize our energy, make clear contact with ourselves and our environment; and, make meaning of our experience in the moment and our lives in a new way. As we build more and more networks of healthy relationship between nature's beings and ourselves, we are more able to create those networks of healthy relationship between people of all sorts. Perhaps then we can stop creating realities in which no one really wants to live and start creating a future in which we all want to live.

The sounds of nature—the rush of the water, the hum of the wind—are more than metaphors. There is a phenomenological language of nature we can learn to hear, therefore learning to better hear each other and ourselves. Nature educates us to see, not to visualize, not to project, but to experience sight. Within the stories nature tells us, we can rediscover and own our past. As humans we need contact and relations with each other, and with that which is beyond human, beyond ourselves into the more-than-human mystery. We need new skills to orient and navigate, and to expand meaning to multiple realities and multiple possibilities. Nature supports the inner building of identity. Again, the rhythm of the natural world has the ability to bring healing and transformation.

I suggested to another client, Rose, that she lead a walk with one of the horses. She asked fearfully, "What if I get lost and I can't find my way? What if the horse does not want to go with me or trust that I know what I am doing? Wait, I have a compass on my key chain, maybe that will help me find my way." As we returned from the walk she said, "It wasn't the compass in my pocket I needed to find my direction, it was the compass within me I needed to learn to use. The horse trusted me and walked with me when I trusted myself."

This experience in nature allowed her to experience herself in a different way. She had always depended on others to lead and to show her the way. Determining the direction of the walk created the opportunity for her to experiment with trusting her senses and self in the moment and to find her own direction. She then can take the confidence and skills she learned from her nature-based experience into her life where she need to make and trust her decisions. Partnering with nature and her horse partner, Rose expanded her personal capacity and range of choice by more fully being herself and daring to be more than she thought she could be.

Inviting people into a relationship with nature and engaging with horses encourages the possibility for them to open to themselves. When people access relationship with the natural world, familiar habitual patterns are often challenged and resources previously untapped become more available.

As we walk in nature, our steps may slow down to watch a bright yellow butterfly or a shiny dragonfly reflected in the glittering water, or to listen to the whisper of a horse; our internal chatter slows, our inside monologue quiets and we hear what is essential for us to hear and know in the moment. As we reconnect with breath, our internal wind, we reconnect with our embodiment.

Dilemmas may not change or go away as we encounter the wilderness and our inner nature, but we change. When in relationship with nature and our own inner nature, with our senses awake, we can make meaning of our world, experience our competency, and respond to the awe and wonder of our humanness and of life.

One afternoon I worked with a bright ten-year-old boy whose mother had been diagnosed with AIDS. He hunted up and down the creek bed gathering stones that caught his imaginative eyes. He brought the stones to the river's edge and I encouraged him to create a pattern with the stones. He carefully arranged them making deliberate choices and changes until he said, "There, done." I asked him if the patterns had a story or any meaning for him. He launched eagerly into a story of a bear and a butterfly. The bear rock protected the butterfly rock while the butterfly rock learned to use its wings to fly to freedom. He said his mom was like the bear rock and that he knew she would always watch over him until he could learn to fly, or maybe he was the bear rock and the mom was the butterfly and he would protect her as she learned to fly. The stones and the land, the forest and the stream gave this boy a safe space to begin to tell his story and find strength and hope. As we returned, walking through the horse pasture, Tess the pony trotted up to him, reminding him he was not alone and that he could still run and play.

> *"In the presence of nature, a wild delight runs through the man, in spite of real sorrows."*
> —Ralph Waldo Emerson

Nature and Human Nature

As humans, if can we see ourselves as an intimate part of the natural world, we are never alone. The "natural" power of nature has the ability to influence our human experience.

> *"Nature always wears the colors of the spirit."*
> —Ralph Waldo Emerson

I believe that the spiritual dimension of people is a strong source and underutilized aspect of our work as leaders, coaches and facilitators of change. The wonder and mystery of the natural world evokes that aspect of our humanness without using words. We as humans are not superior to the natural world but equal with all creation. Utilizing the spiritual dimension requires that we surrender the hierarchal distance between nature and ourselves. If you look, nature will reveal itself; if you listen, nature will speak and you may hear what you most need to hear. Human relationship and vulnerability to nature allows for an expansive approach to well being. Being in touch with and present to our deeper waters, our deeply rooted earthliness, our ancient stone bone memories, and our flow of breath corresponds to a systems-view that is central to an expansive life.

As coaches, therapists or educators in nature-based awareness, we work with change and transition. In nature, the earth is affected by what came before. The richness of the soil is directly related to what grew up and died in this place, much like the effect past generations of a family have on the present generation of the family. When people are invited into relationship with the natural world, the relationships in their own families and communities and businesses can become clearer, more meaningful and purposeful.

As intimate members of nature and as responsible partners with her, we can bring forward the best of our authentic presence and make better choices in and for life.

9
Listening to the Genius of Nature

> *"If you will stay close to nature, to its simplicity, to the small things hardly noticeable, those things can unexpectedly become great and immeasurable."*
> Ranier Maria Rilke, *Letters to a Young Poet*

Indigenous people and tribal cultures have been learning from and with nature for centuries. Architects and designers have been learning from and designing in harmony with nature's incredibly innovative and sustainable designs. Artists and scientists have created many of their best designs and solutions from observing and taking their inspiration from nature.

> *"After 3.8 million years of evolution, nature has learned what works, what is appropriate, and what lasts here on earth."*
> —Janine Benyus

Janine Benyus has given leadership to a field of study, called "biomimicry," which taps into nature's genius and incorporates it to manage human dilemmas. She is a biologist, author, innovation consultant, and co-founder of the Biomimicry Institute. She popularized the term "biomimicry" in her 1997 book Biomimicry: Innovation Inspired by Nature.

Biomimicry (from bios, meaning life, and mimesis, meaning to imitate) studies nature's best ideas and then imitates these designs and processes in solving human problems. One example is studying a leaf to invent a better solar cell, which is sometimes called "innovation inspired by nature." The core idea is that nature, imaginative by necessity, has already solved many of the problems humans grapple with.

In addition to learning about making more earth friendly and sustainable products, biomimicry (or learning from nature) can be applied to earth friendly, people friendly and sustainable leadership, teamwork and the process of human engagement. Observing and learning from horses and their herds about shared leadership, and cooperative teamwork and innovation is a form of biomimicry.

Finding A Champion In Nature

"The lover of nature is one whose inward and outward senses are still truly adjusted to each other; Every natural action is graceful."
—Ralph Waldo Emerson

We can expand and enrich our human identity to an ecological identity by identifying ourselves within the family of the natural world.

Our ecological identity, a natural birthright, is a nature-centered worldview. It is a perspective that places us within the family and interrelated system of nature. Ecological identity broadens our relational field from a human-centric approach to include an awareness of our place as part of nature and within nature, rather than above or outside of nature. This understanding of our identity has a direct impact on our beliefs, values and behaviors in our relationships with people and all life.

> *"Ecological Identity yields a kind of personal awakening which allows people to bring their perception of nature to the forefront of awareness and to orient their actions based on their ecological world view...As you probe the layers within, you might realize that your experiences in nature are now the source of profound wisdom and personal happiness. What are the implications for your everyday life—your job, your personal relationships, your professional goals?"*
> —M Thomashow, Voices of Ecological Identity, 1996

One ecological identity and biomimicry learning experience focusing on the genius of nature, was with the Western Reserve Land Conservancy.

This is a high-performing organization with outstanding leadership. The organizations mission is "to provide the people of their region with essential natural assets through land conservation and restoration." Their vision is that "today, a decade from now, and beyond the time that we can imagine, the Western Reserve will be a stunningly beautiful and healthy place of thriving, prosperous communities nourished by vibrant natural lands, working farms and healthy cities."

The organization had experienced rapid growth in the amount of land they were managing and protecting and in the number of new and talented diverse staff. Many of them were relatively new to the organization—their personal relationships with each other, how their jobs related to each other, and the strategic plan for the organization.

Not only was the growth huge, but so were the organization's many responsibilities. They changed from conserving and preserving mostly rural land to also watching over urban areas, as well as working with the impacts on the environment of oil and shale operations. The organization was moving from one basic strategy to four strategies.

The first time the group came to the ranch was to work with the horses with a goal that the staff would get to better know one another, learn what mattered to each, decide how they wanted to work together, and share what they felt. We spent the day talking, and working with those issues through personal reflection and by engaging in team-building activities with the horses.

The second part of the retreat was a biomimicry project; the Western Reserve Land Conservancy staff partnered with nature to better understand their own strategic plan. And, it was a natural partnership as this organization's goal is to conserve and preserve the genius of nature.

The group of about forty staff was divided into five teams. Each team chose one of the five components of the organization's overall strategic plan.

Their next task was to choose a property, an environment or ecosystem within the Western Reserve Land Conservancy's purview that resonated with them as a team. The team would go to that place, find a champion in nature that somehow represented their piece of the strategic plan. For example, a healthy grove of trees includes young trees and mature trees as well as a variety of species that would allow it to thrive might be a champion for diversity and inclusion, demonstrating the value of diversity and inclusion to organizations. The team would expand their understanding of their part of the strategic plan by learning how nature would approach that strategy. The team would then present to the group what they learned from their particular champion in nature, and from their place in nature.

Each team was required to design a project. They had about two months, during which they were to take an afternoon and go outside with their team to a place or ecosystem of their choice. Some went to wetlands; others went to a mature forest, still others to a meadow. They would ask nature to inspire them, talk among themselves about an idea, then return to the ranch to do a presentation to the whole group.

When they returned, each team did a well-designed PowerPoint with photos, making the connections. They produced pictures of themselves having fun and explained the beauty of the space they entered. They reported on their experiences and passed along to their organization the lessons they were bringing back to it.

One of the champions chosen by a team was the wetlands located on a large conservation farm, a large preserved wetland area.

The group decided the on the wetlands as its champion because the wetlands explained the real purpose of the nature conservancy, which sometimes is not fully understood. A common misconception is that the conservancy protects land, but does not benefit people.

The team created a video first showing how the wetlands are often perceived using images such as swampland, swamp monsters, muck and mosquitoes—all things with negative connotations. Few understand the importance of wetlands because of their bad rap. Sometimes people see the Western Reserve Land Conservancy that way, too, said the team.

Yet, if you look closely at the wetlands, the team wanted to express, you will see that they purify water; they stop erosion; they slow storm surges; they stop flooding; and they provide habitat. Wetlands are essential.

So, the team realized they needed to change the perception of the wetlands.

Changing the perception of the wetlands into a "champion" of nature would also be key in changing the perception of the Conservancy, said the team; they needed to be telling people the good that the Conservancy does as opposed to letting misconceptions about the organization go unaddressed.

At that moment, the strategic plan of the Western Reserve Land Conservancy came further into focus. The teams in the Conservancy began to better understand their own planning needs thanks to the wetlands of nature. They began to see the need for certain strategies, and the role of champions of nature because of a simple, nature-based, biomimicry design.

Got a problem? Ask nature. By partnering with nature, everyone in the organization had become invested in their mutual plan. They had arrived at some doable steps, and they all were working together on it. Why here? Why now? They had invited nature's voice and life's principles to the table as an equal partner. In addition to being nature's advocate and helping nature, nature was helping the organization. Nature was giving back to them something they never could have gotten in their offices.

At the ranch, we champion the concept that biomimicry is about bringing nature to the table as a full partner. Go sit under a tree, and something happens. Maybe part of what happens is that you get quiet enough to use your own senses.

Maybe it's the beauty of nature. Maybe it's the literal gravity from the earth. Maybe it's the wind. Different things impact different people. Perhaps the lack of human-made distractions in nature offers something. There are plenty of distractions in nature, but people out in the natural world are often free of the distractions that interfere in their lives. In nature, your heart opens; you engage your senses.

The Thriving Nature of Horses

Horses have been thriving for millions of years. We can learn from them by observing how they live and adapt. I observe, and I reflect on what horses do that has allowed them to thrive. And over time, what they do has become dramatically clear to me. They work together. They challenge each other to be their best. They adapt. And they prepare.

They prepare for the future by doing what is essential in the present. Being in tune with the weather, they prepare for the deep cold from the time when the weather is warm. As the temperature gets a little bit cold, they grow a little more coat. They begin to adapt. Animals and plants in nature prepare. They react to warning signs that something is coming. They are attuned to the warnings, and their bodies respond, little by little. First, they grow a little oily overcoat, and long hairs begin to sprout over their summer coat. Then a down coat begins to sprout, and as the temperature gets colder, the down gets thicker, and the longer their oily outer hairs grow. By the time winter hits, horses have their regular fur, the down that holds their body heat, and then an oilcloth of sorts to keep out the wetness.

Each evening during the 2013-2014 winter, we, like many North Americans, listened to the news and were told about a weather crisis. We were in a polar vortex. Newscasters said: Don't go outside. We are closing schools. We're in an environmental crisis mode. Some news reports were good sources of information, and offered good advice, such as don't wander around without proper clothing, don't be stupid, dress properly, or don't drive in bad weather. But a lot of the news was fear-based; the energy of the speakers on television, what stories made the news, was fear-based. We were in a crisis.

Well, I was in a warm house, as were many other people listening to the broadcasts. There were folks who were living out in the streets whose crisis was real. But ours? After listening to the news one night and being told not to go outside, I walked outside, where the horses live. I looked around, and the horses were as calm as could be. Their attitude seemed to say, "Well, it's thirty-two degrees below zero, or whatever." They were hanging out, eating their hay, standing close to each other.

The next morning I went out again when it was minus whatever. It was the depth of winter. I watched the sun come up, and the horses were standing in the sun, half asleep. I was thinking, "Look how horses approach this extreme weather relative to how we as human animals approach this extreme weather. The human animal seems to be about surviving: How do I survive? Horses act on the principle of what they need to do to thrive.

In the morning, the horses were covered with frost. At night, they were covered with snow, which did not melt for the same reason that snow on a well-insulated house roof doesn't melt even though the house is warm inside. There was little heat escaping from the horses' bodies. They were not cold because most of their heat stayed within their coat.

When the winds hit, horses as a group turn their butts to the wind. After eating their breakfast, they play, running around, kicking the snow, chasing each other around, rearing, and looking like they are having a party. That generates body heat. After playing, they all come together, and share the body heat that they have created.

The most vulnerable among the herd at Pebble Ledge Ranch that winter was the small zebra. She was in the middle of the pack that especially cold morning. She stayed out of the wind. A horse that doesn't have such a thick coat stands in a tight space between two others. The horses would warm their noses against each other's flanks.

They had worked together. They had all prepared for the winter, and when it came they continued to work together, collaborating, cooperating with each other, and playing. They adapted. In such ways, horses are flexible, resilient, and optimistic. In most instances, they do not panic. They seem to trust that one day, maybe the next one, the sun will come out, icicles will melt off their coats, the wind will dry them off, and they will be ready to prepare for the next season.

 Their bodies adjust, adapt and protect them from the cold. When horses dig under the snow to get grass, the digging pumps blood through their feet, warming their body and their legs. All their blood rushes upward to warm them. They generally don't feel the cold in their legs. Though horses sometimes stand in deep snow, their lower legs and hooves do not suffer from the cold. This is because the legs below the knees are made up mostly of bones and tendons, bone and tissue that can resist freezing. In extreme cold temperatures, blood-shunting mechanisms in their hooves can change circulation patterns to preserve body warmth.

The point is that horses adjust to the cold. Sometimes, I would go out in the middle of the night to throw out extra hay, and the horses were rarely in their shelters because they weren't cold. In extreme cold, horses need an adequate water supply, a place to shelter from the wind, and enough food to burn calories to keep their energy up, according to most veterinarians. As long as owners haven't interrupted their natural coat-growing by using a blanket on them, the horses should be fine. They are hard-wired to adapt. When the occasion arises, horses' bodies are resilient. When they don't need it, their bodies don't grow thick coats.

I wonder how much adapting and resiliency is hard-wired in humans. Humans so quickly change their environments to fit their needs that the body does not often need to adjust itself.

In the hard winter of 2013-14, people would ask, "How did your horses survive the vortex?" I would respond, "They are thriving."

I went out one deeply cold morning to find the horses frosted. Icicles were hanging from their chins. They looked beautiful. The ice was glistening. The scene was amazing. The horses looked like statues standing quietly. They were not agitated, running around, as if to say, "What are we going to do? It's ten below out here!" No, they were just fine.

This fascinates me. If we lived more like a horse lives, how might our lives better adapt to changes and challenges?

> *"Here is your country. Cherish these natural wonders; cherish the natural resources as a sacred heritage, for your children and your children's children. Do not let selfish men or greedy interests skin your country of its beauty, its riches or its romance."*
> —Theodore Roosevelt

Listening to the Genius of Nature

Climate changes are happening, leading to the possibilities of more and more human challenges. The key to adapting is all about how we prepare. It is about how we refrain from panic mode and learn to live sensibly with the forces of nature. I believe that as long as we feel that we can dominate nature, we will be surprised when we cannot. Then, we will feel completely vulnerable. If, instead, we recognize that nature is a stronger force, and we are part of nature, we may choose to use our best resources to adapt, be resilient, and optimistic in the face of great climate change.

What happens when we can't control life, especially nature? The result is often an existential anxiety. Living with an underlying anxiety, all the time, uses a lot of energy. That sapping of energy works against us. It leaves us unable to tap into our strengths and our intuitiveness. We are part of these natural phenomena. There are things that we can do to be more in harmony with our natural environment and thrive over time.

Companies that send their leaders to the ranch are looking for what individuals and families are looking for—ways to thrive, not just survive—and ways to sustain positive change over time.

This is where learning from nature comes in. Nature, for 3.8 billion years, has managed to sustain itself and to thrive in some form or another. Horses have thrived for 65 million years.

How might we as humans learn from horses' and nature's best solutions? How might we be inspired by what we learn with them, and from them, about how our systems and our families might be innovative, might engage in what works and what lasts, rather than creating what is unsustainable in our organizations, our families, and our systems.

Nature is a success. It's a success by continuing to do what works, and letting go of what doesn't work. Horses, for instance, look toward what is. They are not bothered with looking over their shoulders at what has failed. Horses always are moving toward what is life-giving; they always move forward.

Let us look at what is working in nature and with horses. People visiting the ranch may consider: What's working between the horse and me? How can I translate that into my work and my life, both in real experience and in metaphor?

We see moments of breakthrough with our clients. We see changes in perception; they are seeing the world in a different way by seeing it through the eyes and the hearts of horses in nature. People learn to see themselves and their organizations differently, which reveals what might be possible.

As we dwell in nature and enter into silent dialogue with her, we also enter into quiet dialogue with ourselves. As we watch, nature reveals herself; as we listen, nature speaks, and then we may hear what we most need to hear and speak aloud what we most need to say.

Nature emphasizes the interrelatedness of life. Everything in the natural world is in direct relationship to everything else, biologically, physically and spiritually. All is interdependent for survival. Nature encourages diversity, flexibility, innovative, non-linear thinking, and out-of-the-ordinary experiences.

The natural power of nature has the ability to influence our human experience. We as humans are not superior to the natural world but equal with all creation. What is required of us is that we surrender the hierarchal distance between nature and ourselves. Sometimes we are graced by the visit of forest animal—a deer, fox or rabbit. As we watch and are watched by the untamed animal, we awaken to alternatives and have a clearer awareness of the moment. The process of witnessing the mystery of nature encourages us to witness the mystery of ourselves.

Cut off and isolated from nature we are cut off from a vital source of nourishment. Reconnected with nature, we reconnect with our authentic nature and authentic presence with joy, renewed purpose and vitality.

10
Nature and the Wild Path to Authentic Presence

Nature and the wild opens a pathway to authentic presence that is both generous and demanding. This pathway is generous in that we are born onto it and is unconditionally available to us all. The natural world is demanding as it is primary to our well-being and carries with it the responsibility to respect, tend to, and protect this most essential relationship.

I believe there is great value in bringing the natural of the wild world more intentionally and directly into our lives and the lives of others. Humans can learn from the genius of nature how to thrive in our human endeavors, how to understand our challenges, and how to solve our greatest human problems. Inspired by nature's best practices, and our place in nature, we can learn to raise healthier families, build thriving businesses, and create vibrant communities.

When more directly engaged with the natural world, living an authentic presence, we learn to better trust ourselves, feel our rootedness and experience our life flow. When in relationship to nature and our own inner nature, we can make meaning of our world, experience our competency, and respond to the awe and wonder of our humanness and of life.

> *"Nature invites us to be on her side. We couldn't ask for a better partner, and it's up to us to figure what it means to be human and be on earth at this time.... The first living cell came into being nearly 40 million centuries ago, and its direct descendants are in all of our bloodstreams. The living world is not "out there" somewhere, but in your heart."*
> Paul Hawken, Commencement Address, University of Portland, 2009

The awareness of being part of and not in control of the natural world is core to my understanding of being authentically present and guides my everyday decisions and actions. Never do I feel more alive than when I am in the midst of nature. Never do I feel more at home or at ease or authentic with myself than when I am outside in the natural world. Being within the horse herd to greet the sunrise in the morning mist and to listen in the dark to horse snuffles and other night songs, I feel a sense of inner calm and rightness with the world.

We are born into our human family and we are born into the family of nature, the largest living social system. Our first and last most intimate connection with nature and relationship in life begins with our first breath of air as we come into the world and ends with our last breath as we are returned to earth or air. The generosity of nature is that we all belong; we all have a home in nature. We are all essential; our unique diversity contributes that which no one else offers. We all matter; we each are an intricate part of the interrelated whole. We are born into a human identity. Beyond our human identity, we are born with an ecological identity, our identity as part of the natural world.

Nature and the Wild Path

We are born with our own unique authentic presence and natural rhythm, which guides us in the same way other beings of nature are guided. When we are in alignment with our natural rhythm, life seems to be moving in the right direction at the proper pace and we are in the right place at the right time. With our senses awake (coming to our senses), we are able to feel the unique wisdom within ourselves individually and the collective wisdom of the natural world. We feel like we are following a natural flow and living the life we were meant to live. We discover ourselves in nature. Maybe we experience our strength or our humility when mountains surround us. Perhaps walking along the ocean, we slow down to think about what matter to us in our families or our work. In the quiet of the forest, we might hear from within the clarity to make decisions or solve dilemmas we face. Nature can help us rediscover our authentic nature, choosing to be our best selves and live truer to our natures in our family lives, workplaces and communities.

We are most often comfortable bringing nature into our human lives in farming, gardening, planting trees, creating ponds and flower beds, providing bird feeders and bird baths. We may experience less understanding, comfort and care when entering the world of the wild and untamed in nature.

This connection to the wild, while not well understood, is essential to our human nature. The balance and well being of the natural world, and of us within that world, depends on the survival and well being of the wild in nature, not just the tame. Human physical, spiritual and emotional survival is directly connected to the wild in nature. The natural world challenges us to step up, listen to the call of the wild and find it within us, as it carries our passion, creativity, and capacity to love deeply. Man or woman, the wild spirit of nature calls our name and summons us to show up and be present.

> *"Within every woman there is a wild and natural creature, a powerful force filled with good instincts, passionate creativity and ageless knowing."*
> —Clarissa Pinkolas Estes, Author,
> *Women Who Run with Wolves*

I unexpectedly encountered the wild a few years ago in Mexico. I was walking down a beach and was drawn to a man holding a large beautiful cat. I asked if I could see his cat and he placed it in my arms. I found myself holding it against my chest, a warm and furry lion cub. It relaxed against me and I was filled with joyful and gentle aliveness. A beach in Mexico is an unlikely place to meet up with a lion cub, but it is an example of synchronicity, of being in the right place at the right time for something extraordinary and life changing to happen. As I held the cub close to my heart and securely in my arms, I felt the awe and privilege of touching the wild, and in doing so, touched the wilderness heart of the mother lioness in me.

I believe each of us has within us the beauty, freedom and knowing of the wild. That wisdom, which seeks to live in resonance with our true nature, which thrives when we reach for our best and contribute to the best for others, which fiercely protects its young when they cannot protect themselves, that wisdom belongs to the family of the natural world in which we make our home.

I felt a deep sadness that this young cub in my arms would never know the true freedom of his nature or the home of his ancestors, which lives deep within his soul. I also felt a strong connection with him in that we share that place in each of our souls that yearns for freedom and our authentic place in nature.

I have been struggling with the thought that given the rapid climate change and our slower human pace, we could become extinct as a species. But I am an unconditionally optimistic person and I don't feel pessimistic about these thoughts. I believe we have, individually and as a species, been gifted a lifetime. Touching the wild of the cub in that moment touched the place in me that knows the importance of being fully and responsibly present, and I was reminded that in whatever time we have, we must make the choice to live our lives with the utmost care and kindness, conscious of all of nature.

Innovation and technology may save our physical existence, but it is the innovation of respect, responsibility and relationship with each other, our planet and its inhabitants that will save our worth as a species.

My vision and hope is that one day future generations of this young lion will once again run free in their homeland. The pride, dignity and strength of this young cub that touched my lioness heart, gave me courage. I believe that we have the capacity to make choices to insure those future generations of my own children and the children in all of nature's family will one day live in freedom and harmony.

The feel of the wild I got from the lion cub is with me still. I realize that what is important to me these days does not depend on changing a world that it might be impossible to change through human endeavor. Instead, it is important to live with integrity, offer the work that brings us meaning and align with people and beings of the wild that inspire us, open our hearts, offer positive relationships and make us laugh and roar.

Our relationship to nature is buried deep within our psyches and goes all the way back to our prehistoric ancestors. There is a deep yearning in most of us to be connected to the natural world. Nature and the wild embodies and reveals insights to help us move beyond our habitual thought and behavior patterns. Experiencing the wilderness challenges what has become familiar. Experiences in the wilderness can challenge us sufficiently to disorient us, to disrupt the fixed aesthetics and allow for breakthrough moments, more awareness and a reorientation toward what is more productive. The Wild is alive in all of us, an inner instinctual knowing that allows you to be more effective and in achieving your best outcome…let it out to play.

Section III—The Path of the Natural World and Call of the Wild

Pause, Reflect and Respond

Take a Nature walkabout somewhere in the natural world. Notice what captures your interest and what nature inspires in your human nature. How does your inner landscape reflect in your outer landscape?

The Wild is alive in all of us, an inner instinctual knowing that allows you to be more effective and in achieving your best outcome... let it out to play.

What one small thing, one bold thing and one wild thing you will do to bring more purposeful play into your life?

Practice listening and responding to the information of your natural wilderness spirit as you ask the essential questions of authentic presence. Explore the simple: Who am I? How am I to be? What is my unique purpose? What do I yearn for? If not now when?

Take several index cards and write a word or phrase and an image that came from your reflections on each individual card.

Save these cards as you will be reflecting back on them.

IV

The Path of Embodied Presence

Chapter 11
Embodied Presence–The Vessel of Our Humanness

"The body reveals…It is as if the body sees what the mind believes and the heart feels, and adjusts itself accordingly… It is efficient and graceful in its movements, aware and responsive to real needs"
–Ron Kurtz, The Body Reveals: *What Your Body Says About You*

The path of embodied presence is the physical representation and extension of our authentic presence through who we are, how we are and our actions in the world.

Embodied presence is a field of study and practice that focuses on the lived body experience as a vital source of practical information in understanding life experience and in making life decisions.

For me there are five main contributions that the path of embodied presence has offered me on my way to developing a more authentic presence:

- Our embodied presence is the vessel that holds our inherently good humanness. It is me, the temporal and physical boundary of what is me and what is not me. It is the experience of our physical selves, not simply our thoughts about ourselves.

- Our embodied presence exists only in the present while carrying our history and potential future; this both shapes us and is being shaped by us. Tapping into a full body of intelligence, alongside cognitive intelligence and emotional intelligence, provides us a dynamic, present-moment reality of self, others and the environment.

- Being present from the whole body, not just our head and heart, our embodied presence is primary in creating and engaging in relationship as 95% of our communication is through our body language and 100% of our embodied presence.

- Our embodied presence is a miracle of resiliency, healing and transformation, continually adapting, restoring, and revitalizing itself.

- Our embodied presence is a living system of collective wisdom that both influences and is influenced by its surrounding field of possibility. Discovering an embodied knowledge within a lived experience results in the development and choice of a more authentic presence.

We are all born with innate body intelligence as part of our embodied presence. Though it is often not accessed, embodied wisdom is a domain of intelligence equal to cognitive intelligence and emotional intelligence. Alongside cognitive intelligence and emotional intelligence, body intelligence provides us with a collective wisdom and deeper awareness of self and others, allowing us to develop a more authentic presence in leadership and in all life. In a very real way, it is the capacity to talk and provides the ability "to walk our talk." Our embodied presence is an interrelated and finely balanced learning system of collective wisdom within the body, and between the outside realms and ourselves. In a real sense, what happens in any one part of our physical body affects the rest of our body; and, what happens between us and anyone else as physical beings literally affects the other and the whole.

Operating from our embodied intelligence through the information of our senses we engage the world and respond from each unfolding present moment. Our bodies only register information in the present. It is our minds that remember the past or imagine the future. Our physical body only takes information from the reality of the present moment. Coming to and from your senses, you can experience a clearer understanding of what actually is happening, not what you assume, think or fear is happening. From embodied awareness, you can respond with more resiliency, honesty and integrity.

Horses, and all we creatures of the earth, live as embodied beings by physically sensing, registering, and managing inner experience and emotions.

My primary guides along this path have been horses, the natural world and like-spirited people who have contributed to developing this "body" of knowledge. Horses, and all we creatures of the earth, live as embodied beings by physically sensing, registering, and managing inner experience and emotions. Collective embodied intelligence provides information from which the most beneficial action, in relation to the surrounding conditions of the field, emerges. The language of horse is body. Though horses think and problem solve, they are independent of rational processing and imagined reality; rather they are able through their bodies to directly and intuitively perceive present reality. As humans, much of what challenges us–in relationships and in many life dilemmas–is beyond words and rational thought. Much like horses, within our bodies, in the silence beyond verbal communication, lives untapped potential for communicating, adapting and changing in resonance with each other and with our environment.

Horses make sense of their world, communicate essential information to their herd, and make decisions from the collective wisdom of their bodies. The herd tracks and adapts to their present and ever-changing physical realm. Trusting their senses and intuition, and, registering the subtle energy and messages from the field, horses can anticipate and move to the next best place to be...and so can we. Living with awareness of our physical selves expands our capacity to sense, feel, and understand ourselves, each other and our world. Being a more embodied presence deepens the quality of our interior and has everything to do with how we are impacted by the world and the impact we have in the world.

Since I believe that horses are one of the most natural teachers of embodied presence, it seemed only natural to explore how they might be of service in guiding people in becoming more aware, curious and knowledgeable about their own embodied presence and that of others.

Walking in the world is one of the ways we naturally bring our embodied presence into the world and make it visible. I imagined that this might be a place that the horses could help people get more connected to their embodied experience and presence in a playful and non-threatening way. People could also explore their power and ability to influence from a more aware place of embodied presence.

Personally, I have enjoyed and learned from many hours of watching our horses walk and run through their pasture and

Embodied Presence

being interested what it reveals about their embodied presence. I have observed the horses calmly wander through the pasture toward the best green grass or to join a herd buddy at the far end of the field. I have watched them with awe as they gallop, mane and tail flying, as they race each other to be first through the gate or playfully chase each other their hoofs barely touching the earth. Sometimes their walk appears to be in steadfast slow motion as they powerfully hold their ground with each step, commanding respect, or walking fluidly with the strength of confidence, each footstep placed with sure purpose. Paying attention to their way of navigating change and moving around, over or through obstacles, or their way of claiming or giving space, has been of great value to me as I reflected on how I move through life. I thought it might be of value to others to learn more about how people move through life by learning how horses inhabit their bodies and move through their field. If horses can accomplish being coherent, walking with four feet, how might we humans be able to accomplish that by standing and walking with our own two feet?

The very next week I had the perfect opportunity to learn more about embodied presence by asking the question: How do I walk and move through the world when I am performing at my best? I thought that by people having an opportunity to observe, try on, and learn the way of our horses walking in the world, it would bring their attention to their familiar and habitual ways of walking in their worlds. By paying attention to the different horses' unique ways of embodied being, they could learn about their own and could expand the range of ways they might move through life.

A group of managers from Fairmount Santrol, a global corporation based in our area, came to the ranch for some horseplay fun and to build on their leadership strengths by learning with the horses. I designed a "walking in and moving through the world" experience thinking it would be an interesting way to learn about the impact of the horses' embodied presence and how it contributes to our learning about our own authentic presence. As in all our programs, we prepared the group to communicate with and be with the horses through body language and embodied presence. We gave them an opportunity to practice what they had just learned by meeting and greeting the horses that were wandering freely around their native home pasture. Once the people had a chance to meet and greet the horses and the people and horses got acquainted, we divided them up into teams of three people and a horse.

Each team had the task of connecting with their horse buddy and then observing their horse's walk and way of moving. They then were to "try on" and learn their horses walk and way of being embodied. Everyone enthusiastically participated in learning their horse's way of walking and moving and prepared to share what they learned with the rest of the group. We brought the whole group together so that each small group would have an opportunity to introduce their horse partner, embody and demonstrate their horse's walk and then teach it to the others in the large group. After everyone had imitated their horse buddy's walk, we asked them to use words to describe the experience of that walk. We then asked when and where they imagined walking that particular walk, and where that embodied way of being would be desirable and of value.

The first group demonstrated Bea's walk. The large group all tried on the Bea walk and movement and then offered words and phrases that captured their experience of the Bea walk and her way of being embodied. The words used to describe Bea's walk were steadfast, purposeful, connected to the earth, thunderous, and awe-inspiring. When asked when and where Bea's walk and way of being might be useful, the responses were: when asking for a raise at work, when you wanted to show executive presence, when you needed confidence, when you wanted to be a powerful grounded presence.

The next group chose Holly the Zebra. The words for Holly's walk and way of being were light hearted, playful, purposeful, imaginative and quick. They felt that the Holly walk and way of moving would be important in order to be agile, have fun, be creative and be uniquely who you are with whoever you are with and wherever you are.

The Raven group embodied a walk that brought comments like sexy, proud, devil-may-care, nonchalant, bold and brave. They thought that the way Raven presented himself would be great when life got too stressful or complicated and you needed to lighten up, simplify or make a change.

Tess the pony's group demonstrated a walk that brought up the words determined, lively energy, slightly rebellious, and free-spirited. Her group decided that her way of moving and walking would be useful when you felt stuck or confined by yourself or others and wanted to break free.

The Chief Silver Cloud folks described him with the words strength, pride, grandeur, unicorn, nobility, humbleness and majesty. His group liked his capacity to balance his majesty with modesty and noted how we as humans would benefit from the balance of walking with pride and humbleness in all life situations.

Bud's group offered the words gentle giant, big-hearted, friendly, slow going, intimate and welcoming. Walking his walk and moving like Bud would be good when we want to be liked, make friends, be compassionate and engaging and when we want to bring more intimacy into our relationships.

Spirit's group learned from Spirit's distance as each time they got to close to her she threatened to bite them. She allowed them to walk alongside her as long as they respected her space. Words for Spirit were distant, discerning, selective, sensitive, respectful, careful, and "No." Spirit's group appreciated her and even grew to love her–from a distance. They valued her ability to just say no and respected that "no" can be a complete sentence. They thought that her discernment and ability to create clear boundaries led to clear communication and an honest relationship with them. They felt an important part of what she demonstrated with her embodied presence was to remind them not to take things personally and yet still be personable, and that sometimes distance brings us closer.

Toby, in his quiet unassuming way, hardly moved at all despite the lively encouragement of his group, he refused to take even one step. No surprise the words for Toby were strong-willed, contrary, resistant, unyielding, and also friendly, good-natured, and easygoing. Toby's group learned from Toby to honor resistance rather than fight with it, that at times it is best to conserve your energy and not move forward, and that sometimes being good-natured and easygoing and just hanging out is more advantageous than going somewhere or getting something done.

The groups each thanked their horse partner and we left the horse pasture all walking with more awareness of our embodied presence. We have offered this experiential learning opportunity to many people over the years and I often hear back from people months after their experience at the ranch that they used Bea's walk to enter an important board meeting, for example, or Spirit's walk to establish a clear boundary, or Toby's non-walk when it was important for them to hold their ground on a position they valued.

How we humans walk into a meeting, a job interview, into our homes at the end of a long day, along a sunny beach on a vacation or into a challenging conversation or situation has everything to do with a positive result and meaningful outcome. How we express uncertainty or confidence, boldness or humility, calm or nervousness, aggression or peacefulness determines our influence. Being aware of what our walk and way of being communicates long before we speak a word allows us to be more expansive in our relationships. Learning to be more purposeful and intentional in our embodied presence means the message we intend to deliver is more likely to be received in the way we intended. Our embodied presence allows us to feel upright rather than collapsed, powerful rather than powerless and to expand our ways of moving through life.

Why Is Embodied Presence Important?

In today's complexity of living, we are called to go beyond the common or habitual ways of perceiving the world. Embodied presence attends to life from a solid and agile place of listening, thinking, reflecting, experiencing and responding in real time. Operating from our embodied intelligence through the information of our senses, we engage the world and respond from each unfolding present moment. Our bodies only register information in the present. It is our minds that carry memories of the past or imagine the future.

We all have a body, but more than that we each are our body. Our thoughts, emotions and actions come through our body. Our body is the life we live. How we work, play, connect with others, love, discover, learn and achieve is directly related to our embodied presence. Our body carries essential information about the history of our life journey—memories, patterns, genetics, and habits—as well from our evolving life history. This life history shapes how we experience our environment (and how we are experienced by our environment). We are all born with innate body intelligence.

> *"When we are alienated from the wisdom of the body, our lives become theoretical and abstract, and we are distanced from the direct, felt sense of living."*
> –Richard Heckler Strozzi
> (Richard Strozzi-Heckler is an American author, coach, and consultant)

Many of us go through the day without noticing our bodies, and without experiencing what they are communicating to us and we miss essential information. Even when our bodies demand our attention through discomfort or pain, we try to ignore them; we quiet them down with pills, alcohol, and television or by simply overriding our body's call for help.

People, when coming to learn with the horses, often intuitively say to me, "I need to get out of my head, I am just confusing myself." I remind them that our heads are included in the body. We have become dependent on that one-seventh of our body to make meaning of our experience, in the form of cognitive reasoning, Cognition is an essential source of information, but it is not the only, and sometimes not the best, resource we have. The other six-sevenths of us, our bodies from the neck down, provides information our cognitive thoughts require to make sense of our experience and to make decisions in our world.

Embodied Presence

> *"Embodiment: to be more able to engage in more powerful intelligent compassionate ways by living in our bodies not floating around in our thoughts."*
> –Arawana Hayashi
> (choreographer, performer and educator)

Embodied presence, our embodied intelligence and body language, communicates; beyond our thoughts and words we discover the deeper meaning beneath words to understand what is authentically going on between people. The intelligence of embodiment and being aware of our body-self strengthens our capacity to reflect, attune, resonate and empathize with others. Embodied presence is an adaptive, living pattern of self-organization. Attending to and experiencing our embodiment is integral to how we respond to the world, and how the world responds to us. Embodied presence is a way of being and behaving that expands the ability to understand complexity, make informed decisions and find creative solutions. Our embodied presence keeps us true to who we are when engaging with others and while adapting to our environment.

> *"Your body is the ground metaphor of your life, the expression of your existence. It is your life story."*
> –Gabrielle Roth
> (American author, choreographer, musician)

In my professional work, and in my personal life, I pay attention to a person's embodied presence as a way of understanding the whole humanness of them within their particular dilemma and life story. Noticing the physical aspects of their breathing, body postures and how they are sitting; their facial expressions, voice quality and tone; their gestures and their energetic presence are all important clues to understanding them. This information about their embodied presence is as essential to supporting the person's work as what is being expressed through their thoughts and emotions. Our bodies are always honest and they help reveal what the mind has chosen to ignore. The intention of bringing a person's awareness to their embodied presence is always to enrich and deepen their understanding of what they are exploring and to expand their awareness of their present reality. Accessing one's "embodied self," we can bring attention to a more complete perspective of one's life concerns and questions, and thereby expand the potential for possibility, choice and positive change.

Being aware of our embodied presence strengthens our capacity to reflect, attune, resonate and empathize with others and our surroundings in an adaptive living pattern of self-organization. Embodied presence is a way of being and behaving that expands the ability to understand complexity, make informed decisions and inspire creativity. Our embodied presence keeps us true to who we are while adapting and evolving with our environment and while connecting and engaging with others.

Embodied Mindfulness

Mindfulness is not just in the domain of our mind it begins with sensations within our body and is expressed through our body. Unifying the body and mind creates embodied intelligence and embodied presence, which in turn informs our thoughts, emotions and behaviors. Space opens for silence and reflection and deepening our capacity to be thoughtful and mindful. Mindful bodies always tell the truth and move towards that which is positive and life giving. It is intuitively, honestly and non-judgmentally knowing the present moment–the now–through its good senses and felt life experience. Reuniting mind and body is a personal journey of self-discovery that contributes to a more alive and conscious leadership and life.

Embodied Mindfulness and awareness of embodied experience, ours and others, is important in the work of enhancing relationship. When we are mindfully embodied we are most present, responsive and proactive in service of our self, others and our environment. Presence starts with being present, so mindfulness and body awareness is a good foundation for leadership and all life endeavors. The self we are comes through our body in mindful thought, emotional intelligence, purposeful action and compassionate spirit.

Embodied Resonance

Embodied resonance is a vibrational communication and connection, which we may or may not consciously know is happening. It exists as an exchange of resounding shared more than verbal information to and from our bodies when we are in tune with one another. It is the experience of being on the same wavelength. Horses, using all their horse senses, communicate through embodied resonance, connecting via vibrations within themselves, between one another, and in their surrounding field. Coming to our senses through the capacity of embodied resonance, we can deepen our ability to reflect, attune, resonate and empathize with others. An embodied presence resonates with life and allows us to explore and move beyond our previous limitations into freedom of choice. The embodied path to authentic presence is relevant and directly transferable to our family and work relationships.

Embodied Empathy

Embodied empathy is an embodied relational process engaging from the wisdom of the senses in the present moment, and seeing life as it actually is from another's point of view. Empathetically feeling life through our body we can respond to the challenge of each unfolding moment with resiliency, honesty, integrity and wisdom. Horses are gifted with this innate body intelligence and intuitive wisdom. As prey animals, they have developed a fine-tuned survival response to sense and to be aware of the present moment and as relational creatures to be empathetically in tune with other beings. If we are feeling life through our body, like our friends the horses do, we can be more in touch and in tune with whom we care for and what we care about.

Embodied Shape and Structure

Our bodies carry our life experiences, in our musculature, our stance and posture. Over time, we take on a physical shape that moves beyond habit, and into a fixed structure– a character structure. Embodied presence can be visually seen, felt and perceived through the embodied structure of our char-acter and personal identity. When we feel what we have endured as heavy we might physically look like we carry the world on our shoulders. When we feel like it is not safe to be seen, we might physically look like we almost don't exist. If we have grown up always needing to perform or look good we might look great on the outside but feel empty on the inside. Embodied shape and structure can be understood as a field of influence in thematic physical form and patterns. They both serve us in positive ways and limit us in other ways. Our em-bodied structure can be seen as frozen movement, impulse and expression and as is a creative response, adjustment and adaptation over time to the field of our life. Awareness of our embodied structure can help us unfreeze the structure to once more have more range of emotion and motion and flexibility in relationship to others and our world. The structure of our embodied presence is a sculpture of our life and provides information about engaging and being engaged, connecting and being connected with our surrounding field.

Embodied Listening and Horse Whispering

> *"The most important thing in communication is hearing what is not spoken."*.
> –Peter Drucker
> (management consultant, educator, and author)

Embodied listening and horse whispering refers to hearing between the words and beyond what is spoken. This exquisite way of connecting asks that we slow down, sense from a receptive mode, and focus our attention through our senses to the present moment. Horse whispering and embodied listening are states of being awake and aware, <u>softly speaking from heart and silently listening from soul</u>. Engaging with our body awareness and intelligence is a practice of quiet patience, which frees us up from the chatter of inner and outer voices and the desensitizing sounds of telephones, computers and telephones.

The true horse whisperer is the horse. As we enter into silent dialogue with horses and nature as our guides, we also enter into quiet dialogue with ourselves. Through the practice of embodied listening we can feel more our real selves and be more aligned with and authentically presence in our actions. In relationship with horses, we learn to summon our own embodied empathy guiding us into moment-to-mo-ment calm, present-centered focus, heartfelt respect and trust.

Listening to and learning through embodied intelligence brings out an inner wisdom and inherent knowledge, what we know in our bones. How can we learn to pay more attention to our body intelligence and not simply override our body wisdom? Paying attention and aligning our three learning centers head, heart and gut we have a collective wisdom greater than any single way of knowing Being present and embodied is an active process that requires awareness and practice within the competing needs for our attention in the work place and in busy lives. Embodied listening and responding is important in the forming of relationship, living in families, meaningful work experiences and purposeful life.

Embodying Our Personal Power

When we pay attention to and are responsibly intentional about our embodied presence in our daily lives we can free up, access and adjust our personal power for our benefit while doing no harm to others. This awareness is a form of embodied intelligence that tells us when to move forward, when to slow down, when we have crossed over into someone else's space or stepped on someone's toes and when there is too much distance for connection and conversation. How we present ourselves, our stance, our way of taking our space, our manner of moving, are all part of our embodied presence. It is the external expression of what is going on inside of us, be that confidence or uncertainty, being bold or timid, trusting or doubting ourselves.

Learning to trust our honest thoughts, authentic emotions, truthful bodies and spiritual values, we present ourselves in a more believable way whether we are applying for a job, having an important conversation, pitching an idea, or speaking up for ourselves or a cause we care about.

Embodied Presence 277

Our embodied presence makes us visible so what is it we want to have people see in us or notice about us. As we develop awareness and inner confidence and have a good feeling about our embodied presence it shows on the outside. We are more likely to be seen as likeable if we like ourselves and trustworthy if we trust ourselves.

Sometimes we try to make ourselves invisible to not be noticed by playing small or downplaying ourselves but generally we still are noticed we are just seen as small which might translate to inadequate, or not up to the task. If we try to look big by inflating our self or rising above others we might be seen as full of hot air, arrogant or a bully.

Awareness of our embodied presence also requires cultural acuity; as what might be seen as humble in one culture might be interpreted as less than confident. Awareness of context is also important to consider as when it might be appropriate to hug someone and when it might not. In order to have a broad view or good perspective of our life situation it is important to be aware of how we inhabit space and take our space through expansion and contraction of our body.

Sitting in front of our technological devices, be they our tablets, cell phones or desk computers, a narrow focus is required. This results in us generally contracting our bodies and limiting movement. While we need a contracted focus to pay attention to detail, we need a larger focus to see the entire picture or situation in an expansive way as well. It's like the importance of seeing the tree within the forest while still seeing the forest. Research has proved that when we get up from our computers, walk around, stretch our bodies and experience the larger world around us, we are then able to have more clarity of thought and the capacity to be wise when we return to the task.

Chapter 12
Embodied Ways of Being

"Our body is a multilingual being. It speaks through its color and its temperature, the flush of recognition, the glow of love, the ash of pain, the heat of arousal, the coldness of non-conviction...it speaks through the leaping of the heart, the falling of the spirits, the pit at the center, and rising hope."
–Clarissa Pinkolas Estes, author, Women Who Run with Wolves

As we develop specific embodied ways of being and working, we develop a map to guide ourselves and our clients through a lively and mindful journey of discovery. Our life stories are both stored in our bodies and spoken through our bodies.

Embodied presence is not an add-on skill, technique or merely the learning of new concepts. An embodied way of being requires an expanded perception of our embodied selves and body sensations, which only is possible if we are fully in our bodies and live with awareness of our embodied presence. The development of sensation, the experience of our senses within our internal selves and within our environment is necessary for embodied presence. Sensation and awareness is key to embodied presence. Whatever is available through our senses becomes available as information and the basis of how we make meaning of our reality. The more range and depth of sensation through embodied presence we can manage, the more agile in the present moment we will be. The less sensation and awareness we experience, the less adaptation and range of choice will be available to us. Experiencing our senses leads to the development of sensation, which leads to awareness and to the meaning we bring to our situation and current reality.

Experiences taken in by our senses–what we see, hear, feel, taste, smell, touch, and sense–is the direct data from which awareness of our present reality emerges. Sensation is immediate. The meaning we make of the information we take in through our senses, is not objective, its meaning already exists within us, organized in our body. We experience hot or cold, not temperature and it is related to context and culture. What might be cold to a person living in the desert will be different than a person living in the cold of the north of Alaska. The organization of sensation gives meaning within a context; tears at the celebration of a wedding might be an expression of joy, tears at a funeral might be the result of sadness, tears on a windy day might be eyes tearing not from emotion but from wind blowing in the eyes. When basic sensory data is missing or the meaning we make of the information is confused the reality of our actual experience and our relationship to that experience is challenged. Our embodied presence clearly reflects to others what has been well developed in us, what is "owned" and known about us, as well as the less known and disowned blind spots of self. When words fail or interrupt the process of connection, the intimate language of the body can succeed in communicating our sensed and felt experience. The experience of our senses, within our internal self and within our environment is necessary for developing embodied presence.

> *"The body never lies....*
> *The body says what words cannot."*
> –Martha Graham
> (American modern dancer and choreographer)

Awareness of embodied presence, our own and that of others, is important in meaningful relationship, purposeful action and a trustworthy and authentic presence.

We often have a felt sense about someone, but are not aware of the data that led us to that feeling of the person's presence. We can learn to be more aware of the body signals and sense-ability that gives us that insight, so that we can use those skills for more accurate communication, and to experience our selves, not simply our thoughts about our selves.

We can grow and develop our capacity for embodied presence:

- If it is of value to us and we are willing to give it our awareness, intention and attention.
- If we engage in a learning process of developing sensory awareness, listening to our body and trusting what we hear, and aligning our actions with our body.
- If we are willing to engage in embodied awareness practices; we become what we practice.

Through learned practices of embodied presence we can expand our capacity to access the wisdom of our bodies and move more effectively toward the results we intend. An embodied way of being present supports and sustains our ability to:

- Be more comfortable in our own skin and walk in the world with more awareness, respect, trust and integrity
- Manage mood and modulate behavior while standing firm

and grounded, clear and centered and open and receptive in the midst of chaos and stress.

- Be open minded and hearted to new ideas and diverse perspectives, responding with agility and flexibility in response to change.
- Further intuition and insight into issues, concerns, dilemmas and new possibilities and expand range of choice and actions.
- Develop deeper access to relevant information and collective wisdom in the field and create a desired field of influence.
- Increase our range of communication to insure the integrity between the messages we convey and the ones we intend to convey.

Embodied Presence Practices We Can Learn From Horses and Nature

Present Centered: Horses, and all of nature, live in the reality of the present, of the here and now, and being present-centered in their body. Being aware of our embodied presence keeps us centered in present reality.

Grounded: Horses are connected to the resources of their en-vironment. They have all four feet on the ground; it is, liter-ally, how they support themselves in relation to the earth's gravity. We can learn from the horse's gravitas, a weight and depth of character, a relationship to earth through gravity, and the serious responsibility of belonging to something greater than ourselves.

Centered: Horses know who they are, their outer behavior and actions are centered in their inner experience and inner essence. We can learn from the horses to be more true to who we are on the inside, aligning our actions from within with the outer world. Centering in ourselves helps us keep our balance and not get easily knocked off center, and it helps us regain our balance quickly, if we do.

Breath: Horses communicate through breath. If a horse is breathing slowly, the message is that things are probably calm and peaceful and all is good. If a horse is breathing fast and shallow, it might mean it's time to run joyfully to-ward dinner or out with a buddy, or maybe to run away from danger to a safer place. We learn from the horses about breath as a resource for self-support, a way to expand awareness and inspiration, and to manage your energy, ei-ther by raising excitement or lowering excitement. Breath opens the space within and helps us to self-modulate in the outside world.

Management of Boundaries: Horses are skilled at managing their boundaries, choosing who and what to let get close and who and what to keep at a distance. As humans, we can learn healthy boundaries from a horse. What is my responsibility and what responsibility belongs to others?

Movement: We can learn from horses to expand our capacity to be a more embodied presence by watching their natural movement, their physical proximity to each other, the cultural cues of the herd, and the context and circumstance of inter-actions. We, in our human groups, communicate in a similar way through our movements. In the presence of the horses, we can better access a 360-degree multi-directionality, a larger field of perspective. We can be more aware of moving fluidly and effectively in time and space and place, and be more agile in reaching for dreams and visions.

Touch: Touch between humans and horses and between hors-es and horses are important relational contact points. Groom-ing, stroking, soothing are primal bonding patterns in all nature's beings, including human beings from early infancy. Meaningful, healthy touch provides a sense of connection, grounding, rhythm, comfort and well being throughout life.

We can we learn these natural practices from horses in order to be more aware, in touch, and intentional about our embod-ied presence as a path to authentic presence.

The Miracle of Our Bodies

Our body is constantly changing, educating and repairing it-self, and is always in process and transforming. We replace almost ninety-eight percent of all the atoms of our body ev-ery year: a new liver every six weeks, a new skeleton every three months, a new skin once a month. Our body is an ex-pression of our whole being, the container of our spirit, and embodiment of our emotions, the vehicle of our desires and actions. Our body is a self-regulating system, our heart beat-ing, our eyes modulating light and dark, our breathing con-tinuous. Our body is an integrated system and interconnected collection of wisdom, all parts working together in balance for the well being of the whole. Our bodies are hardwired for survival, both striving for independence and interdependence in relationship, and registering safety and danger. Our bod-ies are the center of our emotions; sensation and physical re-sponse creates the physical capacity for emotions, the ability to laugh, cry, and get angry, to feel joy or sadness. We don't feel with our minds, we can only think about what we feel. Feeling our emotions can only happen when we feel with and from our body.

Remembering to appreciate the miracle of each of our bodies, we can focus on its strengths rather than focus on its limitations and imperfections. When we are separate from our embodied self, or are unaware of our embodiment, we become strangers to ourselves. As we learn to experience our body-self, we welcome who we truly and authentically are, and can be at home with ourselves and with others.

Embodied Fields of Resonance and Influence

> *"Embodiment is the way we are. It is how we do. The way we hold the body, move around, attend and intend through the body is a way of managing and expressing who we are."*
> –Mark Walsh, Embodied Training Manager, "Integration Training"

Surrounding our physical body, we have a felt field; this is our field of personal energy; it defines our private space and creates a separation between what is me and what is not me. Clarifying the definition of me and not-me creates a respectful boundary, which allows for personal space and insures our contribution to the collective.

We can become the field of resonance that we want to create through our embodied way of being present, through pace, tone of voice, choice of language, body language, and movement toward or away from something or someone. Being aware and intentional in our embodied presence, we can influence the field toward the emotional resonance we want to create for the best possible outcome. We can create positive field conditions of qualities such as honesty, calm, excitement, trust, kindness, civility and a range of other collective experiences that can serve the greatest good. Embodied presence is the physical container of the emotional, thoughtful and spiritual human being influences the field around us.

Another way to understand embodied presence is through a field of collective wisdom made up of three bodies: our phys-ical body, our earth body, our social body and our . These four bodies (based on the social presencing work of Arawana Ha-yashi) create a field of collective wisdom:

- Our Physical Body can be appreciated as the feeling that we are living in this particular physical body, and we are present via our embodied presence. Awareness through our senses, trusting our senses and sense perceptions, stay-ing open with curiosity and pure experience in present awareness without story; interpretation or meaning we can experience the intelligence and collective wisdom of our physical body.

- Our Earth Body can be appreciated as our physical con-nection to earth, to gravity, to a physical place of belong-ing, to feeling grounded and connected to the earth and all her beings.

- Our Social Body can be appreciated as relationship to our changing field of people and place. We are all intercon-nected people and beings. We are included in the social organism of family, team, herd, and organization. We are always in the social body, moving closer or farther from others, towards or away from them. How we see, hear and feel is a direct experience of the world we live in. Shared knowing of this field can be the source of compassion, courage and creativity.

Our spiritual body is appreciated as the values we live by.

Our embodied presence is able to attune to and resonate with subtle movements in the field. Paying attention to our own embodied responses offers essential information about the system and field that's less available through cognitive reasoning, and it offers insight into our reality and another person's reality.

Embodied presence requires an expanded perception of your awareness of your embodied self and body sensation, which only is possible if we are fully embodied. When words fail or interrupt the process of connection and intimacy, the language of the body can succeed in communicating sensed and felt experience. Awareness of embodied experience, others' and ours, is important in the work of enhancing relationships of all kinds.

Embodied presence is a way of being and behaving that expands one's ability to understand complexity, make informed decisions, and be creatively inspired. Embodied presence is core to being aware and available to achieve and sustain high quality work and life experience. Embodied experience and awareness is important in the forming of relationships, living in families, in work experiences and challenges, and in well being in daily life and in a life well lived.

Our authentic presence is stored in our bodies, spoken through our bodies and enacted through our embodied presence. As a more embodied, sensing being, we can access the collective wisdom from the field and participate more fully in creating the best possible conditions for a sustainable future for generations to come.

Section IV—The Path of Embodied Presence

Pause, Reflect and Respond

Practice using all your physical senses to make sense of your world

Pay attention to your multidimensionality: your grounding what are you most connected to in your world at the present time? Your centering what are you most connected with in your self? Your depth: what deeply matters to you in this moment? Your breath: what inspires you today?

Explore the journey to authentic presence through the realm of your physical body, earth body, social body and spiritual body.

Write on an index card a word or symbol that represents "this is me" in my physical body using all my senses to make sense of the world.
Write on an index card a word or symbol that represents "this is me" in my earth body, my relationship to earth and gravity, the natural world and her elements.
Write on an index card a word or symbol that represents "this is me" in my spiritual body; my values and moral awareness.

Save these cards as you will be reflecting back on them.

V

The Path of Positivity

Chapter 13
The Positive Approach to Leadership and Life

"The difference between what we do and what we are capable of doing would suffice to solve most of the world's problems."
—Mahatma Gandhi, Indian Leader and Social Activist

The path of positivity has informed my understanding and practice of authentic presence. A positive approach expands the range of what we are humanly capable of by opening our minds and hearts and informing our actions. A positive presence builds on our current strengths and gives us courage to face our lives and leadership challenges with inner resource and external support. An authentic positive presence provides an intelligently optimistic guide to living our lives with meaning and purpose.

"I keep my ideals, because in spite of everything I still believe that people are really good at heart."
—Anne Frank, author, Diary of A Young Girl

(Taken from a collection of writings kept while in hiding with her family for two years during the Nazi occupation of the Netherlands during WWII. Anne Frank died in the Holocaust at age thirteen.)

How can we, like Anne Frank, find goodness in the face of evil intention, keep our ideals alive when surrounded by danger, and believe things can get better when we're faced with despair? This is the essence of a positive approach. Positive presence does not deny reality or pretend that all is well, but searches for value, finds courage, and appreciates what can be learned in dire circumstances. This positive stance offers more choice in being and more opportunity for effective action.

A positive approach is not about becoming a "Pollyanna" or living a life without struggle in a state of constant bliss. It is about seeing the world as a place containing challenges and successes, and learning from both. A positive approach does not mean that negativity does not exist. It does not mean that we should trust in optimism to have an inherent ability to vanquish all harsh realities. Unrealistically based optimism can, and often does, result in dangerously underestimating risk and danger. There is negativity in life and in all of us. That negativity needs to be recognized and acknowledged. There are times when it is crucially important to see the negative. It has been my experience, however, that people often dwell on the negative, overshadowing the positive. Shifting self-criticism into discernment and shame into empathy, shifting from despair to appreciation, and maybe even joy, allows for the reality of the challenging experience and for the possibility of something to be learned and more useful to emerge.

I was in the pasture at Pebble Ledge Ranch one morning, thinking about how I might give words to an authentically positive presence and what positivity means to me. My thoughts were interrupted when Holly the zebra nudged me from behind as if to say, "Look up." In the sky were hundreds of monarch butterflies winging their way in a collective migration understood only by them. Holly nudged me again as if to say, "Look down." In the grass was a bright yellow butterfly with black markings. Holly took off on spir-

The Positive Approach

ited chase after the butterfly, which landed in the flowers. As Holly learned down to sniff the butterfly it flew to the next flower. The dance of zebra, butterfly and flower filled me with joy and a sense of peace and well-being. Raven, curious about what Holly had discovered, galloped over, black mane and tail flying in the wind. He joined the dance, following Holly, who was following the butterfly.

What came to me while watching the horses, living with curiosity, joyful wonder and full-hearted exuberance, was that joy is a one of the direct paths to a positive presence. Living a joyful, appreciative life and bringing joy and appreciation into the lives of others in our families, places of business and communities is one of the ways we may experience our own positive presence.

I am not sure whether horses feel happy, but they seem to experience joy. Horses exude joy in their wave of tail and mane in the wind. It is a collective exuberance. We feel that joy simply by watching them live it.

> *"Joy: The kind we feel when we have something that we feel intense about, something that took a risk, something that made us stretch into our best self and succeed maybe gracefully, maybe not, but we did it, created the something, the someone, the art the battle, the moment: our life."*
> —Clarissa Pinkolas Estes, *Women Who Run with the Wolves*

Joy is different from happiness. Happiness is transitory and based on things of life that come and go. Joy is always avail-able to us. It is our essence, the place from which we rejoice. It is an attitude that comes from deeply within, when life has meaning, as we are in harmony and balance with our pur-pose. You can be sad and grieve from your heart and still sense joy. Joy often is found when we are deeply connected to ourselves, to others and to nature. Joy is a lasting internal state of emotion whether we are facing challenges or all is going our way.

I have lived a joyful positive life for as long as I can remember. My world since childhood has been a wondrous place, alive with endless discovery and possibilities. My parents told me, "There is nothing you cannot do, and you don't have to do anything." Their absolute trust in me, unconditional support of my values and their uncomplicated love prepared me to engage in life's challenges with resilience, optimism and faith. My glass always has appeared more than half full to me; when days seem bleak I watch for rainbows. A family of like-spirited optimists nurtured this inherent and preferred style of optimism.

Horses seem to take this even further, approaching life as not half full or empty but always full. A glass half full of water is also half full of air and so can be appreciated as always one hundred percent full. Participating in the everyday life of the horses at the ranch and observing the culture of the herd has expanded my perception of what it means to live with a full glass of positivity and embody a positive authentic presence.

Collectively, the horses create conditions for the best possible positive future to emerge by building on their collective strengths, by adapting to change after noticing what works and lasts, by living in harmony with each other and their environment, and by moving toward what is positive and life-giving. They are always on the lookout for greener grass, a friend to scratch an itch that cannot be reached alone, a way out of a corner or unpredictable dilemma such as a locked gate. They hold no grudges toward each other, carry no imagined assumptions and look for the value and good in one another. They live with an authentically positive presence.

Here is what is required to engage in successful interaction with a positive approach, which I learned by observing horses and the natural world:

- A natural curiosity about life.
- A sense that the world is in general a place that has the resources to meet your needs.
- The ability to live in the present, rather than allowing past occurrences to define current events and determine their outcomes.
- The recognition that engaging from your strengths rather than compensating for your weaknesses is the path to turning challenges into successes.
- Celebrate often, find joy from within

As humans, who have not nearly yet survived the 65 million years of the horses' existence, it is helpful to consider a positive approach to presence as a paradigm of thought and as a realistic approach to being in the world. These are ways to make meaning of life based on the core belief that all beings are inherently good. A positive approach views people, families, communities and organizations as likely doing the best they can in any given situation. It is an optimistic stance that holds that there is always value if you look for it, possibility if you believe in it. There is always the potential that life can get better. A positive approach is a perspective that focuses on strengths rather than weaknesses, on bests rather than worst's, on success rather than failure, and on what works rather than what has failed. It is a worldview that moves toward what life is giving and what is generative. A positive presence deliberately creates the virtues, ideals and conditions enabling people and their cultures to find their sense of meaning and purpose, and the courage to live them and thrive.

When I discovered contemporary theoretical approaches and models that organized from a positive, appreciative strength-based perspective, I was able to take my inherent and learned positive approach from my family and the horses to discover words for it. I could then better direct it into purposeful thought and action in my work and in all my life.

The concept of positive emotions includes contentment with the past, well-being in the present, and hope for the future. Positive individuals look at their personal strengths and virtues. Positive institutions refer to the communal strengths that nurture and support successful interaction of groups and individuals.

Leadership Practices and Theories Point Toward Positive Presence

For me, several contemporary, well-accepted organizational theories and business leadership practices inform the best approach to positive presence: *Positive Psychology, Appre-ciative Inquiry, Social and Emotional Intelligence, Systems Thinking and Theory U.*

Positive Psychology is a school of thought, formally found-ed by Martin Seligman at the University of Pennsylvania. It studies what goes right with people rather than what goes wrong. It tracks positive emotions, character strengths, and life conditions. Seligman's research showed that experiencing life as positive translated into people feeling happier, valued, hopeful, and engaged, with an overall sense of well-being.

The Positive Approach

Appreciative Inquiry is a school of thought conceived of and developed by David Cooperrider and his colleagues at Case Western Reserve University in Cleveland. Theirs is a strength-based, capacity-building approach to transforming human systems toward a shared image of their most positive potential.

> *"Appreciative Inquiry is the search for the best in people, their organizations and the relevant world around them. It is a cooperative search for the best in people, their organizations, and the world around them. It involves systematic discovery of what gives a system 'life' when it is most effective and capable in economic, ecological, and human terms. It involves the art and practice of asking questions that strengthen a system's capacity to heighten positive potential."*
> — David L. Cooperrider, Distinguished University Professor
> (Case Western Reserve University)

Appreciative Inquiry is a collaborative search to identify and understand an organization's strengths, potential, greatest op-portunity and highest hopes for the future. Appreciate means to value and to understand those things worthy of valuing. Inquire means to ask curious, non-judgmental questions, and to search for meaning.

Social and Emotional Intelligence was developed by Rich-ard Boyatzis and his colleagues at CWRU and Daniel Goleman and his colleagues, among others. It is an approach that focuses on developing the capacity to bring out the best in the relational realm and achieve desired outcomes in social transactions through emotional competency. The key com-ponents in Emotional Social Intelligence are: understanding yourself and your emotions, managing yourself and your emotions, understanding others (empathy) and managing yourself in relation to others from a non-judgmental, responsibly emotional place and appreciative perspective.

> *"Great Leaders are aware and attuned to the world around them. They commit to their beliefs, stand strong in their values, and live full passionate lives. Great leaders are emotionally intelligent. They inspire through passion and commitment and a deep concern for people."*
> Richard Boyatizis, Distinguished University Professor,
> Case Westen Reserve University

An emotionally and socially intelligent culture creates motivation, interrupts negativity, encourages the best, and is relevant to all life situations.

Systems Thinking, developed by Peter Senge, reminds us that we are part of the system in our families, communities and institutions creating both desirable and undesirable con-sequences. Systems thinking engages the dynamic interre-lationship of all the parts of the whole to better understand how it operates leading to appropriate positive action for all parts of the system and the system as a whole.

Peter Senge is an American systems scientist who is a senior lecturer at the MIT Sloan School of Management, .

Theory U, designed at MIT by Otto Scharmer, Peter Senge and Joseph Jawarsky proposes that the quality of the results that we create in any kind of social system is a function of the inner quality of awareness, attention, or consciousness within the system from which we operate.

The Positive Approach

The success of our actions as change-makers does not depend on what we do or how we do it, but on inner knowing—the wise place from which we operate. Aligning our thoughts and behavior, we can better create the outcomes that we intend to create. The essence of that view is that we cannot transform the behavior of systems unless we transform the quality of awareness and attention that people apply to their actions within these systems, both individually and collectively.

> *"Presencing is a blended word combining "sensing" (feeling the future possibility) and "presence" (the state of being in the present moment): presencing means "sensing and actualizing one's highest future possibility—acting from the presence of what is wanting to emerge."*
> —Presencing Institute

We are each the author of our life's story and can participate in designing the experience of our journey. We can participate in a story of resiliency, well-being and meaning, no matter what the circumstances, if we live our life with a positive approach and authentic presence.

Positive Approach to Culture Change and Transformation

Our culture can be understood as a set of shared values and beliefs, and behaviors that determine how we do things and how things are done in our families, workplaces, communities and societies. A positive culture is a catalyst for an organization's best performance, future and possibilities for transformational change. It builds on strengths and creates the best possible conditions for the future. When the mind and heart are open and the will engaged, we can embody our human potential for generative positive change. We can live in our uniqueness, communicate effectively and engage in a positive way with others.

A positive authentic presence creates the conditions to:

- Discover, strengthen and focus the best in ourselves and others
- Build on what is working
- Strengthen the capacity of a culture to maintain and generate positive change.
- Inspire an innovative and adaptable change process that results in desired results.
- Expand capacity for success by engaging the whole of the person and igniting passion and commitment from the collective

A positive approach is a practice in believing in the possible.

"I can't believe that!" said Alice.

"Can't you?" said the queen in a pitying tone. "Try again."

Alice laughed. "There is no use trying," she said. "One can't believe impossible things."

"I daresay you haven't had much practice," said the queen. "When I was your age, I always did it for half an hour a day. Why, sometimes I've believed as many as six impossible things before breakfast."
—Lewis Carroll, Alice in Wonderland

Roger Saillant is a person I have been inspired by who embodies an authentic presence with humble brilliance. His teaching extends beyond the classroom and I always learn something from him in his thought provoking and challenging everyday conversations. Roger Saillant is the former Executive Director of the Case Western Reserve University, Fowler Center for Business as an Agent of World Benefit and Sustainability.

He has the amazing ability to ask questions that are challenging and are like "unopened books on a shelf that someday we might walk into." (Rainer Maria Rilke, German poet,1875-1926)

One of his thought provoking challenges that opened my mind to thinking more expansively is called "Follow the Unknown and Lead the Inevitable."

I cannot put into words exactly what that means, but I understand it and know it to be true in my bones like some ancient memory.

Here is another "Rogerism" that resonates with an ancestral memory of tribal life that I know in my heart is true. If we are to thrive and live authentically with positive presence and care for the well-being of all it requires that we: "build community, support each other to grow, tell the truth, and inspire the aspirations of the collective."

When you exhibit a positive approach, you are able to find greater meaning and fulfillment in life and the people around you. The communities, groups, and organizations you inhabit increase in value. A positive approach sets you up to act from your inherent strengths and to recognize past accomplishments rather than to act from a fear of your weaknesses and past failures. It allows you to view the world with an understanding that it contains opportunities to be grasped as well as challenges to be overcome. It is a way of participation that has you stepping forward to engage and share, rather than circling the wagons to separate and protect.

A positive approach can prevent negativity that occurred in your past from becoming the lens of the moment.

For example, let's say that an authority figure from your childhood—a parent, teacher, or coach—constantly pointed out what he or she saw as your shortcomings saying, "You'll never be able to..." And let's say that now, when you find yourself in similar circumstances, the words of that authority figure come back as the lens through which you see your ability to perform. If that's the case, you probably will take actions and make decisions from a negative base. You may even extrapolate that negativity to cover all interactions with authority figures.

I had a client whose boss one morning scheduled a meeting with her for five o'clock that afternoon. It had been announced that the company needed to downsize, and she was afraid that she was going to be fired. By the end of the day she was completely convinced of it. At five o'clock she walked into her boss's office, resigned to being without a job. The meeting began with the boss telling her how pleased the company was with her work and that she was getting a raise.

The boss was a major authority figure in her life; she had assumed the worst when he asked to meet with her. Assuming the worst was a common approach for her when it came to interacting with authority. It was the filter through which everything flowed, and that filter was an assumption drawn out of past experience with authority figures. Had she been able to see the request for a meeting in the present reality of her glowing performance appraisals and many work successes, she would not have spent her day in fear and anxiety.

Instead of using the filter of the present and taking a positive approach, she had assumed the worst. Why? Because an authority figure from her past had diminished her self-esteem so when any authority figure initiated interaction with her, she believed the reason had to be negative, and that she was not measuring up.

We all make assumptions about ourselves, others, and situations in our world. Those assumptions often are based on past experience. The problem occurs when we turn those assumptions into "truths" that govern the present. Those assumed "truths" obscure the actuality of the present. In the case of my client, those "truths" made fear her first response. In turn, the worst outcome that her fear could produce became in her mind the only possible outcome.

Filters that falsely strain events into a purity of negative outcome may not be based only on what someone did to you. Wrongly assumed "truths" can be created out of traumatic situations that were neither directed at you nor caused by a specific person.

For example: Perhaps you, like another client I support, avoid visiting friends who live on a high floor of an apartment building. The reason for my client's avoidance was a fear that if there were a fire he wouldn't be able to get out of the building. That fear was created by having seen an apartment building fire when he was a child; people had died. His adult fear was based on the assumptions that people would be trapped if an apartment building caught fire and that such fires were a realistic major threat. When it came to evaluating apartment buildings and safety, he was caught in a web of assumed "truth" that spun out of assumptions derived from a long ago experience.

Positive approach gave my client an alternative lens through which he was able to view apartment buildings and the danger of fire. Present reality led him to understand that the few hours he would spend visiting his friends combined with safety procedures and modern fire suppression tools and techniques yielded less risk to his life than crossing the street to get to the building.

Positive approach has the ability to eliminate unreasonable negative emotions such as fear, mistrust, or anger as our first and dominate reactions to specific situations. Don't dismiss negative emotions; they may be the most reasonable reaction in certain circumstances. They may be exactly what is needed to maintain well-being. I suspect that we have all been in situations when fear or anger was the reasonable and healthy response. But fear, mistrust, or anger need not become the basis for our rules of engagement with others, and it need not universally determine how we react to challenges and opportunities.

Living like horses, what we do today needs to be based on what is happening in the present, not on assumptions that grow out of past experiences unrelated to the people and specific situations of today. Those past experiences can be integrated into the whole of who we are in a way that gives them justifiable weight. We can say to ourselves, "I've had those experiences. How do I learn from them? How do I let them inform how I am in the world without determining it?" We can recognize that past events occurred in a specific present that is not now. We need not to assume that what is happening now is the same as what happened then.

Positive approach is part of how we can offset emotions and the responses that have a negative impact on our well-being by unreasonably and disproportionately driving our actions. We're inclined to think of emotions such as anger and fear as less positive, but any emotion or emotional reaction can endanger well-being if it is out of balance with reality. There are times when sadness, pain, anger, and fear need to come to the forefront to assure safety and well being. Equally, there are times when trust, joy, and acquiescence need to be placed in abeyance.

Very much like there is dark and light in nature, there is dark and light in emotions. Both have value. Night is needed just as much as day. Your authentic presence relies on the full range of your emotions. The choice is not to focus only on what you want to be true or what you fear to be true, but to focus on the reality of what can be true if we discover the value that exists in any present life reality.

Positive approach allows you to have an authentic presence that says you matter, that you can accomplish what you want to accomplish, and choose the people you want in your life. Positivity reminds us to be appreciative of what we have and grateful for who we are and for those in our families and communities.

Without a positive approach it is possible to have a presence that gives us an outward appearance of success while lacking a positive sense of self-worth. As a result, we can lack a sense of well-being. We are unhappy. People often come to me and say, "I should be happy. Look at all the good things in my life." But the things they point to don't have meaning for them. They may be right for someone else—their father or mother for example—but they aren't the things that would make them authentically happy. They are not in their flow.

Flow, as the term is used in Positive Psychology, occurs when your skills and interests are matched to what you are doing. Put another way: Are you living your life or the life that someone else thinks you should be living? I worked with a client who was enormously unhappy even though his career was a great success. He wasn't in his flow. He was becoming more and more unhappy. His skills were well matched to what he was successfully doing, but his interests and heart were not. In spending reflective time with the horses, he was able to quiet the noise inside of his head and listen to what most wanted to be heard. Envisioning a joyful meaningful life in the mist of nature's natural rhythm of change, he was able to let go of old patterns and assumptions and get closer to his inner nature. As he courageously and cautiously made the decision to shift from his outwardly successful career and began exploring work that had more heart and meaning for him, happiness entered his life.

Positive approach brings ingredients crucial to a well-balanced, authentic presence. It delivers the realization that your strength and purpose is the place from which true success and well-being grow. Our strength is in what works and lasts. It tells us to lead with the best of who we are, rather than by trying to eliminate self-perceived or externally denominated weaknesses. It provides for resiliency. Resilience is having the adaptability and flexibility to grow and respond. It possesses the self-awareness needed to be present in the moment and the ability to call upon our complete emotional range.

Positive approach asks that we each accept and celebrate our "self" and the embodiment of that self in our physical being. Positive approach is not about acknowledging only certain parts of our self. It requires that we call on the whole of our embodied person. Without positive approach, it is difficult for our authentic presence to imbue thoughts, emotions, and actions with the truth of who we are and how we are. With positive approach it is possible to realize the total of all of the parts that comprise the whole of who and how and why we are in the world. A positive and strength-based work environ-

The Positive Approach

ment is a key component in creating lasting success.

Living as an authentic positive presence is a form of spiritual practice, based on beliefs, values, and just actions. It comes from within and is inspired collectively through respect, trust and love.

> "*For it is not too Wondrous for you...
> May we find our life so precious
> That we cannot but share it
> *And not too far away.............
> That light may shine brighter than a thousand suns
> *It is not in the Heavens ....
> With the presence among us of all of the Spirit of light
> It is not on the other side of the sea........
> Before us lies a new day,
>
> *It is very close to you
> And in the distance a new world,
>
> *It is in your mouth and in your heart
> Ours to create, By the strength of our faith
> that you might do it."
>
> —Adapted from text, Deuteronomy 30:11-14
> and meditation from the book Gates of Repentance

Section V—The Path of Positivity

Pause, Reflect and Respond

Bring to mind and heart what you need to leave behind or transcend, transform or make peace with. What do you need to acknowledge, encourage and commitment to be and become more positive in your life?

Take several index cards and write a word or phrase and an image that came from your reflections on each individual card.

Save these cards as you will be reflecting back on them.

VI

The Path of the Eight Intelligences

Cognitive

Emotional

Social

Embodied

Intuitive

Natural

Spiritual

Transformational

Chapter 14
The Collective Wisdom of the Eight Intelligences

*"We must learn to see the world anew....
No problem can be solved from the same level of
thinking that created it."*
—Albert Einstein

Eight Intelligences of Authentic Presence

Authentic presence via the path of the eight intelligences is a way of knowing that reflects a broad and deep ability to comprehend both our inner worlds and our outer surroundings utilizing collective wisdom.

In my relationship with horses, and in engaging with horses and people, I have observed and identified eight primary forms of intelligence that are alive in people, horses, and all the natural world:

1. cognitive intelligence
2. emotional intelligence
3. social intelligence
4. embodied intelligence
5. intuitive intelligence
6. natural intelligence

7. spiritual intelligence
8. transformational intelligence (also called BWI intelligence¬—Beyond [Your] Wildest Imagination)

Each of the eight forms of intelligence offers a unique and interrelated perspective in understanding our inner and outer present reality and possible future. We all have these eight intelligences, as do the horses, some more developed than others, and some that we prefer to listen to and depend on more than others.

The word intelligence comes from late Middle English: via Old French from Latin *intelligential*, from *intelligere*, 'to understand.'

The collective wisdom of these our diverse intelligence is an important pathway to understanding our authentic presence; it expands our capacity to figure out many aspects of our life, and allows us a range of responses and a choice of actions. This collective wisdom of intelligence is about you about me, about us and the world around us, and it is informed by diverse, unique and interconnected information.

We can all further develop our capacity by being aware, exploring through direct experience and responding to life with passion and purpose. Using discipline and practice, we can expand our range and depth of intelligence, build our capacity to listen, be aware, be expansive, and be our best lovable selves. Here at the ranch, we cultivate our collective intelligence by engaging in self-reflection, and by deep relationship with people and horses and the quiet, open heart of nature.

People often ask me if I think horses are smart, do they have intelligence, can they think, what do they think about. I believe that horses are highly intelligent, can think, and most important, can think about authentically important stuff. I might not have the typical research to support my ideas about the intelligence of horses, but what I do have is hours and hours of direct observation, living with and learning from the horses about how they use their range of intelligence. I have observed them use their intelligence to solve concrete problems, to manage their relationships, to meet their basic survival needs, to communicate over long distances, and to manifest their desires in order to thrive. I have observed how horses orient to and engage people through their intelligence and how people expand their human intelligence by engaging with the horses.

Operating from their authentic presence, horses apply their assorted innate and learned intelligences. They focus on what has the most meaning to them and to their herd in the present moment, and what has the best chance of immediate and long-term success. They follow what they love with playful discipline. They practice what they want to achieve in every action they take. They make decisions and take action in the blink of a moment and at the same time seem to pause, reflect, and respond, all in slow motion. They spend long periods of time in what appears to me to be a deep meditative state somewhere between sleep and awakened awareness, what we might call in human behavior "mindfulness." They spend long periods of time resting in harmony so as to be ready for change, preparing to move forward and live intelligently with herd members and within their environment.

One morning while having fun hanging out with the horses, I began to imagine and guess which of the eight intelligences that I have identified seemed to most reflect each horse's and zebra's preferred way of being.

Cognitive Intelligence I connected to Tess the Shetland pony.

Emotional Intelligence to Spirit, our paint mustang mare.

Social Intelligence to Bud, our Montana cowboy horse.

Embodied Intelligence to Chief Silver Cloud, our resident unicorn.

Intuitive Intelligence to Toby, the Gypsy horse.

Natural Intelligence to Raven, our laid-back guy horse.

Spiritual Intelligence to Bea, our fierce lead mare.

Transformational /BWI (Beyond [Your] Wildest Imagination) Intelligence to Holly, the holy zebra.

Cognitive Intelligence (as represented by Tess the pony)

> *"In reality, horses manage not only ordinary daily cognitive tasks but mental challenges as well. In the wild, they must cope with food and water of inconsistent quality or unpredictable distribution, predators that change locations and habits, and a social system in which identities and roles of individuals must be discovered and remembered."*
> —Dr. Evelyn B. Hanggi, President, Equine Research Foundation

Cognitive intelligence can be thought of as the ability to be aware and mindful of our thoughts, organize and make meaning of data from a positive thought process, and appropriately decide and act on thoughtful information. Cognitive intelligence goes on within one's own brain, within one's own mind and within a larger surrounding field of thought.

Wisdom of the Eight Intelligences

I believe that horses are cognitively intelligent; they think in order to solve problems, to complete tasks and to mindfully adapt to changing conditions in their environment. They have the ability to determine the most important thing to pay attention to and they retain essential knowledge.

I chose Tess to represent Cognitive Intelligence because you can almost see her thoughts working to solve the problems that are important to her. As humans, we often get distracted with mind chatter or circular thought that takes us nowhere, but not Tess. She does not, like so many of us less cognitively intelligent humans do, judge herself or blame others when things do not go as she thought they would. Tess simply reorganizes her thoughts in a different direction and focuses her thoughts on what is essential to her in the moment, and figures it out. She is not distracted from her purpose by unintelligent thoughts like "I'm not good enough" or limiting thoughts of failure. She uses her cognitive intelligence to try something, and if does not work, she learns thoughtfully from her mistakes and tries something else. One day I watched Tess figure out how to untie the rope that was keeping the gate closed so she could get into the yard with its delicious flowers and sweet green grass. She used her mouth to pull on the rope and then rubbed against it and almost got it untied. When that did not work as she hoped, she went to the next gate, traveling down the fence line optimistically looking for a gate easier to open or perhaps a gate already open. Not achieving the success she had expected, she resiliently trotted over to the other horses and tried to get them to move toward the gate to help her get it open. When that did not work, Tess came to me, nudging me toward the gate to open it for her. She was on herd time and willing to spend whatever time it took to get to the grass on the other side of the gate. Tess has the benefit of the collective wisdom of generations of herds thinking strategically, and she has endless time and the patience required to reach her goal. Though Tess did not succeed in getting the gate to the green grass open through her own efforts, nor by enlisting other horses or me to help her accomplish her mission; Tess, with optimism and no thought of defeat, turned her hungry thinking in a different direction to get some kind of tasty treat. She knows the exact spot where every horse eats their breakfast, so, abandoning that which was not working, she trotted eagerly to each of seven horse's breakfast spots and happily nibbled the last crumbs they had left. All the other horses had been relaxing in the field. Tess thinks for herself; she had been on a quest for tasty treats, that is, until her thoughts turned to an endeavor of higher priority. Her tummy full, she trotted (as Tess rarely walks anywhere) to join the herd in the field…time for a nap.

Thoughtful Tess has a romantic nature, and just before dark when I bring the horses to their nighttime pastures, she looks for her boyfriend Bud (who stands almost eight feet tall at his ears while she stands just over three feet at her ears). Spotting him across the field, she runs over to him, reaching up toward him for one last goodnight snuggle, nuzzle and nip. She knows it is time to move to her bedtime pasture on the other side of the gate, and with strategic thinking and embodied language, she pauses to say goodnight to Bud.

I learned many useful things from how Tess the pony thinks and reasons that apply to my understanding of developing the best of human cognitive intelligence. As humans we often over-think and lean heavily on intellectual cognition without drawing from our other forms of intelligence. Not so Tess: she balances her cognitive intelligence with her embodied, intuitive and emotional intelligence. We humans tend to get stuck in habitual thinking, outdated mental models and old patterns from our past. Tess thinks strategically in the present and goes with the flow so that she does not get caught in the trap of past thinking that is no longer in service of her. Tess demonstrates that cognitive intelligence takes focus, good common horse sense, and curiosity. She welcomes new ideas and learns from her mistakes. Tess is willing to try something new without the fear of failure, to be flexible in thought and to change direction when things don't work. She is persistent in her thinking, but not attached to her thoughts. She reminds us to think about what's really going on, beyond just "doing things." According to Tess, cognitive intelligence, whether horse or human, means thinking optimistically that things can always improve, and that with time, support, heart and joyful purpose, all is possible.

Emotional Intelligence (as represented by Spirit)

> *"We find that most of the characteristics that differentiate the outstanding performers are these things that we call social and emotional competencies. It's well understood that emotional intelligence (EI) the ability to bring out the best in ourselves and others is a crucial part of a leader's repertoire."*
> —Richard Boyatzis, co-author, Emotional Intelligence

The definition of emotional intelligence as stated by Richard Boyatzis and Daniel Goleman in their book of the same name refers to "the capacity for recognizing our own feelings and those of others, for motivating ourselves, and for managing relationships well in ourselves and in our relationships."

I chose Spirit to represent emotional intelligence. Spirit may not be interested in the definition, but her natural way of being is aligned with and embodies the capacity known as emotional intelligence. Spirit, of all the horses in the herd, is the most demonstrative of her emotions and clear in managing her feelings in her relationships with horses and people. Her emotional intelligence, as with all horses, is centered in present time. She lives in resonance with her inner self, her herd, people that enter her field, and the natural world. Spirit is emotionally discerning, knowing what she wants and what she does not want, and is clear and quick in communicating her requests. Emotion, for Spirit, is simply information that registers through her entire body and outward into her social field.

If we approach Spirit and she is not feeling like being approached or touched or engaged in conversation, she will flick her tail and glare at us. If we do not understand her message and continue to move toward her, she will add pinning her ears back to the glaring and tail flick. If we continue ignoring her embodied language of "What do you not understand about no?", she will swing her head at you and snap as if to bite you. She is not being mean, she is clearly being honest about her wants and don't-wants based on her authentic emotions within her field of reference. Spirit's "no" is not a conditioned response or habitual behavioral pattern, it is based on her present, real-time emotional reality. She will say "yes" to someone if she is in the mood to engage and be social with that person or horse. When Spirit initiates the connection from a "yes" inside of her, she will sweetly approach people and herd members with soft nuzzling and gentle horse kisses. What you see on the outside in Spirit's actions is an honest expression of what she is feeling on the inside. Our human interactions might be less confusing and complicated if we were as congruent and clear as Spirit in being aware of our feelings, in caring about our impact, and in managing and expressing our honest emotions.

Managing boundaries of me and not-me, want and don't-want, yes and no, is important in establishing emotional competency. Spirit is a great teacher of managing boundaries. She is agile in managing her emotions and open to the possibility that boundaries change depending on her mood, her response to a person, to her horse buddy and to the conditions of the environment.

Spirit, like all horses, maintains emotional integrity using only as much power and energy as necessary in the moment. They have developed, as a survival response, a finely tuned and highly developed ability for accurate emotional response. Horses that have been allowed to be horses manage their impulses effectively, and are trustworthy, adaptive, and innovative, all primal skills of emotional intelligence.

If there is conflict within the herd, it is managed at the appropriate time and place, and when it's over, it is over. Spirit manages her internal states and impulses in alignment with the emotional resonance of her herd members. Her emotional presence is authentic, what is going on inside is reflected in her outer behavior and actions.

Spirit is highly sensitive and knows when someone horse or human has an expectation of her or a desire to influence her behavior. That does not go over well with Spirit; she is much more likely to cooperate when it's her idea, or when she is at least patiently asked and her opinion is included in the decision. She does not like to be told what to do or how to do it, but she is willing to be influenced. Spirit is motivated when what is happening seems like fun, and willing to be a herd player when who she is and what she wants is understood and respected.

I believe all horses inherently have high emotional intelligence, recognizing their own emotions and those of others, motivating themselves and others, and responding honestly to emotions in themselves and others. Emotional Intelligence in horses and in people is has everything to do with the quality of relationship. Thankfully, with awareness, discipline and practice, we can improve emotional intelligence, which translates into a more meaningful life experience. In the presence of horses, we humans can attune to our emotional intelligence, and grow more fully into emotional maturity. Emotional intelligence, through honest and trustworthy interaction, can motivate us to engage with one another and with life in a heartfelt way. Being forgiving and compassionate and offering gratitude are all ways to embody and express our emotional intelligence. Spirit forgives my honest mistakes and expresses compassion, being unconditionally loving when I need a friend. I am deeply grateful for Spirit's guidance in emotional intelligence, her commitment to being who she is, and for her abundant generosity in allowing me to be part of her life.

Social Intelligence (as represented by Bud, Big Boy Tamarack)

> *"Today we are faced with the preeminent fact that, if civilization is to survive, we must cultivate the science of relationships - the ability of all peoples, of all kinds, to live together and work together, in the same world, at peace.*
> —Franklin Delano Roosevelt, former President of the United States

Wisdom of the Eight Intelligences

Bud, Big Boy Tamarack, a socially intelligent horse is the FDR of our herd. Social intelligence is the ability to engage effectively in relationships, to get along well with others and to have them get along with you through awareness of the other, and interactions of cooperation and care. Empathy and inclusion are is the cornerstone of this intelligence. It asks that we set aside our beliefs and perceptions of reality to deeply listen to and connect with someone different from us with curiosity and respect and to be influenced in some way in that connection. Social intelligence invites us to pay careful attention to the context, situation and realty of the person or being we are engaging for meaningful interactions to take place.

I chose Bud to represent social intelligence as he is one of our horses with the biggest heart, the most caring responses and friendliest way of engaging. He is the first to step up to say hi to people, lowering his head from his eight-foot height to see them better through his flowing mane. Bud, in his younger years, was a logger in Montana where he worked pulling logs out of the forest as part of a two-horse and human team. Bud developed a strong work ethic and a high level of social intelligence through this experience learning to work in a harmonious partnership toward a shared goal. When Bud arrived at Pebble Ledge Ranch, he was accepted peaceably by the herd with very little chaos or conflict, which is unusual; there is generally some amount of social emotional drama when a new horse arrives. I take this peaceful entry into the herd as a testimony to Bud's high degree of social intelligence, also demonstrated by his empathy, and his ability to understand horses and people from their points of view. One of Bud's most endearing socially intelligent abilities is his way of engaging with unconditional generosity, seeing the best in everyone and helping everyone see the best in themselves and in others.

Bud has earned a place in the heart of the herd, a place of respect, trust and positive regard, and he has won over the hearts of many people as well. The day is always brighter with Bud at your side; a loyal horse of character, he makes sure that someone cares and no one goes it alone, horse or human. He has social emotional intelligence in his sense of responsibility for and sensitivity to the needs of others. He steps forward in his engaging, honest and willing way to be of service to people and his herd. Bud gives of himself without expecting anything in return and what comes back to him is pure love. For some people, when they feel the compassion and love from and to Bud, their heart opens to a new depth of feeling, allowing them to extend their increased openheartedness to others.

You might see Bud standing apart from the horses in the field taking space and time for himself, or he might be standing quietly in the middle of the herd when there is chaos, patiently waiting for the calm and peace he knows will return. What our challenged world really needs now is Bud's good social emotional horse sense, but unfortunately, it's only the horses that have this. Bud sets a high standard of social intelligence for all humans to aspire to in a society crying out for social and emotional intelligence, social justice, healing and loving kindness.

Embodied Intelligence (as represented by Chief Silver Cloud)

> *"Horses are creatures that worship the earth,*
> *they gallop on feet by the sea*
> *Constrained by the wonder of dying and birth*
> *The horses still run, they are free."*
> —John Denver, singer-songwriter

"You have a unicorn," a five-year-old girl shouted with excitement as she pointed her finger toward Chief Silver Cloud who was standing proudly in a field of purple and yellow wildflowers, his silver coat shimmering in the sunlight.

The unicorn is a legendary creature said to have mystical powers, a symbol of purity and grace. It takes the innocence of childhood or child-like innocence to see a unicorn in physical form.

Chief Silver Cloud is our resident herd unicorn and in part that is why I chose him to represent embodied intelligence — an awesome, magical and pure intelligence from which to experience the world. Our physical body, though temporal in nature, is remarkable in its ability to sense, register and make meaning of our inner and outer world. Our embodied intelligence is a living miracle of creation, healing, transformation and collective wisdom. Much like unicorns, our body lives only in the present moment of reality and reveals itself through movement. Embodied presence is the physical container that holds body, mind, emotion and spirit together. Through our embodied intelligence, we take in information with our senses and mindfully make meaning of our inner and outer life experiences. As we connect with the heart of the matter, we begin to know our purpose and can bring our embodied wisdom into the world through our actions. Our embodied intelligence makes it possible to stand our ground for what we believe in and to get moving towards what we value on our path to authentic presence.

Chief Silver Cloud embodies "steadfast" as he takes a stand in the place he feels he belongs, and he is immovable. In addition to standing his ground, he is skilled in moving to the ground where he desires to take his stand. He is often purposefully on the move, mobilizing horses and people in the direction he thinks they should be going. When I first observed his behavior, I thought him to be rude and push, but I have taken into consideration another perspective. During one of our programs, I watched Chief Silver Cloud boldly move a team of executive leaders across our twenty-acre pasture as part of a leadership program. Chief kept giving them gentle and not-so-gentle shoves with his 2000-pound body, keeping them on the move. I ran across the pasture to ask Chief to please be more respectful of our guests and to stop pushing them around as he twice outweighed the total weight of the five men on his team. To my surprise, I noticed that the men were laughing and did not seem to be at all upset about Silver's prodding. By the time I reached the team, they were standing around talking. Chief was just hanging out with the guys, looking respectfully interested in what they were discussing. I asked how they were doing and how they were getting along with Chief Silver Cloud, their horse coach. They told me that Chief Silver Cloud had earned his oats for the day and deserved a bonus for his coaching with them. "Chief delivered the message our team most needed," they said. "He got us moving, kept us moving forward, and would not let us stay in one place for very long. It's just what we needed to have happen. We have been reluctant to move forward and have been stuck doing things the same old way and consequently not achieving our goals." One of the team members remarked, "It's time for us as a team to get moving toward the opportunities in front of us and maybe even have some fun while we are at it. As soon as we came to that realization, Chief stopped and was content to stay in one place with us. Our lesson from Chief is to move forward toward opportunity, stop when you get there and remember to celebrate before moving on." Communicating with his team through the embodied language of movement and stillness in the context of work relationships, Chief Silver Cloud imparted

My ten-minute conversation with this team turned out to be an important lesson for me, and a very important moment in my relationship with Chief. While I have a deep and caring bond with all the horses, I had struggled to establish that relationship with Chief. I assumed, based on what I observed of his embodied presence, that he was a big bully, using force to push people and the horses in his herd around. He was a more gentle bully with people, but could be quite aggressive with the other horses, all except for the horse Toby who is half the size of Chief; he never exerted his power over Toby. Often when the herd was quietly grazing, everyone minding their own business, Chief would come up to one horse or another and chase them away from where they were eating. Sometimes, when the horses were peaceably napping in the sun, Chief would nip a horse on the rump and wake them up. The story I made up about Chief was that not having grown up in a herd, he had not learned the social graces of horses and that explained why he was now a bully in his herd. I dislike bullying behavior and am the first to defend anyone getting bullied, so this disrespectful behavior of Chief's, even though he was gentle with me, made it difficult for me to bond with him. I assumed the herd felt the same way. We all have emotional triggers and when we see something that activates that trigger, we can quickly make an assumption that becomes our "story" and we experience that story as the truth. I noticed that while all the other horses engaged in the intimate touching ritual of grooming one another, no horse ever engaged Chief in mutual grooming. That proved my point of view; the horses, like me, also had difficulty bonding with him. I felt sad for Chief, but I figured he deserved to be left out of this social interaction because of his bullying behavior and meaningless disruption of the herd.

Then something changed in me and in my relationship with Chief. I had a change of heart and mind that day in the pasture, listening to the team talk about their positive experience with Chief Silver Cloud. The guys really appreciated Chief's use of his powerful embodied presence to get things moving. No one was stepped on or run over by him, everyone felt safe and had fun, and they all learned something of value. It was an "aha" moment for me. I realized that there was another story here that carried its own truth. I was able for the first time to understand and appreciate Chief Silver Cloud's value in taking responsibility for getting things moving. I no longer saw him as pushy or being a bully, but saw him using his power "with," not power "over," to provide an essential leadership lesson: sometimes you need to use your influence to get movement. I began to see his behavior in the horse herd and with people in a new light. His leadership job was to make sure the herd was alert, aware, awake and able to respond to unexpected change. He provided the "unexpected change" for the horses to practice and maintain their agility and ability to move quickly when necessary. Chief is good at his job of being a disruptive innovator, and like similar leadership responsibilities, it comes with personal sacrifice, giving up something valued for a worthy cause. As I let go of judging Chief, I saw him with fresh eyes. I could appreciate his positive growth from the time he first entered the herd using aggression and undue force to his now respected place within the herd using assertive power with wisdom. I developed empathy for him as I remembered that he arrived with a big plastic baseball bat with his old name Conan the Barbarian written on it by his former owners. My guess is that Chief was bullied in his last home and learned to bully others. We threw the bat away and changed his name to Chief Silver Cloud, and over time, he has grown into the majesty and responsibility of his new name. Unconsciously, I had still carried the fear of bullies and saw what might have been assertive behavior as aggressive instead of protective behavior. Opening my mind to a new mental image, opening my heart without judgment and letting go of old self-righteous old patterns, I could see the truthful reality of the present and a better future emerged in my relationship with Chief.

Chief Silver Cloud's embodied intelligence, communication and presence are easily recognizable as he is physically so big in body and in embodied expression.

If you walked into the pasture or any place Chief was, his presence would be noticed. His embodied intelligence continues to show up in his engagement and communication with his herd members and with people. Paying attention through his embodied intelligence, Chief knows how and when to get the herd and people moving so they stay alert, agile and ready for unexpected change, and possible good fortune! He seems to sense when someone is feeling small and needs to feel big, whether that person lacks confidence or courage, and he is right there with enormous compassion to help people grow into their potential as he as done here at the ranch time and time again.

Horses (as well as unicorns) are probably best known for their body intelligence as that is the most obvious intelligence to observe and a primary form of communication with their fellow herd members and with us. In the presence of their four-hoofed, well-grounded connection to the earth, we can find our own sense of ground and connection to the earth and to all life. Mirroring their unshakable centeredness, we can experience the stability of our inner center and not get knocked off balance by life events. Within the resonant field of their compassionate hearts, we can experience ourselves as more openhearted. Breathing slowly with them, we can find an inner calm from which to access deeper wisdom. As they enter their meditative horse dream state, we can more deeply enter into our place of human dreams and vision. Horses' embodied intelligence communicates not only through their senses and motion, but also through emotion. They have a wide peripheral vision, a 340-degree wide-view perception, and they resonate to a full spectrum of emotion. Chief, as do all horses, has a way of sensing and registering embodied intelligence, gathering a wide field of information, which results in expanded awareness.

Opening our ability to sense and our perception to a wider range of authentic knowing through embodied intelligence is a valuable resource that we can learn from horses. Listen to embodied presence; it is honest and always tells the truth, and that embodied honesty and truth-telling is essential to living with authentic presence.

Intuitive Intelligence (as represented by Sir Toby)

> *"Intuition is a very powerful thing. Have the courage to follow your heart and intuition. They somehow already know what you really want to become."*
> —Steve Jobs, co-founder of Apple, Inc.

Intuitive intelligence is information and guidance from our inner realm. We all have it, It is independent of rational thought, immediate, positive and constructive; it comes di-

Wisdom of the Eight Intelligences

rectly from within and is always available. When we listen to our intuition, our entire being hears a wholehearted "yes," an inner sense that confidently tells us what feels true for us in that present moment. Though sometimes challenging to discern, we know it when we feel it¬—that aha, in the flow, synchronistic and immediate inner certainty.

I chose Toby to represent Intuitive Intelligence as he has an invaluable talent for helping people discover, develop and advance their intuition. Being with horses is one of the best ways to cultivate intuitive intelligence because this is a primary intelligence, which the horse depends on to survive and to thrive in its world.

Intuition, sometimes called the sixth sense, is not more important than our other five senses, nor does it stand alone as a sense but is instead part of (and depends on) the collective wisdom of all our senses. Intuition comes from the word intuitio, 'consideration' or 'contemplation' in the ongoing collection of experience that comes together in a moment in time. It is related to but different from our instinct, which comes from the word instinctus, or "impulse," meaning, it's an automatic biological tendency experienced in a moment in time. Both intuition and instinct come from within and depend on the direct and honest communication received from our embodiment to make sense of our world.

Interacting with horses can help us strengthen our connection to both our instinct and our intuition by helping us:

- Bring our attention to our physical sensations and embodied wisdom
- Be more in the present moment, experience silence and stillness within

- Resonate with our true emotions, making our inner experience consistent with outer behavior
- Trust our inner knowing and believe magic is possible

Toby is a champion in living intuitively and in helping people experience intuition for themselves.

Sir Toby is the Gypsy horse that was born in the United Kingdom and lived with Romany people, sometimes disrespectfully referred to as "Gypsies." For Romany folks, also known as travellers, horses are considered members of their families and communities. The Romany relationship with the horse is deep and ancient and it is said that a Romany person without a horse is not a true Romany. Sir Toby's horse lineage is interwoven with the Romany nomadic tradition, a way of life unchanged for generations. The Romany culture is deeply connected to intuitive intelligence through their traditions of everyday ritual, magic, myth, storytelling, and through their freedom of expression and trust in intuition. Many of these inner ways of knowing and practices were passed down from family to family and community through the generations. Toby, being part of that rich tradition and ancient horse lineage, inherited the amazing gifts of inner knowing, instinct and intuition.

The Gypsy horse by Romany tradition was involved is every aspect of family and community life. Toby, as a prized family and community member, listened to their legends and mystic tales and participated in their ritual celebrations of protection, love and healing. Toby's flashy black-and-white coat; long, flowing mane and tail, and the elegant furry feathers around his hoofs matched the beauty of Romany dress and made him every Romany's dream horse. In his youth, Toby proudly pulled their colorful caravan wagon from camp to camp, and faithfully carried their children on his generous back. Not only was he valued for his gait, which seemed to "float and fly on air itself," he was loved for his good nature, gentle temperament, hardiness, and adaptability. His instinctual and intuitive knowing was of ultimate value to his Romany family, warning them of physical danger or spiritual threats. Many of these qualities inherent in Toby are readily available to all of us when we are loyal to our selves and others, trust our instinct and intuition, seek beauty and harmony, and live with authentic presence.

> *"It was the travelling, rather than the arriving that was important. Every lane and the surroundings were a part of a Romani's life, and they knew every road."*
> —Mr. Henry Elliot, Romani Traveller

The Romany are a proud people and especially proud of their horses. There is a mutual affection and honoring between the people and their horses. You will never be allowed to see their best horses if you do not belong to their community, but you will see a good horse. When Toby was six years old his life changed dramatically. A woman from Arizona visited the Romany encampment in the UK in search of a Gypsy horse to buy, bring home to the US and start a Gypsy breeding program. She wisely chose Toby. It was a difficult decision for Toby's family to sell him, as Gypsy horses, in addition to being valued, are very loving and relational with their families, and especially the children. It was painful for Toby to leave the only home he had known, but being a good horse, and being hardy and adaptable, he made the best of his unexpected journey to life in America.

Toby, of the traveller people, boarded a ship and traveled across the ocean to his new home bringing with him the wisdom of the Romany culture and the gift of intuition. He lived in Arizona and then Montana, charming people wher-ever he went. It was through Toby's intuition, and mine, that he was brought to Ohio and Pebble Ledge Ranch. Coming from a culture that commonly travels, works, and lives in ex-tended family groups that offer companionship and mutual support, much like horse herds, Toby easily found his way into the herd. In his Romany family, togetherness had been important and the males were the protectors responsible for keeping family together. Toby quickly established his place as the lead stallion and like the men in his Romany family, he became the defender in the herd. He took on the family herd leadership job of making sure that everyone was safe, there was order among the horses, and no one would ever get left behind. In addition to that sixth sense of intuition, Toby also brought with him to the ranch his own mysterious Romany powers. Having always lived close to nature, roaming freely across the countryside with his family, Toby learned from his Romany tradition and heritage of the herd to be true to his word, sensitive and generous, and in tune with the forces of nature. Like the Romany people with whom he lived, Toby listened to the wisdom of his inner nature and found magic in all the world around him.

Toby's Guide to the Collective Wisdom of Intuitive Intelligence

While we all have intuitive intelligence, we often depend and trust logic over our intuitive way of knowing; or, we are unaware of how to access or listen to this way of knowing. Intuitive intelligence can be strengthened though awareness, commitment, practice and the support of a trustworthy guide. Toby has been for me, and many others, that guide. According to Toby and other wise elders, ways to expand your Intuitive Intelligence follows:

1. Seek times of quiet and solitude to engage the deepest inner wisdom.

   "See how nature grows and moves in silence…
   we need silence to be able to touch souls."
   —Mother Teresa

2. Listen deeply from deep within; to hear what most needs to be heard.

   "There is a voice inside of you that whispers all
   day long," I feel this is right for me,
   I know that this is wrong."
   —Shel Silverstein, American writer

3. Trust in the heart of your inner knowing with courage and confidence.

   "Go confidently in the direction of your dreams!
   Live the life you've imagined."
   —Henry David Thoreau

4. Engage in creativity; art, storytelling, music and dance as expressions of your life.

   "Let the beauty we love be what we do".
   —Rumi

5. Release judgment and negative thought and emotion and embrace positivity.

   "What lies behind us and what lies before us are
   tiny matters compared to what lies within us and
   when we bring what is within out into the world,
   miracles happen."
   —Ralph Waldo Emerson

6. Experience your embodiment and come to your senses.

> *"The physical world, including our bodies, is a response of the observer. We create our bodies as we create the experience of our world."*
> —Deepak Chopra

7. Practice, practice, practice.

> *"We can do anything we want as long as we stick to it long enough."*
> —Helen Keller

8. Connect deeply and humbly with all life and notice everything that makes you feel most alive.

> *"Seek out that which makes you feel most deeply and vitally alive, along with which comes the inner voice which says "This is the real me, follow it"*
> —William James

We all have intuitive intelligence; we just need to seek it and follow it. We know from our inner being without knowing why or how we know. It begins as an unconscious process of knowing that gathers and instantaneously brings together knowledge from diverse and unrelated experiences in the moment as collective wisdom.

> *"There is a growing body of anecdotal evidence, combined with solid research efforts, that suggests intuition is a critical aspect of how we humans interact with our environment and how, ultimately, we make many of our decisions,"*
> —Ivy Estabrooke, Program Manager, Office of Naval Research

We are born with the ability to immediately sense, feel and quickly know without conscious thought or reasoning. Intuitive intelligence is a hidden genius and a gift that lives within us just waiting to be opened to awaken the best in all of us. Accessing this unique inner intelligence, we can be of service in creating a better world for the coming generations.

"Intuition is a sacred gift."
—Albert Einstein

Natural Intelligence (as represented by Raven)

I chose Raven to represent Natural Intelligence, the knowing we have; from an understanding that we are part of the natural world, and by learning to trust our natural common sense. All horses draw on this type of natural intelligence as their primary source of information as did we when we lived a lifestyle that depended more directly on our relationship with the natural world and our natural senses to survive and thrive in life. Our natural intelligence is the ability to perceive ourselves as part of nature and to be able to understand the language and information from the natural world. Nature is practical, and part of our natural intelligence is the genius of nature and of our common senses. This intelligence offers confidence and a feeling of competence. It provides us with an internal compass so as to know the present best place to be and how to move to greet the best possible future place. When we are connected to the natural world as a part of the family of nature we are more connected to our natural self and natural abilities. Cut off from nature we feel a sense of loneliness, unease with ourselves and our life and a disconnection with from our common sense natural knowing.

Raven is my opinion the most "natural" horse, the most "horse" horse of our herd being less influenced than the rest of the herd by human culture. He had little human interaction or bonding from birth to six months of age and was without any real human interaction from the time he was six months old till he was two years old, some of the most formative times in horse and human growing up. Raven had the creatures and forces of the natural world for companionship, a stray cat to play with, resident birds to sing to him, the wind on his back and sun to warm him, trees for shelter and sweet grass to graze. When I first met Raven at two years old he was alone in his pasture hanging out with his cat buddy and munching dandelions and clover. He lifted his head, ears alert, sniffing to sense what had entered his field. He seemed more curious than afraid, me too, as we walked toward each other meeting half way between. We slowed to a stop, Raven extended his nose and I reached out my hand and we greeted each other with cautious curiosity. What followed was a game of approach and retreat, each of us moving towards and away from each other in a meeting dance of closeness and distance. It was a good beginning to what has proved to be a friendship between us, with Raven just being horse and me just a human being with him. When I brought Raven to Pebble Ledge Ranch to join his real horse mom Bea, and the herd, he knew little about horse culture. He had no real time knowledge of the horse rules of engagement or code of herd behavior. Over time the horses, especially his mom Bea, and grandmotherly Rojo helped him remember how to be a horse and responsible herd member. Toby, our resident stallion engaged him in vigorous horseplay teaching him to be a guy horse. Spirit offered him friendship and taught him first horse love. She would patiently wait for him while he and I, for an hour each day, negotiated the lessons necessary to live in the human world. Lesson over the two of them would joyfully gallop across the field to join the rest of the herd.

One day it came time to introduce Raven to the saddle and blanket in preparation for him to learn to accept a person on his back. I dragged the saddle and saddle blanket out of the barn and put it in the middle of the paddock for him to check out and to realize it meant him no harm. Raven in his customary innocent, fearless, playful and devil- may- care attitude, sniffed the saddle and stepped on it and then picked the saddle blanket up in his mouth and waved it around. He took a step toward me and looked down on me as if to say "what's up?"

What I knew in my heart was that if I asked Raven to learn to be ridden by people he would say yes but the cost to him and to all of us who knew him would be great. Horses were not physically or spiritually meant to carry people on their backs, though most will accommodate that request with training and preparation and some might even grow to like that job. The intuitive message that I heard from Raven was, "Naturally, I'd rather not be a riding horse, I just want to be a natural horse." I put the saddle and blanket back in the barn and honored his request to just be a horse. A year later when Raven was about three years old, my three-year-old special needs grandson who has Angelman syndrome came to the ranch to visit. Joshua cannot speak but communicates much like the horses through gesture, thought pattern and emotional resonance. He walked up to Raven and reached his arms up toward him. Raven stood still as a statue and slowly lowered his head to reach back to Joshua. I sensed a deep connection between them in a language of the heart and soul. They nuzzled each other and looked into each other's eyes and then Raven walked next to Joshua and leaned against him looking back at me. It seemed that Raven and Josh were working something out that included Raven inviting Joshua onto his back and

Joshua saying yes, yes. I slowly lifted Joshua onto Raven's back, holding him to see what was going to unfold. Raven sighed softly, looked gently back at Joshua and stood quietly while each felt the warm and loving presence of the other. After a few magical minutes, I sensed that Raven and Josh were ready for me to bring Josh to the ground. Raven lowered his head, and nose to nose with to Joshua, they shared breath. Raven with a horse grin and Josh with a little boy grin, each turned to walk away to the next adventure. This meeting of the hearts and bodies is an expression of this extraordinary but most natural friendship that has happened for five years now each time Joshua and Raven renew their friendship and join up.

I often see Raven lift his head and sniff the wind to check out what is happening in field, or see the quiver of his skin as he senses a coming storm, or know just what grasses and plants to eat with his whiskers and muzzle. He has an intimate knowing of the natural world and the forces of nature around him. Like most beings of the natural world his reality exists in sensing intuitively and registering in his body the ever-changing present moment. From this place of natural being in the present he is able to sense and anticipate impending change just before it happens. He can then move instinctually, intuitively, gracefully and naturally toward the best possible future and then be there to greet it.

Natural intelligence is also about making responsible and sensible decisions for your own well being and for the well being of others. Raven's closest relationships from birth were not humans like the rest of the herd but with the natural world. He had to depend on his natural instincts and natural intelligence for information on how to live and survive. In Raven's presence people seem to most naturally know how find to their purpose and place of belonging and help others do the same.

I had an experience with Raven and a coaching client at the ranch who learned from him to trust her natural intelligence. We were in the pasture and she was sharing with me some of the recent developments in her life as Holly the zebra grazed nearby. She was talking about feeling like she did not belong anywhere and that she felt lost about her place or her purpose. She felt that others seemed to always know what was best for her and she did not trust her own decisions. She said that she often made decisions that were not her own and that she backed down and found herself in situations that made her doubt herself and caused her to be unhappy.

Right at that moment that she was sharing her dilemmas, Raven charged right through the space in between Holly the zebra and the woman and it was clear he wanted her to move. Rather than get knocked off balance or stepped on by Ravens youthful and bold moving energy she did not argue. Her natural common sense and physical sense said "just move" and she did. She and Raven had a good relationship, and she didn't mind that in that moment that he caused her to move. She respected him, but she also respected herself. She moved and kept herself safe. This was not the appropriate time to argue or stand her ground. If she had tried to fight for where she was standing she might have been stepped on and hurt.

Raven's actions and the meaning she gave to them offered her an important insight and the reinforcement she needed. She realized that she had not lost her place nor did it mean that she did not belong there or was not valued it simply meant that she had to take responsibility to move out of harms' way to the next best place of her choice. She knew that in taking care of herself she made a powerful move and took back her power of self-confidence. She valued herself enough that when given a choice to stay or move she chose the best natural choice given the situation and moved to a place of well being. She realized that in order to belong and to find her place, she needs to be free to move in the direction of her choice. She re-alized that a place of belonging did not depend on the actions of others but on her own actions and reactions. In moving in a direction of her choosing, she reclaimed her sense of purpose. In the company of Raven's natural actions and presence, she began to better trust her own natural intelligence.

One of the best places to develop your natural intelligences is in the natural world. We are all part of nature and as we re-claim that part of who we are we reclaim more of who we are. In the presence of horses and within the realm of nature sur-rounded by trees or alongside a river or gazing at the ocean we remember who and what we are both as humble beings of the natural world and powerful beings who can live fully and freely according to our natural and authentic presence.

Spiritual Intelligence (as represented by Bea)

> *"If I am not for myself, who will be for me? But if I am only for myself, who am I? If not now, when?"*
> —Hillel, Ethics of the Fathers 1:14

I chose Bea as the relentless ambassador of spiritual intelli-gence as she always finds the divine presence in everyone and reflects it back insisting that they see it in themselves. She is a leader of spiritual adventure challenging us to share our di-vine presence through our way of being (or Bea-ing) and our commitment to action for the greatest good of humanity and the entire living world.

Wisdom of the Eight Intelligences

Our spiritual intelligence is a source of collective wisdom that incorporates many perspectives with a common core value of believing in inherent goodness, connecting to a power beyond ourselves and living a purposeful life for the greatest good. This intelligence, a sacred way of knowing, defines our way of being and actions in our day-to-day life. It is the domain of our values and their alignment with our behavior and actions, the cultivation of this domain and state of being and doing requires inner stillness, self-contemplation and outer actions of love and compassion. Spiritual intelligence as a pathway to our authentic presence builds a foundation for a loving and just world for all life based on the divine presence of the human spirit.

I often see Bea in what seems to be a deeply contemplative or meditative state of spiritual experience. She is still as a statue, in the center of the herd in the middle of the field, her eyes softly focused as if seeing from within, standing relaxed but absolutely connected to the earth. Her breathing is slow, long and deep in an intimate exchange with the outside air as she listens from within. As our ambassador to the spiritual realm she is preparing herself to go out into the world as a prophet, oracle and spiritual warrior. It is a tough assignment requiring fierce dedication and discipline and fearless courage and commitment. Lead mare of the horse herd and of our human herd she sets the direction on the path of Spiritual awareness, guidance and activism. Within the massive black beauty of her sturdy body she embodies a strong moral code that reflects her inner quality of tough compassion and unconditional love. She tends to the heart of relationship, manages the complexity and chaos of herd life, and makes a divine difference by being the divine difference. Bea loves ceremony. Whenever people gather in her pasture to share their heartfelt stories and meaningful experiences or to offer gratitude for the honor of giving and receiving, Bea is right there standing between people or moving to the center of the circle to grace us with her wise and generous presence.

The Bea Pathway to Spiritual Intelligence

Bea invites people to journey with her on the "Be," rather than the Not-to-Be path of spiritual intelligence and authentic presence. Upon entering the "Be" path, Bea gazes at us with a soulful eye asking us to reflect on the questions; "Who am I? What is my unique value, contribution, and destiny? What is the greatness of my purpose and of the divine presence that is me?"

I asked Bea if she could offer some guidance on these questions. She replied, "The knowing is already within you. Be unlike others so you can be good at being you. Pay attention to how you take your place and space in your relationships. Do not be too big, feeling superior to others, or powerful over others. Be careful of being too small, feeling inferior to others or powerless under people. Take your place and space in your life with powerful humbleness and humility, thinking less of only yourself and more of your only self."

As we continue along the path of spiritual intelligence, Bea asks in a silent message from her heart to our heart that we consider the question: "If I am only for myself what am I? What is my place and purpose in the world? Who am I as part of the greater whole?" Bea's spiritual guidance in regard to these questions: "Put your unique gifts in service to the lives of others. Be involved, fully invested and share yourself with others."

On her next step on the path of spiritual intelligence, Bea stomps, drumming her foot on the earth, demanding attention. It's a call to action. From the heartbeat of the earth comes the question, "if not now, when?" It says, "Step forward, show up, be more conscious and less self-conscious, and then act by leading the way, always moving forward toward being more of what you already are."

The last step on the journey of spiritual intelligence is the domain of our values and their alignment with our actions. Horses live their spiritual intelligence in the way they care for each other and live in harmony with their environment. In their presence we can discover inner calm, care fully for each other and live the message of our divine selves. The compassion that horses offer each other and us is contagious and helps us bring forth the best of who we authentically are. Completing our journey takes us to a spiritually present and divinely confident place of being our humble best and most lovable, noble selves. When faltering on the spiritual path, we forgive self and other, we make amends, we return to the path of loving kindness, justice and righteousness. Spiritual intelligence is a practice of repairing and perfecting oneself, repairing and perfecting the world and repairing and perfect-ing love.

Transformational Intelligence (as represented by Holly the Zebra)

> *"We're here to take you to the river; are you ready to be transformed? There's a world of love and it's standing right in front of you..."*
> —Bruce Springsteen

Holly the Zebra reminds us there is nothing standing in her way or ours, and she challenges us with the question: "Are you ready to be transformed? Are you ready for the world of love standing right in front of you?" This is a big question of deep faith in the possibility of humanity transforming into its best whole and holy self, and it can happen in an instant.

Holly, for me, is the most obvious choice to represent transformational intelligence as her life journey took a radical change, which transported her beyond her present possible into her future potential.

Transformational intelligence is inspired by profound, irreversible changes in beliefs, behaviors, embodied form, perspectives and paradigms. The worldview of a caterpillar crawling along the ground or an immobile pupa is radically different and irreversible from the worldview of the transformed butterfly flying from flower to flower. Transformation is distinguished by profound change in form, appearance or inner knowing, and is both spontaneous and a process of metamorphosis. It is generally a radical change that bears little resemblance with the past, orients to a different future and moves to a new level of what is good and useful. This is why we sometimes call it intelligence "beyond your wildest imagination." In some ways, it is coming home to a place we have been before and knowing it for the first time or coming to a place we have never been before and knowing it as home.

Holly's outer transformation was not as physically dramatic as the caterpillar's journey into a butterfly. But like the butterfly as she changed she remained the essential same self though the world in which she found herself and her needs in that domain had changed. Her profound change was inner and created unexpected possibility in her outer world. Holly is my hero of transformational intelligence and change in her courageous quantum leap into the journey of the unknown and in her extraordinary ability to land on all four hoofs in a new place of opportunity. It required her to let go of all she had known in order for her best possible future to emerge and come forward. Her life path as a zebra, a herd member of 10,000 zebras living on the desert plains of Africa, was radically changed to life as a zebra in a herd of seven horses in the forest of Northeast Ohio. She had to let go of and what would have worked in her African culture and life on the plains. Her transformational intelligence provided the wisdom to let come that which she would need in her new life in America. She was still a zebra but she had to make sense of things from a totally unknown point of view. At the heart of Holly's transformational intelligence was her innate wisdom that what was more important than surviving, or maintaining the status quo, was thriving and moving to a better place. Holly's transformational intelligence opened the path to her innate abilities to recreate her life in a new and resourceful way. Holly said yes to being transformed and yes to being authentically present as a zebra, and yes to a world of love standing right in front of her.

Holly's Hints to Transformational Intelligence
Trust the Process

Transformational intelligence is a leap of faith believing that from the improbable and impossible emerges the best possible. Holly befriended the unknown and embraced the mys-tery of her life with fierce curiosity. We all intuitively know what we need to know. Holly knew absolutely nothing about living in a herd of horses. She did not know how she was going to do it, and was uncertain of the outcome, but she ab-solutely trusted she could do it.

Let Something Die So Something Can Be Reborn

Transformation intelligence knows there is no going back and we need to let go of the old so something new can come forward. Holly shed her expectation of being in a zebra herd and the fear of not being accepted. She confidently and courageous took her place as a zebra in herd of horses. Since then she has been a champion of diversity and inclusion challenging people to make room in their hearts to accept differences and be kind and generous to all. She inspires those who are afraid to bravely show up by freely expressing who they are and openly loving who they love.

Adapt to Being Better and Better At Who and What You Already Are

Holly's adaptability and resiliency is amazing and through it all she never hid her stripes or gave up being a zebra. She came into a herd of horses, into the human culture, and into a physical world that is quite different from her original zebra life. In Africa she did not have to thrive in snow and extreme cold. Here in Ohio she has thrived by adapting innately to frigid cold and snow up to her belly. She grew a thicker coat and, as zebras can do, she grew an extra layer of fat and muscle under her black stripes. Her black stripe absorbed sun and whatever heat was in the air. The white stripe of her coat reflected the warmth back, which worked thermodynamically like a layer of heat above her body. She manifested, from her long ago ancestral capacity, a long oily coat to keep her dry, and a kind of a down underneath that. In spring, she rolls on the ground and rubs against trees to release her Ohio winter fur and bring back her African coat.

In summer, her body absorbs the fat of the black, so it goes low, and the white stands out. The white reflects the heat, working as a cooler. The stripes also keep insects off her, as flies think that she is moving. Most flies and insects prefer to land on a plain surface rather than a striped surface, which was the zebra protection in Africa from the tsetse fly. Zebras with the most stripes survived, and it works for Holly now. Sometimes, when the horses are out in the pasture, with flies on them, Holly is standing with no flies. That is part of her physical adaptability.

The physical transformational adaptations are relatively easy to see. What is less visible is the internal change, the intuitive inner knowing Holly and we all have to draw on to thrive in our relationships and within the fields of our life.

The ability to adapt to changing conditions relatively quickly is a huge plus for Holly and animals in the wild. Humans might be able to adapt, but the question for all of us is, how fast and effectively can we adapt? We might be able, over several generations, to adapt to cold, to an ice age. But if we can't figure out how to do that relatively quickly, our solution may be too late. True transformational adaptability is very quick, very much in the present, to present conditions in order to be prepared when the future arrives.

Be A Rebel with A Cause

When it's your time, step up. Holly like any good rebel accepts the risk to be the change she desires to create. As true rebel she digs in her hoofs to stand strong in her position, is willing to kick out to disrupt the peace and take off at a gallop to fight for her cause. Holly knows who she is; she does not hide her individuality nor abandon that for which she has passion. She is steadfast and straightforward and fair and feisty. The big cats in the wild are the major protagonists of the zebra. One dark evening with a full moon rising, Bobcat our resident barn cat, was out hunting, creeping through the pasture in search of wild game for his dinner. Holly was calmly grazing in the pasture with the herd. As Bobcat ran by he cast a large shadow giving him the appearance of a large wild cat. Holly lifted her head; ears pointed forward and with a fierce snort ran toward what surely looked like a cougar in her pasture. Piercing the night with a rebel cry, Holly putting risk aside galloped, teeth bared, after the cat. Bobcat looked over his shoulder once and bounded for the nearest tree. Safely on a limb Bobcat looked down at Holly with a Cheshire cat smile. Holly realizing it was her pal Bobcat from the barn stepped back to invite him down from the tree. Bobcat climbed down from the tree and dropped to the ground by Holly's feet. Together they walked off peaceably into the night. It is easy to conform under pressure, not listen for what is right for us or to become comfortable with the usual ways of thinking and doing. Transformational intelligence does not conform it reforms and performs. Holly the rebel was committed to her cause; she was the super hero defender of justice, and a zebra fully engaged in being the life she wants to create.

Being Positively Present

We all possess ideal forms, the signature strengths—being social connectors, for example, or being able to see the positive in any situation—that we use naturally in our lives

Holly has an unbridled wilderness of spirit with a wide band of emotional depth and breadth. She is not afraid of losing control or needing to know the outcome. She has a large capacity to authentically feel and respond without cutting off the experience before it reaches completion. She is quick to try something new and stay with it if it works and quick to let go and try something else that might work better.

Creatively Championing Change

Holly has a vision whether it's to bring all the horses closer together in the pasture when they have spread out to far for her liking or to round up the horses and start them moving when she senses danger. She does not attach to an expectation of how her vision will unfold but she holds true to her vision of the herd gathering and moving together as a coherent whole. Holly's overall goal in transformational intelligence is not to execute a well-defined plan, but to be innovative and passionate for her vision of the future. From this approach obstacles can be transformed into opportunities and all mistakes are essential learning in the change effort. Tapping into her transformational intelligence Holly releases all need to know how it will happen, intuitively knowing the improbable is absolutely possible, trusting that it will happen it quickly comes into being.

Rising Up and Lifting Each Other We Are One

All of us together are better than anyone of us alone. We can transform the improbable into the possible rising up together and uplifting each other's hearts up. We can get things done in herds, families, communities and organizations in higher and higher degrees of wholeness and holiness. Transformational in-telligence integrates all personal and communal perspectives, and ways of understanding into robust collective wisdom as a platform for spontaneous, profound and positive change. "Ris-ing up and uplifting," implies an essential change within our-selves as individuals and as a collective that extends our poten-tial to bring forward greater compassion, purpose and integrity.

We are living our human history in a time of rapid and unexpected change while facing global challenge of unprecedented magnitude and crises of our own making. Am I willing to be transformed and are we willing to collectively transform ourselves to meet the challenges facing our people, and raise the quality of life for all living beings.

"Beyond your wildest imagination," or BWI, as we call it, is when the impossible becomes possible, and it's at the heart of transformational intelligence. It was beyond my wildest imagination to ever have the unexpected honor of touching the wild simply by saying a resounding yes to caring for Holly. What I am learning is that transformational intelli-gence is not a change brought about by simply doing good in the world, though that is important. Genuine transformation is different. An inward change takes place in our being as divine life flows within us and between us. What is real-ly needed for sustainable, positive transformation is within our wildest imagination. It is a deep commitment to genuine change resulting from an individual inner life process and a collective herd and community process of becoming more and more responsibly, compassionately human and grateful-ly and lovingly humane.

Cultivating Multiple Intelligences

> "Despite my irm convictions, I have always been a man who tries to face facts, and to accept the reality of life as new experience and new knowledge unfolds. I have always kept an open mind, a lexibility that must go hand in hand with every form of the intelligent search for truth."
> —Malcolm X

In our search for the truth of authentic presence we have multiple intelligences and a collective wisdom to guide our journey. Each of these abilities informs how we observe, reflect, make meaning, and respond. The ways in which we know the world through our many intelligences influences who we are and how we perceive and engage the world. We know, through our collective intelligence, where we belong and how we can best contribute in our families, communities and places of work. Horses have thriven over time in their families and herds intuitively living their collective intelligence and with collective wisdom. Through this inner knowing they focus on what brings pleasure, and what is of most value and interest with the least amount of stress and effort. If we, like horses live with whole hearts the collective wisdom of our intelligences we too might thrive. Following the path of our eight intelligences and the collective wisdom of our herds, we just might find our way to a more authentic presence and to a more just and peaceable world.

Section VI—The Path of the Eight Intelligences

Pause, Reflect and Respond

Explore your journey to authentic presence from the viewpoint of each of the eight years intelligences. Give each an equal voice and place of importance.

Take several index cards and write a word or phrase and an image that came from your reflections on each individual card.

Save these cards as you will be reflecting back on them.

VII

The Path of Indigenous Culture

Chapter 15
The Wisdom of Our Indigenous Way of Being

"The Indigenous way of life is based on a holistic worldview that sees everything—the land, the people and all living things—as vitally connected. The fundamental purpose of this way of life is sustainability. Indigenous social, political and economic models are designed to keep our families, communities, and natural environment in balance, not just for the present but for generations to come."
—First People's Worldwide (http://www.firstpeoples.org/)

The wisdom of Indigenous culture is one of the pathways that has led me to a deeper understanding and practice of authentic presence. The awareness of the essential connection of people, the land and all living beings across generations offers a perspective that is a key to being who we are and bringing our best forward.

There seems to be no universally agreed upon definition for Indigenous people, but there are common ways that Indigenous cultures perceive life. One definition of Indigenous people is those people who inhabited and belonged to a place or a region when people of a different culture arrived. The Indige-nous culture incorporates a tribal, community -based and col-lective identity rather than an individualistic perspective and identity. Indigenous people tend to live in close relationship to the land and in harmony with the natural world, which results in their reverence for the land and forces of nature.

I honor and respect the people who specifically identify as Indigenous. While most of us are many generations removed from living an Indigenous lifestyle, at one time in our histories, all of us had ancestors who lived an Indigenous way of life. All of us have the heritage and legacy of Indigenous people deep in our bones.

What is important to me about Indigenous culture is not who is or is not by ancestry considered Indigenous. The value is in the knowledge and wisdom ways that are clearly different from more pervasive ways of being in our world. Being Indigenous is a state of mind, an attitude of heart and a way of behaving that is in harmony with the earth and all earth's beings, including human beings. Indigenous culture in this way can offer a pathway to develop our authentic presence.

Horses and Indigenous Culture

Many Indigenous cultures were horse culture communities, people of the horse from Mongolia to the plains of the Americas. Horses transformed and were integral to daily life of these nomadic cultures. Horses were and still are revered as spiritual beings. They increased the mobility and hunting capacity of the nomadic tribal cultures. There was a strong partnership and heart connection between the tribal people and their horses. Horses were honored in their artwork, dances and ceremonies. For Native Americans today, horses endure as an emblem of tradition and a source of pride, pageantry, and healing. For those of us striving to live the Indigenous values of living in balance with people and all of nature, the relationship with horses and their herds can guide our way. If we lived more like horses, we might live more intelligently with our surroundings and in more harmony with one another. Living like horses, we would work cooperatively with our herd mates, we would adapt quickly to unexpected change and could create the most positive conditions for the next generation to thrive.

Horses represent a spirit of freedom for me and for people of many cultures. When we are free to be who we authentically are and free to support others in being authentic, we contribute to a free world. When we are free to be who we are and disciplined about following a practice that frees us to be our authentic selves, we can find and follow a life path of purpose, meaning and joy.

Guided by Indigenous Ways

Four important life experiences and intimate encounters with Indigenous culture guided my pathway to authentic presence. Three of those experiences were with Native American Indian culture, one in Montana, one in northern Michigan and one in Ohio; and one was with the culture of the Bedouin tribes living in Israel's Negev desert.

The culture, landscapes and traditions varied but there were guiding principles that the Indigenous cultures had in common.

Indigenous Principles

We Are One: Respecting Community—Tribe, Herd As Pri-mary

The collective is primary with a high degree of connection, social cohesion and interrelationship and is the place of belonging for the individual. The individual thrives as the community thrives and as the individual thrives the community thrives. The community is a web of all life and an interconnected web of relationship.

We Are One: Trusting Nature As A Source of Great Wisdom

We are part of the natural world. Learning from the shifting patterns of nature and the constant laws of nature we can learn to live with more respect in our human world, to be more responsible to the earth and her creatures and to the forces of nature.

We Are One: Living In Harmony and Balance

All members of the community are equally deserving of equal access and distribution of the physical, emotional and spiritual resources needed to thrive within the flow of present life and for generations to come.

We Are One: Gathering Collective Wisdom

A relationship of respectful cooperation, trustworthy collab-oration and commitment to gather and share information of all forms of knowing, unique perspectives and diverse points of view contributing to the good of all.

The practice of these four Indigenous principles can strength-en our authentic presence as we live with the integrity of who we are within our families, communities, and places of work, and as responsible members of the natural world. Guided by these four principles we can think of ourselves as Indigenous stewards of our planet with a responsibility to protect the nat-ural environment on which we depend. We can accept a collective responsibility for the physical and cultural survival, and thriving, of all peoples and species. Then, we will be living an authentically present life. This perspective and these guiding principles have intuitive resonance for me within my bones. I believe this comes from a deep soul memory instilled before anything I consciously remember. This way of authentic living makes ultimate sense for us today and provides a guide for authentic presence as we live into our future.

Indigenous Roots In My Own Backyard

My initial journey within Indigenous culture did not begin intentionally, but became deeply rooted and inherent in how I live my life. When I was a kid, I had the good fortune to have inherited a grandmother, Rhoda, a warm hearted, play-ful and wise woman who helped raise me in a grandmotherly way. She was employed by our family to help my working parents care for our household, my siblings, and me while my parents were away at work. She brought me into to a way of being with nature that was alive and relational. Garden-ing became knowing the language of plants, trees and but-terflies, rather than their names. The beings of nature were my playmates; nature was family. Sometimes when I came home from school, Rhoda would be chanting beautiful songs in a language I did not know but understood. These ancient songs became my childhood lullabies and the melodies have followed me into my grown-up dreams and visions.

What I didn't know as a child was that Rhoda was a Native American of Cherokee descent. Later when I was an adult, she shared with me some of her journey, and I came to realize that a lot of my early, formative life was based on what I had absorbed from her Indigenous belief system about the sacred-ness of life, its people and all beings of nature.

Then, one summer when I was about 40 years old, I began an important journey on remote Garden Island in Lake Michigan. When I arrived with camping gear, I learned that I was on a traditionally Anishinaabe island called MinisKittigan. The Anishinaabe people also are known as Ojibwa or Chippewa. I was one of the few on the island who was not Native American. I met an Anishinaabe medicine woman, Grandmother Kee, who lived on the island each summer to immerse herself in the "old ways" and to teach them to the young members of her tribe. I was among a few who serendipitously found our way to her.

As a medicine woman, Grandmother Kee was not a healer in the sense of a Western M.D. or an Eastern herbalist. She was among the tribal elders who bring healing to individuals and communities by bridging the natural and spiritual worlds. Their "medicine" is their knowledge and wisdom, which is "privileged" because it develops and is offered only to those called to and blessed with the capacity to offer its power for the benefit of the tribe, its members and the well-being of all life.

Concepts taught by Grandmother Kee took me back to my childhood memories and a deep inner knowing of a way of life that cherished aliveness in all of nature. I recalled the values of balance and harmony and a tribal way of living with collective wisdom that had been communicated to me by Rhoda, my Cherokee "grandmother." She and Grandmother Kee shared an approach to the world that was about living a humble life that consisted of living fully in the present, honoring the past, and preserving a desired future. I had absorbed aspects of that view as a child. Decades later, as Grandmother Kee introduced me to her Indigenous practices, I could understand how Rhoda was following their wisdom and sharing them with me.

From Grandmother Kee, I learned Anishinaabe ways on how to create a shelter from nature, harvest medicinal herbs, and find profound meaning in daily community life. I also learned from her an old tradition that is part of many tribal cultures. It is called the Medicine Wheel.

The Medicine Wheel is a cosmology, a storytelling and visioning process, a conceptualization used for understanding life in the context of its whole from a variety of perspectives. At the evening campfire, Grandmother Kee told stories that shared the ways in which the Medicine Wheel could help guide all of us in living relationally responsible in community life and to appreciate the interconnectivity of our individual and collective impact. The Medicine Wheel is used by tribal cultures to explore and teach the unity of the physical and spiritual in all things, thoughts, and actions. It is a way of understanding the significance and the insignificance of our daily lives and our place in the universe. In a sense, the Wheel offers a guided journey of one's authentic presence, beginning in the center and bringing in the wisdom of the eight directions to guide our path of authentic presence.

It represents the circle of existence and carries wisdom from many perspectives to inform and bless our daily journey through life.

The Medicine Wheel has become part of how I reflect on and understand the process of change from a diverse and inclusive perspective. It offers an appreciative understanding of the wholeness found in nature, sought by humankind both individually and in community, and required for fully integrated living. When I explored the concepts of the Medicine Wheel, I gained new insights into what I have come to understand as authentic presence.

In Search of Call of the Wild

> *"Sounding the old wolf-cry, seeking the mysterious something that called -- called, waking or sleeping, at all times, for him to come.... Deep in the forest a call was sounding, mysteriously thrilling and luring."*
> —Jack London, The Call of the Wild

Hearing the call of the wild I yearned to find it in my own nature. In search of the wild, I journeyed to the mountains of Montana. I traveled from my home, which was feeling much too tame, to seek out what lived wild and free in my heart. I was looking for adventure and ready to fully live this one precious life I was granted. I decided to engage in the sacred journey of a vision quest. This ancient ceremony brought to modern time is a process intended to open one's heart and soul to life. There are four core components to a quest:

- Community

- Solitude in nature

- Focus on being present

- Blessings of gratitude

While it is a solo endeavor, it always takes place in and is held within the circle of a community that sends you off on your quest, watches over you from afar and welcomes you back when you return. There is generally someone assisting, often an elder who is responsible for tracking your well being on the vision quest. Solitude removes you from your everyday world and invites being in touch with self. Nature offers a wealth of wisdom in both modest and profound life messages. Gratitude allows the wisdom of the quest to find a place in your life. I was blessed to have a teacher and dear friend, Brooke Medicine Eagle, guide me in the process of my vision quest. Within the four-day quest I had many profound experiences and returned from my quest with the gift of clarity about the direction of my life. The natural world would be the context for my life work. Horses and nature would be my guides and partners. Family comes first in my heart and life. I was to be a protector of the earth and her family. In the mountains of Montana overlooking the Continental Divide, I found the call of the wild in my Indigenous heart.

Bedouin Tribal Life: My Home Away from Home in the Desert

> *Only in complete silence, will you hear the desert...*
> *Only love knows how to marry this space.*
> – Bedouin poem

My experience in the Israeli desert with the Indigenous people of the Bedouin culture gave me another perspective of what it means to live authentically: aligned with one's values and actions, interconnected to one's community and in harmony with one's environment.

I spent seven summers, while I was Director of the Mandel Jewish Community Center in Cleveland, supervising a cross-cultural identity program with Jewish Israeli and American youth, and Arab youth. All these young people were seekers exploring their personal and cultural identity through the wilderness of the Israeli landscape and its people. We lived as a nomadic Indigenous tribe for the summer. We began the adventure in the deserts of Israel shedding the dust of Western culture and gaining the dust of the ancient desert. The simplicity of the landscape was breathtakingly beautiful amidst the challenges to survive in a harsh and unforgiving environment.

The young people became a tribe of desert dwellers. One of the first lessons the youth learned was that those who competed to be first up the mountain hillside had to wait for the others at the top in the hot sun. The next time they went up the hillside, rather than running ahead, they helped those who were slower and struggling to get up the hill until all arrived at the top together. They learned that "all of us are better than one of us."

While camping and hiking in the desert, we lived for a time with an authentic Bedouin tribe, the true modern-day desert dwellers. The word Bedu in Arabic refers to people who live in the open space of the desert. They live in tents of black camel and goat hair, which protects them from the intense heat and sand storms. They have a strong sense of kinship critical for survival, which is an ancient tradition passed to the following generations through story telling around the campfire. These traditions ensure the safety of the families and their way of life.

One day, a member of my staff and I traveled ahead in preparation for taking the newly formed tribe of kids for an overnight stay with the Bedouins, and to set up the logistics for their visit. The Bedouins move around in the desert following their goat, camel and horse herds and the source of water, so we were not sure of their exact location; we only knew the general area where they were likely to set up encampment.

We began our trek by army jeep in the cool mysterious dark of desert night before the intense heat of desert daybreak. We arrived at the Bedouin camp mid-day. We had engaged with this tribe to host youth over the past several years, so they basically knew who we were and what we were going to offer to them and request of them.

Even so, Bedouin desert ritual was expected. We were greeted warmly as strangers wandering through the desert. First we were offered water from a goatskin jug to drink. They brought out an intricately woven rug for us to sit on. They took off our sandals and washed our dusty feet even though in a few minutes our feet were again dusty from the sultry and constant desert winds.

The ritual was not about physical cleanliness but spiritual cleaning before we entered their living space. We were first served a light tea made of plants that were gathered from a dry desert wadi (stream bed). In the tent, we sat on the sandy and rocky earth, which was now covered by an intricately designed and colorful ancient carpet, and we were surrounded by a circle of members of the Bedouin tribe. In front of us on a small fire pita bread was prepared on hot rocks. We were served something milky looking and a curdled and green goat cheese, which we ate with the warm pita and with our fingers. You can say no to the food and drink offered, but it is better to say yes. After about an hour the greatly respected tribal chief called the Sheikh joined us in the circle around the fire. Bedouin culture is loyal to family and tribe, which values solidarity, honor and harmony. The responsibility is first to the collective and it holds a place of value above the importance of the individual in the tribe.

We were welcomed as honored as guests. As an important ritual of hospitality and respect, strong sweet Arabic coffee was served in small egg shaped cups called feengal. The first cup of coffee was filled half way and given to the host to taste to let us know we were safe. The second cup was poured by and tasted by us. The third cup was poured for us by our host for us to drink. Once this ritual was complete it was our turn to show gratitude and respect by offering gifts.

We brought bags of flour and herbs from the Arab market in Jerusalem for them to prepare pita, and brightly colored scarves for the women.

The Sheikh returned the honor by bringing out beautiful tapestries to show the artistry of the tribal women who had woven them from goat and camel hair, with vibrant colors from the pollen of desert flowers.

Next the Sheikh carefully, and with ceremony, unwrapped his special collection of handcrafted knives and swords. As it began to get dark he walked us outside to see his goat and camel herds and, most precious to him, his Arabian horses. His pride in the wealth of his tribe was expressed by the number of goats, camels, excellent breeding horses, and the craft shop of swords and tapestries. We knew we were accepted as their honored guests when they brought out their prized Arabian horses.

More than 4,500 years ago, the Bedouins were the first to breed horses—what we know today as the Arabian horse—verbally passing the mystery of the breeding and ways of training the horses down through the ages from one generation to the next. The Arabian horse evolved like the Bedouin, adapting to and living in harmony with desert. The horse was essential to the physical survival and spiritual traditions of these nomadic people, and the horses were often brought inside the family tent for shelter, securing the physical protection of the horse, and the spiritual protection of the people. In Bedouin culture, the horse is considered a gift of life from Allah to be cherished and revered.

When a desert traveller outside the tribe touched the pole to the entrance of the tent, the tent dweller was required to provide food and water for up to three days for all the people and animals that arrived. The most revered horse would have its decorative bridle hung from the center pole of the tent to indicate its owner's authentic presence, letting those inside know who he was and that he came with good intentions. Residents of the tent, with generous hospitality, would share stories about their finest, fastest and bravest horses.

> *"And Allah took a handful of southerly wind, blew His breath over it, and created the horse.... Thou shall fly without wings, and conquer without any sword. The wind of heaven is that which blows between a horse's ears."*
> —Bedouin Legend

As the dark of the desert surrounded us, and stars became clear in the black of the sky, we returned to the family tent. In the glow of the campfire, we sat again in a circle of the tribe. The elders smoked the traditional hookah, filling the tent with the sweet smell of herbs. It was then that the chief (the Sheikh) who spoke some English asked about the purpose of our visit.

He had waited eight hours after our arrival to ask the reason for our visit. We then asked permission to bring our group of youth to visit their camp and learn of their Indigenous culture. Because we honored their traditions and were patient with their "way of doing business," they generously agreed to the visit.

That night we slept on the ground in the area of the tent reserved for guests, lulled by the sultry hot breeze, dreams of the desert and the magic story of its people. In the morning as we prepared to leave, the Sheikh offered the man I was traveling with three goats for me in exchange for permission to marry me. I was disappointed not to be important enough to warrant camels or horses, but I was excited to be worth at least three goats. Was it Bedouin desert humor or a real offer? It was probably both.

There is no room for anything but authentic presence in this ancient tribal culture, which, like the horses, lives in harmony with its environment, work together for the benefit of all, adapts quickly to changing environmental conditions, and honors its traditions by passing them on to the next generation.

I believe that the code of honor, the kindness and generosity of spirit found in the Indigenous culture of the Bedouins, can be of great value to the cultures of our families, organizations and communities who also are the challenged by living in unpredictable times. The modern world is more challenging for the Bedouin culture than the desert and harshness of nature in the desert. Maybe that is true for us as well as we strive to journey through the challenges of modern life.

I learned much about harmony, balance and flow from the Native American tradition. I learned from the Bedouin culture the importance of solidarity and comradeship, standing strong together and for each other. I believe experiencing our personal harmony and flow and the solidarity of companionship supports us in being authentically present, being who we are meant to be and being at our best in all situations

Coming Home

> *"The world of relationship is rich and complex... With relationships we give up predictability and open up to potentiality... We would do well to ponder the realization that love is the most potent source of power."*
> —Margaret Wheatley, Leadership and the New Science

Meeting One White Horse Standing

The creation of authentic presence in relationship is a sacred heart quest. In exploring the power of relationship and intimacy, we can discover the known and unknown possibilities in others and ourselves

My most intimate relationship with Indigenous cultural experience is more current than childhood and closer to home than the island in Lake Michigan or the desert in Israel. It is within my relationship with one man.

This part of my journey began in my hometown when I was just a few years shy of being forty years young. I attended a workshop close to my home, presented by the Foundation of Shamanic Studies, on listening to and learning from the voices and spirit of nature. On a beautiful sunny spring day in Northeast Ohio, I parked my red top-down Jeep Wrangler and was walking to the workshop when I noticed a pair of long legs in blue jeans coming out of a white Mercedes. The car did not impress me but the man with the long legs did. He looked a bit like a tall, rangy wild west Montana cowboy in his boots and leather vest.

My Annie Oakley spirit from childhood immediately recognized him as a soul mate and my grown-up, adventuresome spirit as a man to meet. I was a happy, independent, single mom of ten years and in no way interested in romance. But my renegade heart had other ideas. I waited for him and learned his name was Herb, which fit for a nature workshop, though not for a rugged cowboy. I decided to get to know him anyway.

At the end of the two-day workshop we were saying goodbye and discovered some interesting coincidences. I learned that though he lived four hours away and could have attended the same workshop closer to his home, he had followed his intuition and participated in this particular place. I discovered that on the day before the workshop he had spent time on a farm with a yurt on it. I thought it a bit strange since I have a yurt on my farm, and even stranger when I learned he had been at my farm with the workshop leader who was using my yurt for nature-based healing sessions. Herb said he felt a kinship to the land and that he could make his home there. A year later he was making his home on the farm with the yurt and me, and our romance was in full herb bloom.

What happened next was an interesting transformation. The cowboy began to look more like an American Indian. Herb, being of Cherokee and Shawnee lineage, began a quest to recover his native heritage and reclaim his ancestry. He grew his hair into a long braid and was given the Native name of One White Horse Standing. As part of his transformation, a large, dramatic Native American mask beyond my wildest imagination appeared on the wall of our bedroom. Soon there were eight fierce-looking Native American warrior masks on the walls surrounding our bed. It looked kind of scary to me and I asked Herb if we could hang them somewhere else. He replied simply, "Those are my ancestors, here to watch over us." Seeing them from that point of view I felt a kinship and warmth toward them. It was ten years before I asked Herb what the images and energies of the masks meant to him,

He stood in front of each one for a few moments and shared with me what he heard. "The first is the protection of gentle strength and strong gentleness. The second mask is saying, stand your ground. The third is a bear shield to protect in the darkness. The fourth mask is a reminder to balance compassion with courage. The fifth is the wise elder old one watching over us. The sixth is the call of the ancestors calling forth our wisdom, the mask Buffalo Chief visioning the future. The seventh is opening to the light. The eighth mask is dancing with darkness into deep healing."

Being fiercely proud of Jewish ancestry, I never would have imagined I would one day be married to a Native American. Though both of our lineages are of tribal descent, Herb and I came from very different tribes. Mine is from the Levis of the twelve Hebrew tribes of the desert and his of the Shawnee and Cherokee tribe of the Americas. In many ways this union of spirit, soul and Indigenous culture is a perfect fit for us both. Our family has grown from the two of us to include a tribe of three outstanding grown kids and spouses, many amazing grandchildren and a community of like-spirited friends. The tribe includes beings of the wild; a pack of wolf-dogs who share our home, and sing us to sleep and wake us with a soulful pack howl, a herd of wise horses and one lively zebra, and the abundant wildlife that have made their home on this land. Herb and I are partners in the family of nature and all life. We share a love of the land and all its beings. We see magic and knowledge in all of nature and we feel most at home, alive and inspired in the natural world.

Herb and I have a partnership of heart and life work as we each in our own ways bring people and nature together. We offer opportunities for individuals and their families and organizations to awaken to their authentic inner nature, and in Mother Nature, we find balance, purpose and a life worth living.

We, like all couples, face the challenges and stresses of the world around us and the challenge to maintain intimacy. Together we support each other to strive to be who we are at our best.

> *"So, just as rocks in a stream accentuate the force of the water rushing against them, the obstacles to perfect romance can help us realize the power of our capacity to love. They force the heart to stretch to embrace all of who we are."*
> —Adapted from John Welwood, Love and Awakening

We are who we are with each other and strive to create a relationship that has its own rhythm of authentic presence. Marriage and family life with the complexity of children and grandchildren and work/life balance is a perfect place to craft authentic presence. Living authentically with unconditional love and acceptance and the spirit of adventure makes what we might have believed impossible become possible.

Herb and I, in the spirit of Indigenous ways, respectfully and passionately approach relationship as sacred power. Indigenous relationship is inspired and guided by nature and the abundant life force that flows in ever-changing balance through the circles of the seasons, day to night, in the interplay of the elements, beauty of rainbows and within the compassionate opening of the human heart. Relationships approached in this way can dance with change and deepen the relationship throughout its journey over time. Everyday life can be lived in this flow of sacred connection with each other and all life.

Weaving Life Together

> *"When you know who you are; when your mission is clear and you burn with the inner fire of unbreakable will; no cold can touch your heart; no deluge can dampen your purpose. You know that you are alive."*
> —Chief Seattle, 1780-1866

My entry into the wisdom of Indigenous culture and the gratitude I have for the meaning it has given to my life did not happen in any sequential or chronological order. Common strands wove a pattern of Indigenous wisdom.

We Are One: Respecting community, tribe and herd as primary, trusting nature as a source of great wisdom, living in harmony, balance and solidarity, gathering the gift of collective wisdom.

Living with authentic presence, we can inspire a high quality of life and integrity in relationship with all life. Each of us has the opportunity to awaken to conscious relationship and choose to embody and live by our guiding principles and values, which supports our authenticity and well-being, and the well-being of all.

Our challenge is to discover our way home, more and more often, to our connection to sacred relationship, to shared Spirit, and thereby to authentic presence for the benefit of all beings.

Chapter 16
Cross Cultural Guide to Authentic Presence

"All my life's a circle, sunrise and sundown
The moon rolls through the nighttime,
Till the daybreak rolls around...
Our love is like a circle
lets go 'round one more time."
Harry Chapin, American singer-songwriter

The spirit of authentic presence can exist only within a circle of true relationship. The quality of our authentic presence is determined by the radiating circles of integrity, intelligence and action within us and within in all our relationships in life.

I created what I call the "circle of authentic presence" as a process to explore, engage and embody the essence of authentic presence. The honored tradition of the Medicine Wheel was the inspiration, starting point and guide in my creation of this circle. The foundation for the circle of authentic presence came from the designs of sacred geometry, the wisdom of Indigenous culture and the intelligence of nature's patterns.

Sacred geometry is a perspective from which we learn by experiencing our world through universal symbols and patterns. The circle has appeared for thousands of years in many forms and generally symbolizes wholeness and unity. Nature shows us the repeating shape, symbol and pattern of the circle in the sun and moon, in the shape of the Earth, and in the nests of birds. The landscapes in the natural world inform us of our internal landscape, help us understand the shape and pattern of our own lives, and the many forms of life around us.

All Indigenous cultures have myths, life stories and cosmologies to understand the meaning of the universe, make sense of daily life and as a guide for how to live within the circle of life. In the Bible, described in the book of Ezekiel, cherubs hold Ezekiel's sacred wheel representing the path we travel through life. In Hindu life, the wheel is the symbol of human spiritual experience. The mandala, which means "circle," and the labyrinth, often are created as a circle, are spiritual symbols of sacred space and a path to a more conscious life.

I learned about the African Medicine Wheel tradition from Malidoma Patrice Somé, West African elder, author and teacher from a village in Burkina Faso, West Africa, who travels to share the ancient wisdom and practices that have supported his people for thousands of years. I had the honor of attending a workshop with Malidoma where I learned about the African Medicine Wheel and its power as a process for awareness, connection and change. I experienced the cosmology of this wheel as a model for creating sacred space, relationship, and ritual. It connects the circle of present life in the village with the life of the ancestors. The African Medicine Wheel's main purpose is to strengthen personal identity, community identity and ancestral identity to help inhabitants understand how to live a sacred life that is focused, motivated, and purposeful.

In my primary spiritual tradition, Judaism, circles are central in sacred practice. The Hebrew Biblical word for circle is chuwg. The meaning of this word is translated in a variety of ways; sphere, circle of the earth, compass of direction, horizon connecting heaven and earth, and as container of all creation. The circle is central in Jewish dance, weddings, religious holidays and celebrations. The circle reflects Judaism's positive perspective on the unending circle of life, from birth through death to life by way of the continuity of generations.

The Native American Medicine Wheel is a symbol of great spiritual significance representing the never-ending circle of life and the unity between the human realm and the realm of the Great Spirit. The wheel was most often created by stones upon the earth but also was painted, beaded or sewn onto blankets, clothes or ceremonial objects.

The Medicine Wheel represents the natural flow of change: season to season, day to night to day again, birth to death to rebirth, all within nature's life cycle. The wheel, sometimes called "the sacred hoop" or "circle of life," is a spiritual tradition central to most Indigenous peoples. The sacred geometry of the circle of life in diverse forms can be found in nearly all spiritual traditions. Although aspects vary from culture to culture, its basic meaning and process is similar in intention. For those who utilize it, the Medicine Wheel is both a sacred representation of life's journey and a practical system for maintaining balance and direction for individuals, families, and communities. The Medicine Wheel, as a circle of life, can provide guidance on our quest for our authentic presence

The word "medicine" as used here refers to a person's wisdom, personal power, essence and unique spark of the divine, one's authentic presence. To learn the wheel is an opportunity to approach our lives from divergent perspectives, and to integrate the wisdom and truth from each in our pursuit of wholeness. Thomas Jefferson learned the system of the Medicine Wheel from the Six Iroquois Nations and incorporated some of those ideas into the U.S. Constitution; specifically, incorporating a system of checks and balances into the basis of government.

Thousands of years before the advent of European settlement, North American tribes created physical representations of Medicine Wheels by using stones to outline their pattern. Sometimes called the "sacred hoop," these stone structures date back 4,500 years. Today, those Medicine Wheels remain on the land and consist of a central cairn with radiating spokes that reach out to one or more encompassing circular rings. For Indigenous peoples, the sacred stone circles connect people to the ancestral realm of those who come before them and those generations yet to come.

Designing the Circle of Authentic Presence

One early spring morning when I was in the field with the horses, I noticed that all eight equines, seven horses and the zebra, were standing in a perfect circle equal distance apart. Around the circle of horses was a circle of wildflower daisies. Around the flowers was a circle of glacier stone almost buried by the very tall sweet-smelling grass. Around the circle of horses, flowers and stones was a circle of trees, and above the trees, a circle of wind.

I imagined being high above and looking down upon nature's sacred geometry of concentric circles. From this vantage point I began to see patterns to explore, rhythms to reflect on. I began to wonder if nature's incredible designs might provide a map of discovery for us to seek what it means to be a more conscious and intentional human being.

My feet back on the ground, I picked up a stick and in the paddock next to the field I began to draw in the sand circles within circles, which had no ending or beginning. What came to me, as I stepped back to take in the sand painting, was that this might be a personal mandala symbolizing life's journey. The circles of life in nature might provide a natural guide on my quest for authentic presence. Picking up my stick, which now felt more like a staff, I carved in the sand the title of the drawing: The Circle of Authentic Presence. That night I dreamed of circles and when I awoke in the morning my understanding of the Circle of Authentic Presence emerged with clarity.

In the tradition of sacred geometry and the Medicine Wheel, I designed the Circle of Authentic Presence in four concentric circles, radiating from the center outward. The circle, much like the circle of horses, was divided into eight equal places along the circle. Each of these eight positions, like the eight horses, embodied diverse qualities. The polarities and unique differences between the eight diverse positions provide a creative tension at their integral meeting points. With the strength, beauty and intricacy of a spider web, it captures and contains collective wisdom.

The eight positions, representing eight perspectives can be called "lodges." In Indigenous tradition, a lodge is a dwelling of home, hearth and heart. It is a nomadic habitat, often a natural shelter of foliage covered by tree bark or branches, or posts covered by animal skins. The lodge created a shelter for the physical and spiritual wellbeing of the family and was at the heart of community life. I adopted the concept of lodge from the Native American Medicine Wheel to be the abode or dwelling place for the different positions and perspectives that make up the circle of authentic presence.

The design of the Circle of Authentic Presence provides a nature-inspired process of interdependence and interconnection from which to consider life's most important questions, and provides a form of direction in the quest for authentic presence. The circle serves as a compass to indicate cardinal (North, East, South, and West) and sometimes ordinal (NE, SE, SW, NW) physical direction, and also represents life direction. Each of these directions represents a "lodge" or "place of unique perspective." Each diverse perspective informs and balances the other.

The first and inside circle of authentic presence is drawn from the eight lodges of the Native American Medicine Wheel:

- Masculine Lodge
- Peacekeepers Lodge
- Warriors and Children's Lodge
- Storytellers and Prophets Lodge
- Feminine Lodge
- Council Lodge
- Wisdom Lodge of Elders
- Dog Soldiers Lodge of Humility

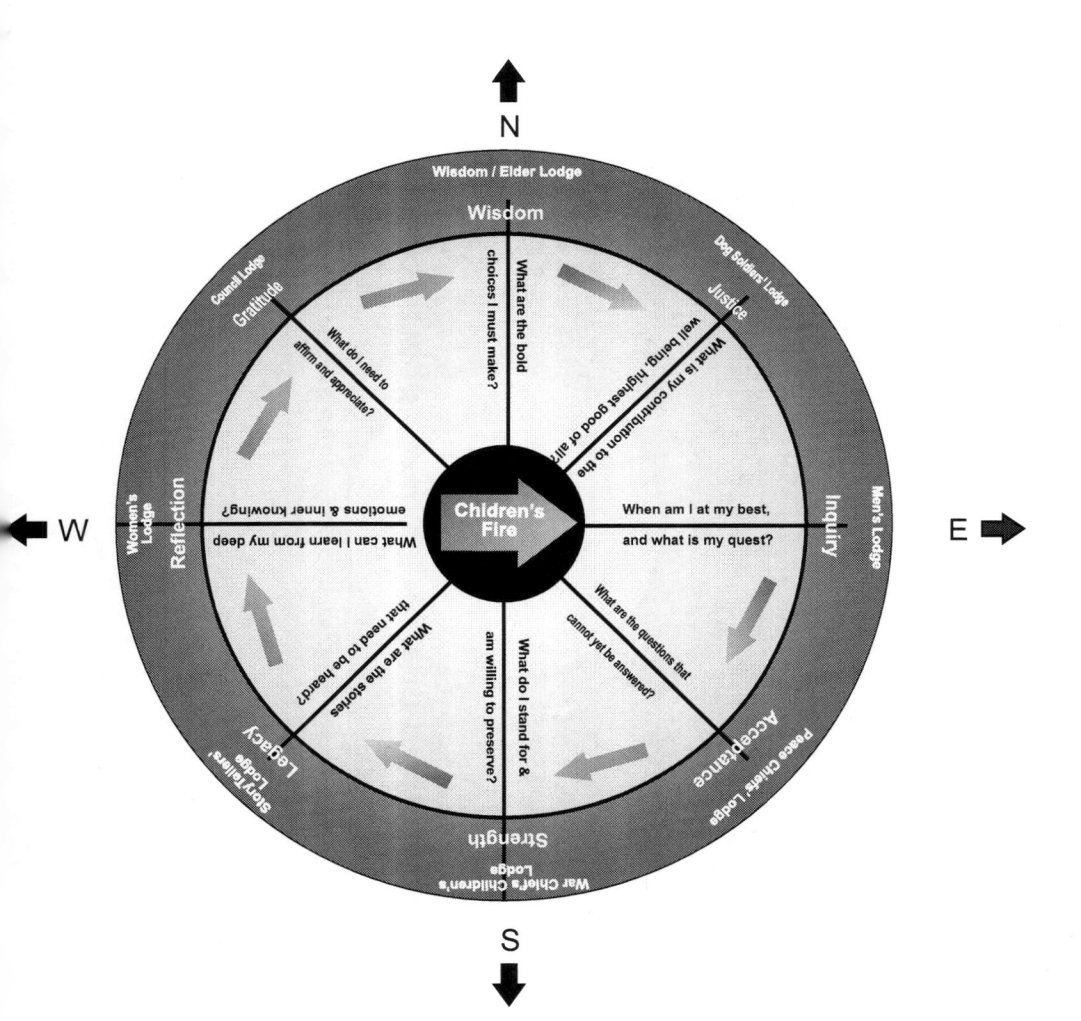

Medicine Wheel

N (North) — Wisdom / Elder Lodge — **Wisdom**
- What are the bold choices I must make?

NE — Dog Soldiers' Lodge — **Justice**
- What is my contribution to the well-being, highest good of all?

E (East) — Men's Lodge — **Inquiry**
- When am I at my best, and what is my quest?

SE — Peace Chiefs' Lodge — **Acceptance**
- What are the questions that cannot yet be answered?

S (South) — War Chief's Children's Lodge — **Strength**
- What do I stand for & am willing to preserve?

SW — Story Tellers' Lodge — **Legacy**
- What are the stories that need to be heard?

W (West) — Women's Lodge — **Reflection**
- What can I learn from my deep emotions & inner knowing?

NW — Council Lodge — **Gratitude**
- What do I need to affirm and appreciate?

Center: Children's Fire

In its center is the Children's Fire. This circle aligns the elements of air, fire, water and earth with the eight compass directions and other aspects of nature and human nature.

The second circle radiating outward describes eight aspects of our spirit, character and way of being. These eight ways of being are guiding principles on the path to authentic presence:

- inquiry
- acceptance
- strength
- legacy
- reflection
- gratitude
- wisdom
- justice

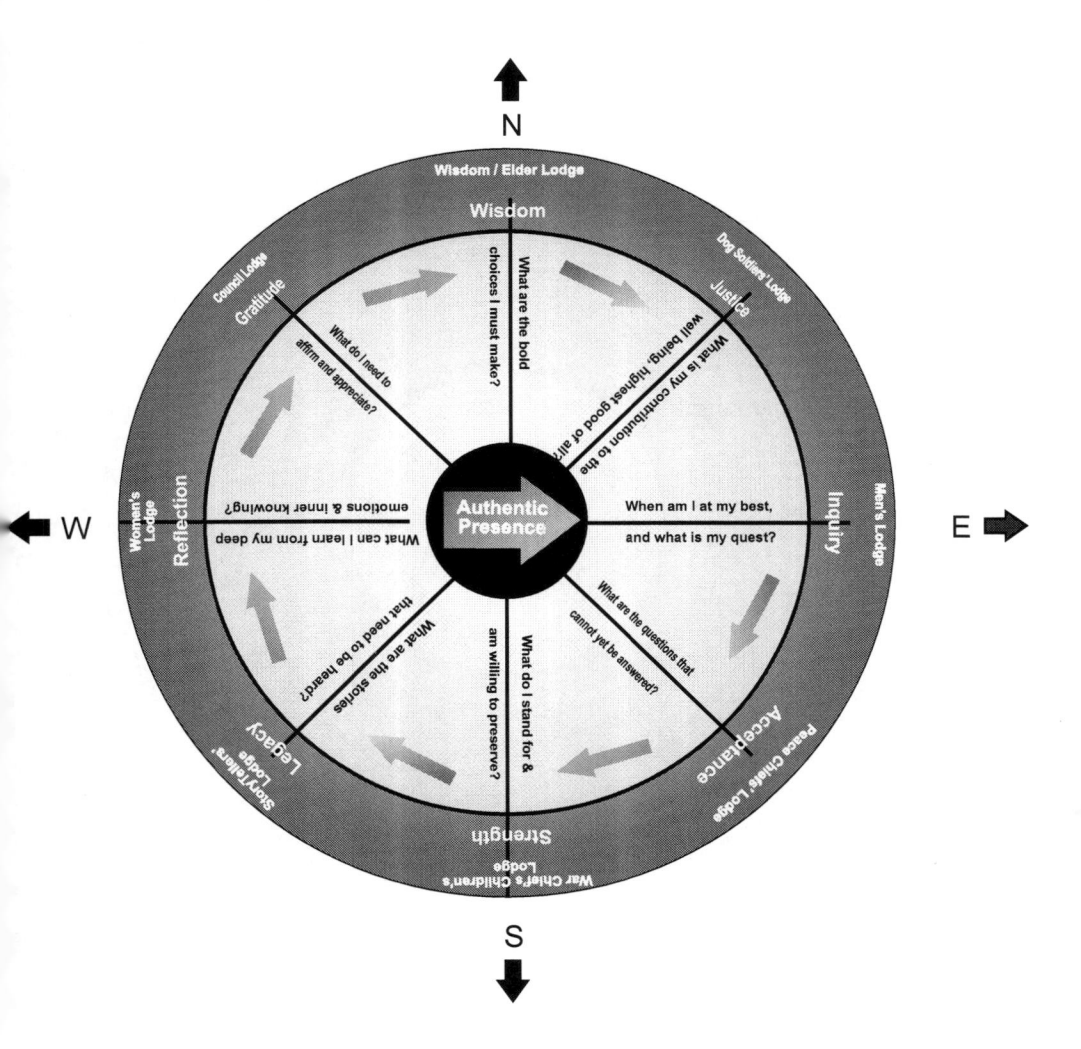

The third circle moving outward includes what I have identified as the eight forms of intelligence as described in Chapter 14:

- cognitive
- intuitive
- embodied
- social
- emotional
- natural
- spiritual
- transformational (beyond our wildest imagination)

Join me to begin a journey around the Circle of Authentic Presence.

Compass of Authentic Presence

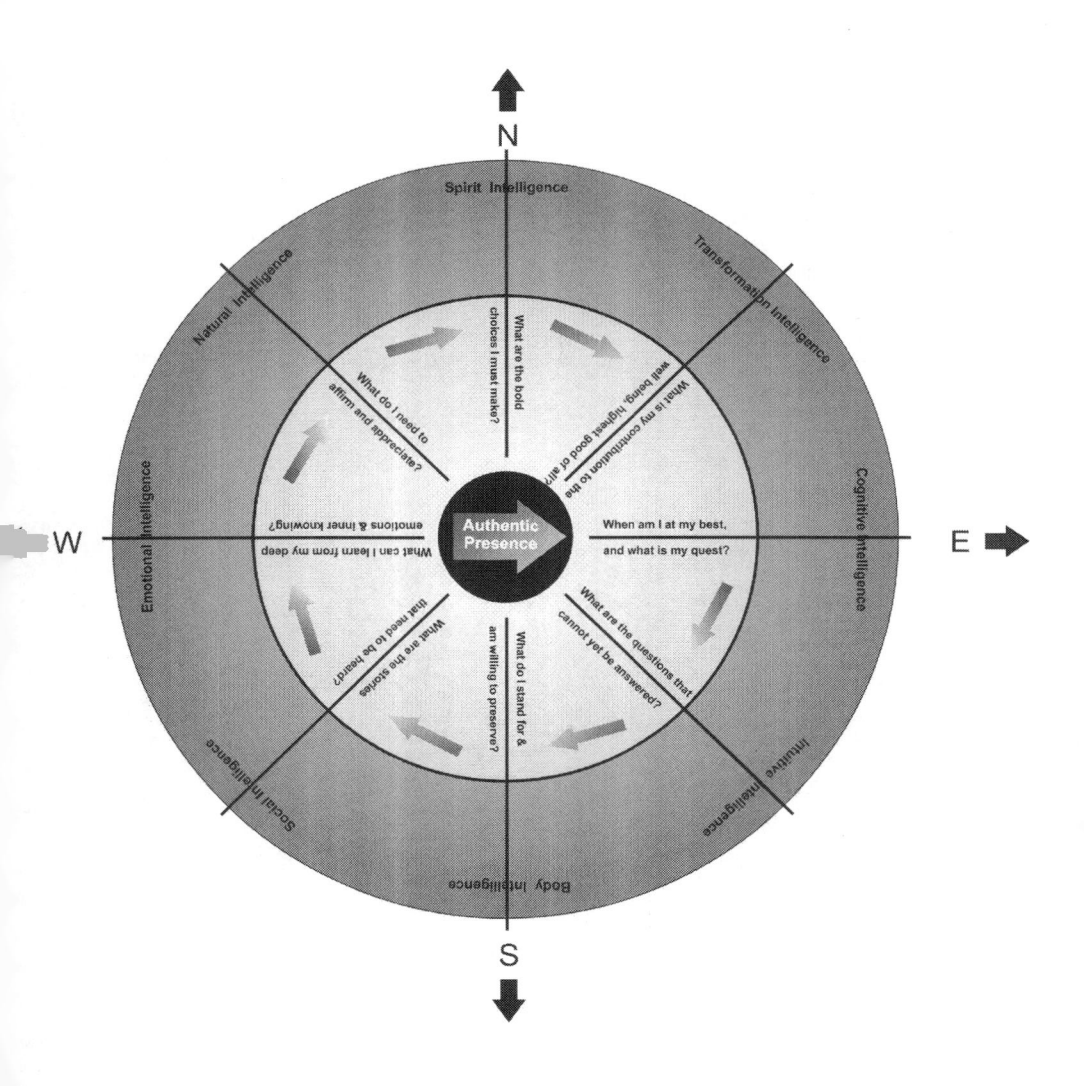

N — Spirit Intelligence
E — Cognitive Intelligence
S — Body Intelligence
W — Emotional Intelligence

Outer ring (clockwise from N):
- Spirit Intelligence
- Transformation Intelligence
- Cognitive Intelligence
- Intuitive Intelligence
- Body Intelligence
- Social Intelligence
- Emotional Intelligence
- Natural Intelligence

Inner ring questions (clockwise from N):
- What are the bold choices I must make?
- What is my contribution to the well being, highest good of all?
- When am I at my best, and what is my quest?
- What are the questions that cannot yet be answered?
- What do I stand for & am willing to preserve?
- What are the stories that need to be heard?
- What can I learn from my deep emotions & inner knowing?
- What do I need to affirm and appreciate?

Center: **Authentic Presence**

In the fourth outer radiating circle are eight key behaviors, or ways of taking action:

- creativity (Creativity is the energy of beginning)
- cooperation (Cooperation brings diverse parts together)
- courage (Courage protects and defends that which is vulnerable)
- collaboration (Collaboration integrates all the best)
- compassion (Compassion opens the heart)
- celebration (Celebration brings gratitude)
- challenge (Challenge strengthens purpose)
- consciousness (Consciousness commits to the highest good for all)

These eight attributes or behaviors *are to be cultivated on our journey to authentic presence.*

N

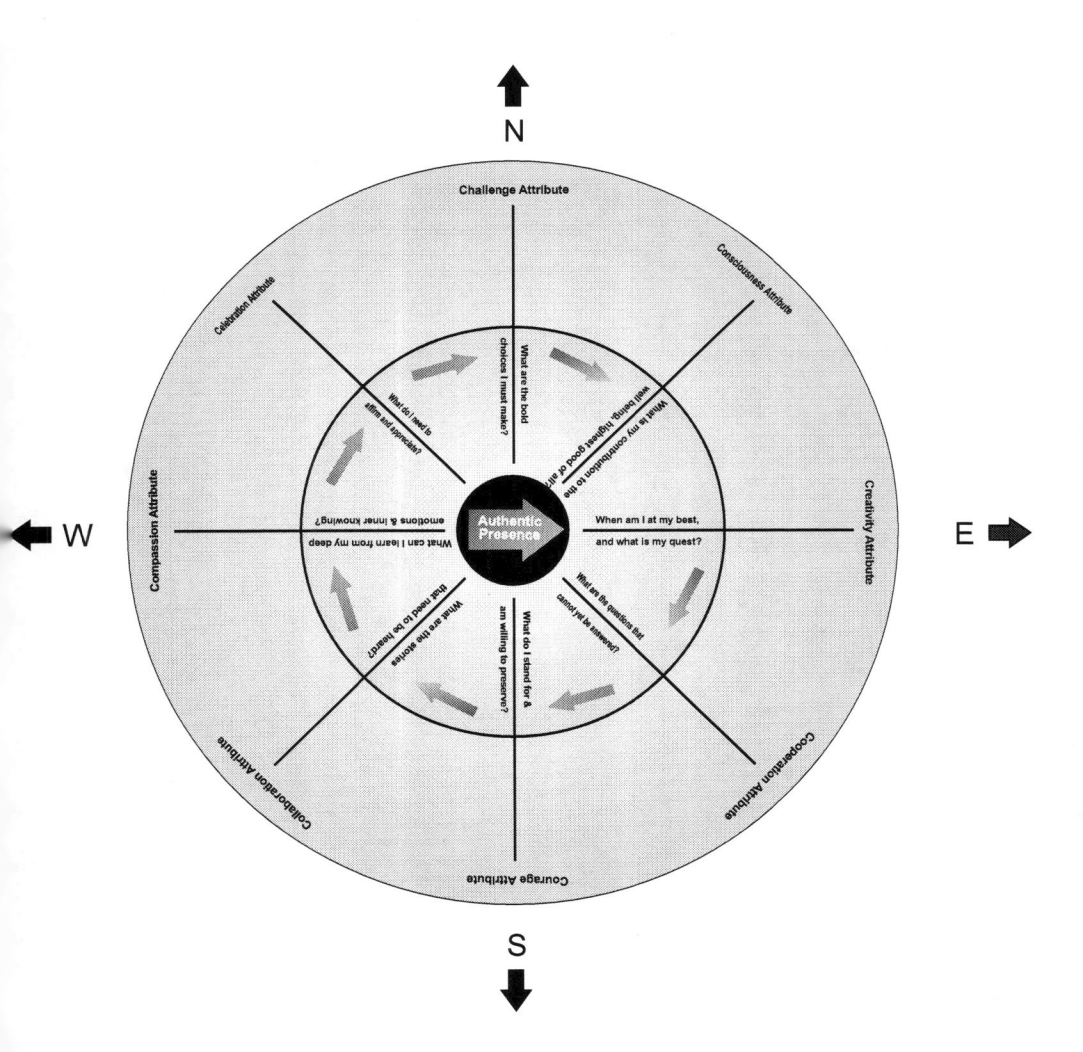

Challenge Attribute

Celebration Attribute

Consciousness Attribute

What are the bold choices I must make?

What do I want to celebrate and appreciate?

What is my contribution to the well being, highest good of all?

Compassion Attribute — W

Authentic Presence

Creativity Attribute — E

What can I learn from my deep emotions & inner knowing?

When am I at my best, and what is my quest?

What are the stories that need to be heard?

What are the questions that cannot yet be answered?

What do I stand for & am willing to preserve?

Collaboration Attribute

Courage Attribute

Cooperation Attribute

S

The Circle of Authentic Presence involves a holistic approach. The circle offers an integral map of the physical, emotional, cognitive, and spiritual realms, and an opportunity for personal discovery, balance and healing.

The interrelated directions and perspectives of the lodges in the circle offer us spiritual teachings and practical life lessons as a path to authentic presence and a pathway to transforming ourselves and our communities.

Beginning the Journey

We begin our journey around the Circle of Authentic Presence with the Medicine Wheel.

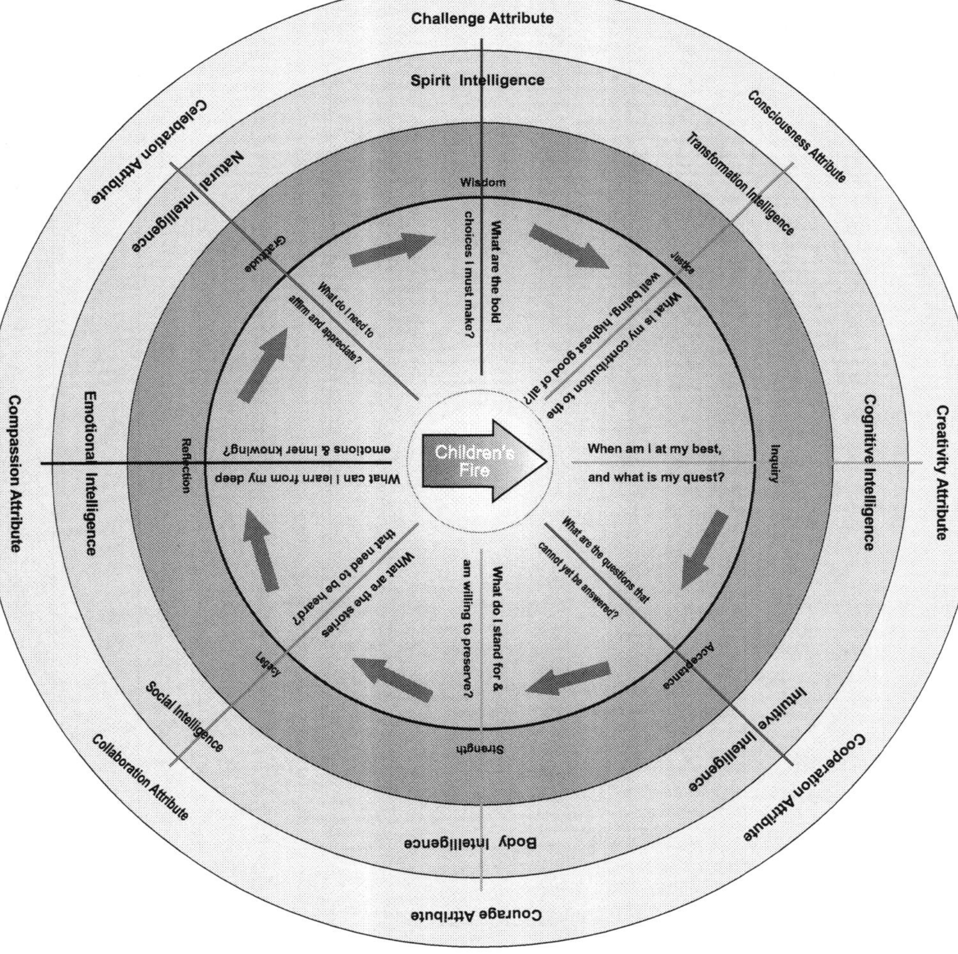
Challenge Attribute
Spirit Intelligence
Wisdom
What are the bold choices I must make?
Consciousness Attribute
Transformation Intelligence
Justice
What is my contribution to the well being, highest good of all?
Creativity Attribute
Cognitive Intelligence
Inquiry
When am I at my best, and what is my quest?
Children's Fire
Cooperation Attribute
Intuitive Intelligence
Acceptance
What are the questions that cannot yet be answered?
Courage Attribute
Body Intelligence
Strength
What do I stand for & am willing to preserve?
Collaboration Attribute
Social Intelligence
Legacy
What are the stories that need to be heard?
Compassion Attribute
Emotional Intelligence
Reflection
What can I learn from my deep emotions & inner knowing?
Celebration Attribute
Natural Intelligence
Gratitude
What do I need to affirm and appreciate?

Center of the Circle: The Children's Fire

> *"Start where you are ... Use what you have ...*
> *Do what you can."*
> –Arthur Ashe, professional tennis champion

We begin in the center of the circle, in some traditions this is called the Children's Fire. The center is a place of great power, because no one is closer or farther from the center of power no matter where they are on the circle. Each person can benefit mutually from the circle's diverse strengths, which lead to a stronger whole as well as stronger parts. The center of the circle is a touch place for and is the essence of our authentic presence.

The center or hub of the wheel is the place of unity where each lodge or perspective begins, and to which it returns. It is the place where all differences can come together; separation becomes togetherness and converges naturally in a promise of collective wisdom. It is both the center of self and the center of the community. This represents the center of our being, the place of heart—equal distance between heaven and earth—and the relationship to All Beings. This place in the wheel is the spark of the divine that shines forth from our soul. It is the place where we rest in the perfection of our "self," where we are perfect just as we are. Within this space, we refresh ourselves, and restore our vitality and energy. From the ancestral realm, we open to receive courage and comfort, strength and gentleness, grace and gratitude, forgiveness and compassion. We yield to receive the ancestral gifts that intuitively we know are most needed in the moment. There are no questions to be answered, nor any work to be done; all is just as it should be in this place of peace and wholeness.

Living like a horse from the center of the circle in deep quiet and protection, we replenish our bodies and souls. We are connected to our hearts as hoof beats echo the heartbeat of the earth, inspiring our spirits to be free. We move both outward from the center to each of the eight compass directions, and back inward to the center in an interconnected dance of collective wisdom gathering. Again, here there are no questions asked and no answers given...it is simply a place of being where we are.

East: Lodge of Masculine Energy

"Go confidently in the direction of your dreams.
Never look back unless you are planning to go that way.
Live the life you have imagined."
–Henry David Thoreau

From the center of the Medicine Wheel, we journey to the East Lodge, the Lodge of Masculine Energy (or Men's Lodge).

The cardinal direction of the East represents dawn and illumination of creation, and the morning light. We awaken to the nature of light and the **element of air** that gives us our first breath of life. With dawn light, we awaken to the beginning of our journey. In the **season of spring,** life renews its promise, opening to a life of new adventure; this is a chance to bring light to a relationship or insight to a dilemma with which we have been struggling. The **place of mind** and cognitive thought, it is where we begin to ask questions big and small, and to analyze problems and discover our purpose.

In the second circle we explore the **spirit of inquiry.** This process of discovery opens our curiosity to find deeper meaning and expanded potential and possibility. This expansive cultivating of information and collective wisdom reveals pathways to solutions for the highest and best good of the whole, and is also a path for authentic presence to emerge.

The intelligence in the East lodge of the third circle is **cognitive intelligence.** This gift of mindfulness offers the ability to question, make sense of information and organize thoughts into purposeful meaning.

Within the fourth circle, the essential behavior or **action is creativity,** where we innovate and give birth to ideas. This is an inspiring place from which all life begins and begins anew. Creativity is an essential quality of authentic presence that resides within all of us, and tapping into this vital resource creates a vibrant and meaningful life.. The East calls forth the leader in us to ask the essential questions and take the essential first steps to begin our journey, a quest that moves us toward a more spirited and sacred life for all.

Living like the ancestral horse of the East, we sniff the delicious spring air, bringing our inner world of spirit and vision into the dawning of springtime and a new day. Flying without wings into realms of experience where we cannot travel on foot, we find new life.

We ask: What are the questions that have no right to go away?; Who am I? When am I at my best? What is my purpose and what is my quest?

South East: Lodge of the Peace Chief

> *"Be patient toward all that is unsolved in your heart and try to love the questions themselves. Live your questions now, and perhaps even without knowing it, you will live along some distant day into your answers."*
> –Rainer Maria Rilke

We turn to the right to the Southeast quadrant, the Peace Chief's Lodge. The responsibility of this lodge is to create harmony between opposites or polarities, to maintain the peace within complexity. We pause to resolve what is essential to resolve. We move on acknowledging what is unresolved without needing resolution in order to allow the process or journey to move forward.

Here, in the second circle, with the **spirit of acceptance** we acknowledge and make peace with the unknown or yet to be known aspects of the journey. We solve what is essential to solve to engage our journey and accept peaceably what is currently unsolvable.

The third circle, the intelligence of this lodge, is represented by **intuitive intelligence** as it reminds us to listen to our inner knowing and trust that which we know, and trust that which is uncertain in time becomes clear. This place of inner knowing inspires our curiosity and motivates innovation.

The fourth circle is the essential **behavior or action of cooperation,** bringing diverse parts of the whole together. We learn to bring unresolved differences together by cooperating, so we can move forward. Cooperation is the process of working together to the same end. This requires the skill of teamwork with the goal of mutual benefit, understanding that we are all in this together, managing different perspectives, and not knowing all the answers. Authentic presence asks that we accept what we cannot change and learn from the value of curiosity that comes from not knowing.

Living like a horse we flow from one moment to the next with curiosity and peaceful acceptance, not needing to know, just needing to be.

We ask: What do I need to make peace with that which is unresolved in order to move on? What are the questions that have to be answered, cannot yet be answered or have no answers?

South: Lodge of Children and War Chiefs

> *"I learned that courage was not the absence of fear, but the triumph over it The brave man is not he who does not feel afraid, but he who conquers that fear."*
> –Nelson Mandela

We make a quarter turn to the South, the War Chief's Lodge, the place of children, warriors as they reflect our readiness to defend what is young and vulnerable. A new blade of grass, a newly sprouted flower, a baby, a fresh new idea–all need care until they establish their own power to exist. In the warmth and abundance of **summer** growth, our hearts fill with courage to defend our new beginnings. The **element of fire** informs this lodge, offering warmth and passion and fierce protection.

This lodge in the second circle represents the **spirit of strength,** the lodge of our body, the **physical realm** of our five senses, and of our body's well-being. It is the place we made a stand for our beliefs and ideals and offer protection for the beliefs and ideals of others.

The third circle of the South is the **embodied intelligence;** an intelligence of primal survival, beyond verbal communication, and knowing one's place in the present moment and one's place in life's journey.

The fourth circle of the South is the commitment to **behaviors and actions of courage,** a way of protecting and defending that comes not from a place of oppression or gain, but from a place that preserves innocence and integrity. The South also is the lodge that champions childhood innocence, exuberance, joy and play. It is the place of the inner child of the adult and of new beginnings in adulthood.

Living like the ancestral horse of the South, we remember our first language, the honesty of body language and the embodied communication of movement. Standing strong with courage of heart and a fiery spirit, we protect our young and defend our herd. When all is well, we kick up our hoofs in passionate play and irreverent childlike enthusiasm.

We ask: What do I stand for and what am I willing to preserve and protect?

South West: Lodge of Singers, Storytellers and Mediums

> *"A bird does not sing because it has an answer*
> *a bird sings because it has a song... Love jumps*
> *hurdles, leaps fences, penetrates walls to arrive at it*
> *destination full of hope."*
> –Maya Angelou, American poet and teacher

Turning to the Southwest lodge, we listen to the stories of our ancestors meet the stories of the prophets in a lively conversation between the past and future. We begin to remember our own stories and find the courage to speak our truths.

Within the second circle, we find the **spirit of legacy;** we listen to the stories of our history and the patterns of the past to know how to better live in the present. We craft our story, living our future legacy by how we live in the present.

The third circle of the Southwest offers **social intelligence,** the intelligence of empathy, of valuing relationship and respecting "all my relations." This lodge on the circle pays attention to possible consequences of our current actions in relation to our future.

The fourth circle is the collective **action of collaboration,** a social relationship that engages and moves everyone together toward a common story, purpose or goal. Finding our authentic voice, we proudly sing out and humbly speak the most important song and story of all, our own.

Living like a horse, we live our story in the field of life, finding joy in our relationships, moving together as one herd and creating a living legacy.

We ask: What is my unique story and what is our story? How do I remember who I am and how I want to be, and how I want to be remembered?

West: Lodge of Feminine Energy

> *"Women have to summon courage*
> *to fulfill dormant dreams."*
> –Alice Walker

Traveling west, we reach the Lodge of Feminine Energy, a place of dreams and vision. West is the direction of the setting sun, and symbolizes moving into the dark and into the **night time** of dreams. The season is autumn, when nature shows her colors and sheds leaves and whatever else is no longer needed as she prepares for winter. It is the place of **water,** where **emotions** deepen and flow, the water of healing tears, of sorrow and of joy. Emotions simply exist and then move on the tides of change.

Within the second circle of authentic presence the **spirit of reflection** takes its place. In its stillness and quiet, the inner voice is invited to be heard; the sound of silence for contemplation, remembering and visioning is embraced.

The intelligence of the third circle is **emotional intelligence,** the balance of emotions. In this lodge we learn to expand our range of feeling, to be aware of and experience our emotions, and to manage them internally and externally.

This lodge, in the fourth concentric circle, holds the **acts of compassion,** which opens the heart. Diving into the deep well of compassion and depth of forgiveness, we return to the surface bringing loving kindness to a planet much in need of healing, peace and wholeness.

Living like the ancestral horse of the West we walk gently into the dark, slowing down to listen and going within for knowing. Traveling into the cave of our soul we learn from the images within, like petro glyphs on cave walls. Nudged gently by our fellow herd members we enter into the flow of life, diving deeply into our inner realm to heal and coming back up to life.

We Ask: What are my dreams and visions that are emerging? What can I learn from the depths of emotions and inner knowing to heal myself and others?

North West: Council Lodge

> *"The best way to show my gratitude is to accept everything, even my problems, with joy."*
> –Mother Teresa

The Northwest offers us a place on the wheel to pause, bless and affirm the integrity of our journey and its teachings.

From this direction we acknowledge and offer gratitude for the quest, the new beginnings, the emerging visions and ideas, the struggles and pain, the tears of sorrow and laughter, the clarity and the confusion.

The **spirit of gratitude** rules this lodge, within the second circle, and holds us together. We have much for which to be grateful from the smallest blessing to the grandest gift of life. When we choose to offer gratitude and appreciation, we create a world of positive connection for ourselves and others; one that we would want to live in.

The intelligence of the third concentric circle is **natural intelligence.** One of the best places to develop your natural intelligence is in the natural world. In nature nothing is taken for granted; the natural resource of generosity of sharing is always available. In the presence of horses and within the realm of nature we can remember and appreciate how and what we are as humbly powerful beings of the natural world. Sharing gratitude, we can live freely according to our natural and authentic presence and help change the world for better.

Celebration is the behavior and action of the fourth concentric circle. Life is to be celebrated with all of its expected and unexpected gifts and challenges. Celebration is the process of gratitude and appreciation, and is even better when it is a shared experience in community. Saying yes to all experience moves us closer to the possibility of authentic presence. Council Lodge offers blessings of gratitude for the journey of life.

Living like a horse we overcome obstacles and greet challenges with grace, the spirit of gratitude setting us free and freeing others.

We ask: What in my life do I need to affirm and appreciate? For what can I be grateful?

North: Lodge and Place of Wisdom and the Elders

> *"The ultimate measure of a man is not where he stands in moments of comfort and convenience, but where he stands at times of challenge and controversy."*
> ¬Martin Luther King, Jr.

We journey to the North, direction of the element of earth, in the place of elders and wisdom. In this place of the elders, we explore the truth underlying all things. We struggle to make clear the teachings of our quest and find the strength to carry out the spiritual work that has been given to us.

The North carries the **spirit of wisdom** with the courage and commitment to take on life's challenges. It is the ultimate domain of belonging, essential being, and meaning by mattering in the world.

In the place of **spiritual intelligence,** on the third circle, we are asked to be wise enough to be who we are and brave enough to be responsible for our place in the circle of life. Spiritual intelligence is the knowing of the wisdom of the soul, which results in a sense of deeper meaning and life purpose.

Within the fourth circle of authentic presence we accept the **challenge** of finding our inner strength to meet the adventures of the soul and to find deep peace to understand the mystery of life. This lodge offers us strength and stamina, and courage and heart, guiding us through the complexity of our journey and bringing us safely home to our Spirit.

Living like the ancestral horse of the North, we venture into the heart of the circle of elders to discover our inner strength, to meet the challenges of the soul, and to be humble in the presence of the great mystery of life. As a majestic horse of the North, we meet life with a clear mind, resilient body, courageous heart and free soul. We trot along through the complexity of our journey and return safely home to our Spirit.

We ask: What are the bold decisions I must make, what is my soul work, what is my responsibility to creating a better world?

Northeast: Lodge and Place of Dog Soldiers

> *"A very great vision is needed and the man who has it must follow it as the eagle seeks the deepest blue of the sky."*
> –Crazy Horse, Sioux Chief"

> *"In our every deliberation, we must consider the impact of our decisions on the next seven generations."*
> –Iroquois Maxim (circa 1700-1800)

The Dog Soldier's Lodge in the Northeast is the position on the circle that is the guardian and the check-and-balance of the journey. It has the final say whether the journey and its teachings are to be accepted. In this lodge we design our priorities and actions in alignment with who we truly are as our authentic best selves.

The Northeast in **the second circle** is the **spirit of justice.** This direction is one of an impeccable warrior who protects the best interests of all life, and especially the good of the children, and the children of generations to come. In this lodge of movement, before the journey can move forward, we pause to consider if the decisions and actions of this journey are in alignment with what is best for us, our families, and our communities: and, for seven generations to come and the ancestors seven generations back. If the answer is yes, the journey moves forward; if the answer is no, the journey begins again. This lodge requires us to examine the consequences of our quest in the present and future; we do this for ourselves, our human community and the community of all life.

Within a flow of conscious behavior and action we can stretch into our **intelligence to transform** the world "BWI"—beyond our wildest imagination.

The behavior and action here is **consciousness,** living closer to the truth of your heart and the heart of collective wisdom within every moment of your life. In this lodge of the fourth circle, we are asked to commit to moving the vision of the journey forward only if it is in the best interest of all now and for generations to come.

Living like a horse is a gateway to justice, a life well lived and victory of the human spirit.

We ask: Is this in the best interest of you, your family, your community, and all life? Is this in the best interest of the children for seven generations to come and the ancestors that came before?

Coming Full Circle

> *"To everything (turn, turn, turn)*
> *There is a season (turn, turn, turn)*
> *And a time to every purpose, under heaven."*
> –Pete Seeger (from *Kohelet*, Ecclesiastes 3)

We all have a precious portion of time, a season we cannot prevent or alter in which to enjoy and to share our earthly gifts. There is a season, our time of purpose, will and desire, to do the right thing. Wisdom is to know the right season of time, purpose and action. There is a season under heaven, the high dwelling place of reason, righteousness, and revelation. Reason is the heart, soul and spirit of right conduct. Righteousness is the pursuit of justice and the doing of good deeds for their own sake. Revelation is where wisdom is revealed and the awe and wonder of life becomes known.

We are living in a complicated time that calls for creative approaches to gain personal insight, open our hearts and bring our communities together in harmony. The teachings of Indigenous ways, cross-cultural practices and ceremony offer us a unique perspective to expand our awareness of ourselves and others in the present moment. This exploration supports creative, adaptable and meaningful change. The Indigenous path to authentic presence is a sacred quest of ever-evolving circles, collecting wisdom and living consciously in our personal and professional lives.

Living like a horse, we set our soul free, travelling fiercely across time and space and running with the wind in wild abandon. Gathering the collective wisdom of the herds, following ancient rhythms in circles of life, and living with authentic presence, we return to a place of free spirit, an Indigenous home and hearth we never left.

Chapter 17
A Journey Around the Circle of Authentic Presence

The Circle of Authentic Presence is a cognitive and intuitive process for deepening personal discovery, making decisions, solving dilemmas and bringing dreams to reality.

There are no simple answers to our ordinary and extraordinary life questions. Engaging these questions with curiosity and compassion through an intentional process is an opportunity to strengthen our character, and our awareness of our authentic presence. The Circle of Authentic Presence is a way to gain personal insight and gather collective wisdom.

What follows are two real time experiences in which I turned to the Circle of Authentic Presence as a process of inquiry.

"All In": A Circle of Authentic Presence Initiative

One experience of incorporating the Circle of Authentic Presence within the context of my professional work was with a large healthcare system, MetroHealth. Established in 1837, the oldest hospital system in Cleveland, it is dedicated to creating changes that ensure high quality patient care, as well as ensuring that it's a good place to work.

I was hired by MetroHealth to help facilitate a transition process intending to merge two long-standing hospital departments, the Social Work department and the Nursing department, into one integrated, smooth-working department. The goal was to bring the best of both departments together to better serve the well being of the patients, staff and total hospital system.

I met with the leadership of the two departments to learn what was important to them in the change process and its outcome.

After listening to their hopes and concerns, I created an approach that would encourage collaboration, cooperation and creativity and would be inclusive of all in the two departments. I applied the Circle of Authentic Presence as the first initiative in the process. Staff from the two departments came together for three half-days to participate in creating a meaningful change process. The two departments were integrated, then divided into teams of eight people. The model of the Circle of Authentic Presence was presented. Each team chose a lodge on the circle to explore, from that perspective, the question: who are we and how can we be at our best as one integrated department?

The first day each lodge team met to discuss the question, "Who are we?" From the perspective of their lodge on the circle, each team discussed their thoughts on the meaning and significance of MetroHealth's new change initiative; and what effect it would have on them personally, on their individual department, and as one new department; and, how it would affect the hospital system as a whole. At the end of the first day each team presented their key thoughts, feelings and collective learning to the whole group.

The second day each team addressed the question, from their lodge perspective, "How can we be at our best as one department?" Their task, based on the discussion of the question, was then to design an initiative or ceremony from the vantage point of their lodge that would contribute to a good present and a future of well being for their department.

The third day each team presented their initiative or ceremony and engaged the whole group in a conversation about what interested them about the perspective offered. The teams then shared what they learned in the process of working together as an integrated team and how that might serve them in the transition process going forward.

The team from the East Lodge, launching the quest, took the lead. Their initiative was to create a new draft of a mission statement, goals and objectives as a clear direction for their department to move forward in a positive light.

The team from the Southeast Lodge, making peace with the unknown and the contradictions, designed a ceremony where each person would bring a representation of something they personally needed to make peace with, or their department might need to make peace with, to come together in acceptance of one another and cooperation with each other. Each person would say something about why they chose that artifact and what it represented in support of a positive transition process.

The team of the South Lodge (of children and warriors) took responsibility for identifying something physical and practical that would protect the identity and value of each department as they merged into one. Their hope was to have the courage to collectively create a new title, logo and image for the new department rather than have someone outside the department do that for them. The idea was to create an authentic presence contest, with a grand prize, to be determined for the group that had the most compelling and popular branding initiative. A democratic vote would be taken to select the winner and choose the best approach. The idea would then be sent with the new departments blessing to the administration for their consideration.

The team from Southeast Lodge (of stories and legacy) came up with a project whereby each person would have an opportunity to tell a true story to someone in the other department about when they, within the realm of their professional responsibilities, made a difference in someone's life. These stories would then be collected and placed on a website commons for all to read. They also suggested a white board where people could write their hopes and dreams for themselves within the department, for their colleagues, patients, hospital and for humanity.

The team from the West Lodge (of reflection, deep emotion and healing) decided to transform one of the hospitals fountains into a "healing and well-being" well. They would place a plaque explaining the purpose of the well, which was for people to pause and reflect and toss a coin in the water for healing and well being for themselves or others, and even for the planet.

The team for Lodge of the Northwest (in the spirit of gratitude) proposed an initiative where at the start of each department meeting, each person would pick a name of someone at the meeting and offer appreciation and gratitude of and for that person.

The team from the Lodge of the North (wisdom) asked each person to create a personal shield out of paper and other materials that were provided that captured the spirit they wanted to be pres-ent in their new department. All the shields would then be placed together in the form of a collage representing the col-lective spirit of the people in this newly formed department and would be displayed in the lobby of their department.

The team from the Northeast Lodge suggested there be a group of rotating representatives from each area that would meet over lunch each week. The responsibility of this group was to connect with one another and to come up with one practical idea, one bold idea and one "beyond your wildest imagination" idea that would keep the departments lively, innovative and moving forward in good ways.

The team that was responsible for the Center (the Children's Fire) committed to organizing four all-department celebration events, one for each season. The purpose was to keep communication open through connections that included fun, food and a meaningful learning experience.

In bringing the process of the Circle of Authentic Presence as an approach for their transition and change process I had three core intentions.

The first intention was to build a space and place within the heart of the hospital setting and within the hearts of the people of respect, trust, compassion and care.

The second intention was to encourage the people in the department to take responsibility for creating their desired reality in which to work and live.

The third intention was to help the people create a culture of collective wisdom that was fun-loving and loving; one that valued diversity and practiced inclusion and that honored each of their professional traditions and personal visions.

This was the beginning of a change process that would have many challenges and offer many opportunities, but I felt that the three days we worked together provided an inclusive and solid foundation of good will, good hearts, and good spirit for these good people.

"What's in a Name?" A Circle of Authentic Initiative

One of the most difficult tasks is for parents is to choose a name for their new baby or for an entrepreneur to choose a name for his or her new business start-up. Sometimes we struggle with our own names wishing we had a different name or wondering how to live up to the promise of the name we were given.

In my family we gave our three sons biblical names, David, Joseph and Jeremiah. Interestingly, who they are as adults in many ways reflects the ancestors and ancient archetypes for which they were named.

David, being our first son and the first grandchild in a large family was often fondly referred to as "David a Melich" Hebrew for King David. This majestic beginning to his identity had its benefits and its challenges for him. David, in claiming the strength of his name and of his authentic presence, lives freely as a married gay man with a beautiful family of three children, Joshua, Ethan and Aria. He, like King David, his namesake, is wise and just in his life and life's work. In his professional role of lawyer, David defends those who have been unfairly treated in business based on their social status, age, gender identity or on unfair labor practices. He is active in the human rights movement and takes on the challenges and fights for those who cannot protect or defend themselves.

Joseph, being the second born, has always lived like his namesake as brilliant dreamer. As an architect he dreams awesome designs of green buildings into reality and dares to dream the impossible into possible. As a father he has taught his son Jaren to dream big and dream often.

Jeremiah, the youngest, has embraced his namesake with the fiery audacity to call out injustice, with a passionate voice proclaiming the honest truth and the spirit of faith and hope in humanity. He and Sarah and daughter Natalie are at the front of the race for a cause or first in line to speak out for that which they believe.

What's in a name? Who were you named for? What story does the name of your business tell? How does your name reflect or reject your authentic presence in some way?

A "What's in a Name" Journey around the Circle of Authentic Presence

I invite you to have your own experience in a journey around the Circle of Authentic Presence by exploring "What is in a name?" Simply pose the question you are interested in exploring and visit each lodge in the circle, reflecting on and then responding to the inquiry of each lodge.

East: Lodge of Masculine Energy

As I think about my name, how does it relate to the inquiry, "What is my purpose and what is my quest?"

South East: Lodge of the Peace Chief

As I wonder about my name, how does it relate to the inquiry, "What do I need to make peace with that which is unresolved so I can move on?"

South: Lodge of Children and War Chiefs

As I take a stand for my name, how does it relate to the inquiry, "What do I stand for and what am I willing to preserve and protect?"

Southwest: Lodge of Singers, Storytellers and Mediums

As I remember the story of my name, how is it related to the inquiry, "What is my unique story? How do I remember and want to be remembered?"

West: Lodge of Feminine Energy

As I reflect on my name, how does it relate to the inquiry, "What are my dreams and visions that are emerging?"

Northwest: Council Lodge

As I offer gratitude for my name, how does it relate to the inquiry, "What in my life do I need to affirm, be grateful for and appreciate?"

North: Wisdom Lodge

As I take responsibility for the honor of my name, what does the wisdom of my name require of me?

Northeast: Lodge and Place of Dog Soldiers

As I commit to what matters to me about my name, "Is this in the best interest of me, my family, my community, all life and of the children for seven generations to come and the ancestors that came before?"

Children's Fire
My name is simply my name, a gift to me from those who named me. How might I be the gift by simply being me?

"What's in the Bag" Journey Around the Circle of Authentic Presence

People all around the world have been carrying bags for cen-turies; bags of skin and cloth, bags made out of clamshells or coconut shells. Whether big or small, a bag needs to be able to carry stuff: fancy evening bags, book bags, paper lunch bags, sports bags, doggie bags. The requirement met by a particular bag might be its price tag, weight, size, versatility, or its beauty or efficiency.

I have often wondered if those responsible for inventing the plastic bag had journeyed around the Circle of Authentic Presence what the final outcome would have been. The plastic bag might have made sense from each perspective until it reached the last lodge. In the very last lodge where the question is: is it in the best interest for the seven generations to come and for all life? I believe the answer would be a big no. What alternative bag might we have created that had all the benefits of plastic bags but not the negative impact on our environment? In this case, it is all in the bag,

Your Journey Around the Circle of Authentic Presence

I invite you to choose a question you would like to ask or an inquiry that you would like to engage in and take your own journey around the Circle of Authentic Presence. You can approach the journey from any one of the four concentric circles or from all of them. In this quest, we offer ourselves up to a higher purpose, aligning unique perspectives and weaving diversity into a collective intention for the good of the greater whole. The culmination of our journey around the circle of authentic and collective presence reveals wise action and abundant possibility for the good of our lives and for the good of all life.

Section VII—The Path of Indigenous Culture

Pause, Reflect and Respond

Be curious about your place of belonging, the ancestors who could support your inner knowing, where are you most at home and who is your tribe and are the people with whom you can be most yourself.

Take several index cards and write a word or phrase and an image that came from your reflections on each individual card.

Save these cards as you will be reflecting back on them.

VIII

The Path of Greeting the Emerging Future

Chapter 18
The Collective Wisdom of the Emerging Future

"'We'll meet on edges, soon,' said I,
proud 'neath heated brow.
Ah, but I was so much older then,
I'm younger than that now."
—Bob Dylan

When I was younger the future seemed so far away and the older I get the closer the future has come. The path of greeting the emerging future informs authentic presence within the limits of a lifetime as we create the best possible conditions in the present for our most positive future to emerge.

"All things originate from one another and
vanish into one another according to necessity in
conformity with the order of time."
—Anaximander, early Western philosopher

The natural world lives within an ongoing process of beginning and endings in each moment. In the present the future exists waiting to happen. In the acorn exists the tree waiting to grow if the present conditions allow and no squirrel eats it for breakfast. The caterpillar shows no signs of being a butterfly but all that is needed for that transformation is within it, preparing for its future to emerge from its cocoon. There is a circular and emergent natural order of movement through time and timelessness. The past darkness of night becomes present light of day to future dark night to present daylight. The seasons arrive and return fulfilling their annual promise. Within that rhythm of time there is much uncertainty but also the faith of certainty.

> *"How we think about the future and the past determines everything about how we think about our situation as human beings."*
> —Lee Smolin, American theoretical physicist,

In the realm of physics, the naturalists have been debating whether time according to the laws of nature is timeless and determined, or is, unfolding moment to moment in real time. According to physicist Lee Smolin, if we perceive the laws of nature evolving over time, the future may be less predictable but more open to possibility. This way of understanding time and space gives us the freedom to imagine what can be and the responsibility to make wise decisions that influence our collective and individual futures.

The future may not turn out like we hope or expect and yet we persistently imagine the future world we want and a vision of how to get there. Transforming hatred and greed into loving kindness and generosity in the present, we might become the people the future needs for a better world. Building on our strengths, working together for the good of all, and with a little bit of luck, the present may emerge into a positive future in which we all want to live.

> *"The distinction between past, present, and future is only a stubbornly persistent illusion."*
> —Albert Einstein

Greeting the Emerging Future

We can choose to live more fully in the present; it is a reality that we can directly engage and embody. The present contains our past memories and future thoughts and we can experience both directly as alive within the present moment. From this place of present awareness, we might not be able to change the past or future, but we can change our perception of them and so create a more satisfying and authentically positive life.

The horses have been wonderful guides for me in opening this path of the emergent future. In observing their behavior and engaging with them in the herd I began to notice how it is that they live in the present and create the conditions to be ready to greet an emergent future of collective well-being.

They seem to sense the reality of the present moment and sense their way into what is emerging, moment by present moment.

> "Real generosity toward the future lies in giving all to the present".
> —Albert Camus, French philosopher

Horses sense the present moment: The unfolding future emerges from the present moment as they listen with open eyes, hearts and through their embodied presence.

The horses, without knowing the current theory of Otto Scharmer's "Open Heart, Open Mind and Open Will" approach to change, nor Aristotle's historic theory of Open Mind, Heart and Will, are able to tune into the most essential and relevant present reality. Being present to their world with all their senses prepares them to be aware and ready to take the actions required to greet the most promising future. By slowing down and deeply listening, seeing and registering through their bodies the reality of the present moment, they are not distracted by old, useless habits, past judgments, or future fears. What they pay attention to, and how they pay attention in the present creates their future reality.

Horses are curious, opening their minds to discover what is essential to their well-being. How might we humans open our thoughts and curiosity to surprise, imagination and creativity? Horses live with open hearts by experiencing their world through honest, relevant emotion. How might we as humans open our hearts to be more compassionate and caring? Horses are free from worry about what will happen and can therefore focus on moving forward towards what life is offering. How as humans might we move forward with resiliency and optimism towards what life is providing for us?

> *"Sometimes what seems like surrender isn't surrender at all. It's about what's going on in our hearts. About seeing clearly the way life is and accepting it and being true to it."*
> —Nicholas Evans, The Horse Whisperer

Horse Whispering

"Horse whispering" is the act of slowing down and permitting inner stillness and quiet listening within to reveal the "whisper" of what needs to be heard. Horse whispering and deep listening allow people to connect to their best selves, to an authentic presence that wants to emerge. In the presence of the horses, we can better know who we are at our authentic best. We can create space in our lives to acknowledge the good that already exists and open the space for something incredible to emerge.

> "We keep moving forward, opening new doors,
> and doing new things because we're curious and
> curiosity keeps leading us down new paths."
> —Walt Disney
> Curiosity, Exploring and Experimenting

Horses are inherently curious. They learn what works and what lasts by trying new things. Sometimes what they try works and they move forward with success, and sometimes what they try does not work but leads them to what might be the next best success. Each new step forward in the present moment leads to a new discovery that can be adopted, adapted or discarded. When we allow ourselves to explore and experiment one step at a time without fear of failure, we can move toward untapped inner wisdom and innovation.

> *"Tuning must come first...his head bent to the
> vibrating string and his lips slightly open,
> breathing quickly, as over the body of a lover."*
> —Ann Wroe, Orpheus: The Song of Life

Collective Resonance and Wisdom

Horses tap into the flow of life within them and life around them. It is an embodied and intuitive awareness, coherence and flow with life force, which positively influences engagement toward a common positive purpose. Strengthening our capacity to sense information through collective resonance, we expand our capacity to be in harmony with one another and with life around us, and the possibility of better solving the complex dilemmas we currently face on our planet.

Most often when I have experienced the path of the emergent future, it is in the horse field through an unplanned, unexpected magical moment.

One warm summer evening in 2016 as I was giving the horses their night meal, I noticed that Chief Silver Cloud, a horse with a hearty appetite, sniffed his dinner and walked away without eating. When a horse is not interested in dinner it generally means that they are not feeling well. I watched as Chief Silver Cloud walked away nipping at his side and then he lay down. Horses lie down to rest but when they lie down not feeling well it generally is a sign of colic, a possibly life-threatening illness.

I coaxed Silver to his feet and began walking him to try to relieve his discomfort. I called our vet, Doc Hepner, who was at a baseball game but said he would be there as quickly as possible to administer medication to try to relieve the painful digestive condition. I walked Silver for about five hours while the amazing Doc administered aid to him till 2:00 a.m. in the morning. We stabilized his condition but he still would not eat. Doc said, "We are not out of the woods with him until he eats." Doc was back at 7:30 the next morning and back again that evening. Silver was no worse but only a bit better. Day three he was still not eating. Doc said that each day that he does not improve the condition becomes more dangerous but he would do what he could. It was about 5:00 in the afternoon when Chief Silver Cloud decided to walk out to the far end of the field to join the rest of the herd. I hoped that this was a sign that he was feeling better but soon realized that was not the case when instead of lowering his head to eat he lay down in the shade and cool grass. I was on my way across the field to check on Silver when a man named Daniel, who had been on the ranch the previous few days at a men's retreat with my husband Herb, called out to me to wait for him. He knew Silver was in trouble and asked if he could walk with me. During his time on the ranch he said he had connected with Silver in a deeply heartfelt way and wanted to help if he could. When we approached Silver it was clear he was in distress as his breathing was labored. I called Doc to let him know that I thought Silver had taken a turn for the worse and he said he'd be there in about an hour. Daniel and I got Silver to stand and slowly walked the quarter mile back to the cool of the shelter to wait for Doc. It took us about twenty minutes as we had to stop often to let Silver rest. When we got to the shelter I told Daniel that I was going to play Silver some Native American flute music on my phone as it helped calm him and bring his heart rate down. Daniel told me that he was a musician that played cello for the Cleveland symphony orchestra and at other classical music venues. He said he had come directly to the ranch from a music gig and had his cello with him. He asked if he could play for Silver. I have learned that when the Great Integrity is at play, the smartest thing to do is to simply say yes. Daniel returned with his cello, a chair, and four other guys from the men's retreat and four of the horses that had followed Silver back through the field.

Daniel sat in his chair and began to play Strauss's "Alpine Pastoral Concerto" and some of his own original music inspired by Chief Silver Cloud. At first Silver was startled by the unfamiliar sound and vibration and moved away from Daniel. He then turned, faced Daniel and walked toward him stopping about eight feet away. As Daniel, a beautiful, magical young man from Venezuela, played his heartfelt music, Silver, a seemingly magical horse from mythic times, began to slowly sway to his music. Daniel, his eyes closing, played for about twenty minutes, deeply connected to his music and to Silver. Head lowered and eyes closing Silver, listening to the music being offered, seemed to be deeply connected to Daniel.

I took a few pictures with my phone camera and then stopped, realizing I was witnessing a sacred moment and perhaps even a sacred ceremony.

Daniel brought the music to a close and as he opened his eyes, Silver opened his eyes. The horse stretched up to his full height, yawned and walked over to the nearest pile of hay and took his first bite of food in three days. I looked around and all the men had tears in their eyes, all the horses were quietly watching and the horse in the middle let out a big sigh joined by the soft snorts of the surrounding horses. What I felt was the resonance of interconnected hearts, the harmony of heal-ing and the felt experience of the field of the Great Integrity.

A few minutes later Doc Hepner arrived, and taking one look at Silver chowing down on hay, he just smiled. Learning about the impromptu concert and Silver's unusual healing process and recovery, Doc quipped that next time he had a horse with colic at 3:00 a.m. he would be sure to call on Daniel and his music.

I made a copy of the two pictures that I had taken of Daniel and Chief Silver Cloud. I gave the pictures the title "Healing One Heart At A Time." As I looked at the pictures a second time, I wondered if it was Silver healing or Daniel healing and renamed the pictures "Two Hearts Healing." I gave the pictures to Daniel and he told me something old, perhaps pri-mal, had healed in him via his connection through music with Silver. He knew that Silver was deeply listening to his music and actually hearing the love that came through. In Daniel offering his music in a pure way of being with no agenda or "doing," and Silver receiving the music within the purity of his heart, a sacred bond of collective resonance was created. The power of the connection extended from Daniel and Silver to the surrounding field of horses, humans, birds and breezes. In this co-created field of the emergent future, Daniel began to hear his music from deep within himself in a way he had always dreamed possible.

> *"Music acts like a magic key, to which the most tightly closed heart opens."*
> —Maria Augusta von Trapp

The path of the emergent future is both a solitary path and a collective journey. Horses in their herds each have their respective individual destiny while sharing the collective wisdom of the herd in the present moment. The heart-and-hoof-wide web can bring forward the wisdom of their ancestors and call to the wisdom of the future generations to thrive in the present moment. Without the barrier of time and confines of space, they can access essential information to thrive in unpredictable situations and through unexpected change. Their ability to drawn on past and future to inform the present is centered on trusting their inner instinctual knowing and the collective knowing of the herd. This integral and generative information of past, present and future is informed through the brilliance of their physical senses: sniffing the air; seeing the whole of the field; listening to what is most essential; being in touch with themselves, each other, and their world; tasting what nurtures life; and getting the feel of their present experience.

The knowledge that horses and all of nature carry from past to future, which lives in the present moment is integral in that it takes the most vital information from diverse perspectives to create an expansive perspective that is balanced and in harmony. It is generative in that the wisdom of the current moment grows and evolves with the change of times and changing fields of experience.

Entering the world of horse and herd, I began to observe the path of the emergent future as walked by the horses and sometimes as a participant, I felt included on this path as their guest.

There are several human herds that opened a way to understand the emergent future from a human perspective.

The first human herd was my family. They instilled in me an appreciation for our past lineage and my Jewish ancestral line through shared values and a code of behavior built on respect and loving kindness for all.

The Gestalt Institute of Cleveland is a learning community that offered me a way to continue my personal and professional growth. Visiting a childhood friend in her garden shed home in Sausalito California, I saw on her table a book with the title Gestalt Theory Verbatim: In and Out of the Garbage Can by Fritz Perls. Waiting for her to return from work, surrounded by vines that grew up the walls inside her garden shed home, I read the book and found words that I felt had been written in my heart. Returning to Cleveland, I discovered that there was a learning community based on this theory called Gestalt, inspired by Fritz and his wife Anna Perls. The timing was perfect and at twenty-two years of age I discovered a learning community that I could call home. Now almost fifty years later, this continues to be a place for me to learn and teach and grow from the inside out. Gestalt is a great theory and practice that has guided me in life and work and has many commonalities with the innate wisdom of the herd. This theory is present-centered, like the horses, bringing the past and future into a lived present. Learning by experimenting is another common approach as we literally try on situations to learn from them. The third commonality between horses and Gestalt is that the wisdom of the moment comes from the direct, embodied source of the senses, which leads to awareness, mobilizing energy, taking action and learning from what works and what lasts. The word gestalt means patterns. Nature lives and evolves through changing patterns, not getting stuck in irrelevant assumptions, past fears or future concerns. Gestalt invited us to be aware of our individual patterns and collective family group and societal patterns so as to appreciate the information held in those stuck places and to be able to get unstuck to move forward. Gestalt, like horses and nature, views resistance as important information of opposing forces pushing for resolution. As we honor, move toward, and learn from and with the resistance, we can move to the next best place on our way to the emergent future. I hold in my heart deep appreciation for the theory and practice of Gestalt and my many colleagues and student learning communities at the Gestalt institute of Cleveland.

The CWRU Weatherhead School of Management has also been a home herd in which to learn from within, stretch intellectually towards my emergent future and find a vibrant and welcoming learning community. Within this community I have found thought partners who in their generosity of heart and spirit have challenged me to think beyond what I thought possible and supported me in getting there. Diana Bilamoria offers unconditional encouragement to find my voice in my writing and to follow my dreams in my work and in all life. Richard Boyatiz challenges me to think and reach beyond. His ability to listen thoughtfully to the heart of the matter and for the ideal self that is waiting to emerge is a rare gift. Melvin Smith is a champion for our leadership and team-building work at the ranch and a spokesperson for what the horses offer in helping us be better leaders and human beings. Ellen Van Oosten, Mindy Kinnard and Jen Carr are wonderful partners in collaborating and creating executive education programs at the University that expand our ability to stretch into our professional and personal best selves.

The EAHAE, the European Association for Horse Assisted Learning and Horse Dream community has been my like-spirited horse and people herd community. Gerhard Krebs of HorseDream Inc. founded this global organization in Germany as a platform to support its members to develop their own horse-assisted education businesses. I trained with and joined this organization as it adhered to certain values that matched my own.

"Above all is trust. Further, we encourage caring, collaborative business and not competitive business. We collaborate on an equal level. Regarding our horses, we consider them trainers not tools," says Gerhard Krebs, founder of EAHAE.

I first met Gerhard at an Equine Guided Education conference in northern California. The hotel at the conference was overbooked so I had rented a SUV and was sleeping in the back of it in a sheep pasture on the ranch where the conference was held. Surrounded by sheep and the newly born spring lambs, I didn't count sheep in my dreams but I did have profound and somewhat troubling dreams. In the early morning I went into the cottage next to the sheep pasture to shower and snag a cup of coffee. Sitting at the table in the early morning light were two people who introduced themselves as Karin and Gerhard Krebs. We got to chatting and I shared with them one of my troubling dreams. Karin, the deeply wise woman that she is, suggested that the horse in my dream had a profound message for me and that I might benefit from listening to that horse in my dream and to listen more carefully to the horses in my life. Gerhard silently confirmed this with a nod of his head and twinkle in his lively blue eyes.

I knew then that these two people who had traveled from Germany for the conference and listened in the early hours of morning to my dream as I sat with the smell of sheep on me would be important guides on my learning path. Over the next year I traveled to Germany four times to learn with Karin and Gerhard and their Friesian horse herd, preparing myself to be worthy to engage with and partner with horses.

Essential in each and every learning opportunity, whether it was at the Gestalt Institute of Cleveland, or the Weatherhead School of Management at Case Western Reserve University or HorseDream Partners in Germany, was learning to be worthy to guide people in their personal and professional journeys. What I learned was that beyond understanding what to do was learning how to be: humble and honest, respectful and trustworthy and in integrity with myself and others. Being present in each of these vibrant and different learning communities prepared the path to my emergent future of bringing horses and humans together to learn, heal, grow and thrive.

A strength and challenge of the emergent future is that it is generative—each step opens to the never-ending next. That has proved true for me in writing this book. Just when I think I am done and the book is finished, another story that wants to be told emerges from the last story.

One year and one month from the time Daniel and Chief Silver Cloud discovered a heartfelt friendship through the healing nature of music, Daniel was at the Ranch for a program with the herd. In the morning, we had learned from the horses a deeper and more profound way of listening with our ears and with our hearts. Quieting within and being present without inner chatter, we practiced a heartfelt and appreciative listening within ourselves for what most wanted to be heard from the horses and from each other. At our lunch break Daniel told me that he had brought his cello and would be pleased to play for the group. His choice of where to play his music was in the horse pasture. After lunch, on this beautiful sunny fall day, our group of sixteen brought their chairs into the pasture and prepared for the impromptu concert against the backdrop of abundant fall colors. The horses were napping in the shade some distance away, resting from a morning of human engagement. Daniel began to play, and with our heightened ability to listen, we were soon mesmerized by the classical music carried on nature's gentle afternoon breeze. A few minutes into the Bach concerto I noticed Chief Silver Cloud in the distance no longer sleeping; his head was held high and his ears forward, awakening to Daniel's music. Slowly he walked away from his herd buddies who were still resting in the shade and toward Daniel. Silver stopped in front of Daniel, lowered his massive head and quietly and gently stood listening. Heart to heart, Daniel played and Silver listened. Each of us had our own experience as the beauty of the music and the magic of friendship, and maybe even love, touched our hearts. The music came to a close. Silver took one step closer to Daniel softly touching him with grace. Daniel and Silver sighed as if sharing one breath. Silver gracefully turned around and walked slowly and ceremonially back to the herd to join them in their afternoon nap.

> "Out beyond ideas of wrong doing and right doing there is a field. I'll meet you there. There is a community of the spirit; join it and feel the delight."
> —Rumi

Join your community of spirit, listen for its music, feel the delight.

The path of the emergent future lives within each of us: it listens to the music of our spirit and it leads us to our most positive authentic presence.

Section VIII —The Path of Greeting the Emerging Future

Pause, Reflect and Respond

Write the words: The best possible future is waiting to emerge and I am already there waiting to meet and greet it.

Close your eyes and spend a minute in thoughtless mindless quiet.

Take a minute to invite an image or picture to come to mind. Write it or draw it.

Save these cards as you will be reflecting back on them.

IX

The Path of the Great Integrity

Chapter 19
Entering the Field of the Great Integrity

"We learned about honesty and integrity—that the truth matters... that you don't take shortcuts or play by your own set of rules...and success doesn't count unless you earn it fair and square."
—Michelle Obama

The path of great integrity is core to a positive authentic presence. A person can be authentically present but without integrity can be corrupt and intentional in doing great harm. The great integrity is the moral compass that guides a life of truthfulness and trustworthiness, virtue and valor. It is a value system that informs our beliefs and behaviors.

- Integrity comes from within and is learned through relationship and engagement with the outside world.

- Integrity requires that we act in an honest, consistent, reliable and visible way at all times in accordance with the values and beliefs we hold.

- Integrity is a firm commitment to our principles no matter the consequences, and no matter who is or is not aware of our actions. It is about doing what is truthful and good, even in difficult situations and even when no one will know about it.

- Integrity asks us to stand up for what we believe and to be advocates for justice and the well being of all.

- Integrity is the discipline and resiliency to act in alignment with our values for the good of the whole, no matter the circumstances.

- Integrity is incorruptible, has a reverence for all life and is forever.

We all have wandered off the path of integrity. We can find our way back through courageous acts of humility, compassion and forgiveness. The steps back are to be aware of our failings, to find the humility to admit we are wrong and to have the wisdom to make it right. In taking responsibility for repairing mistakes within ourselves and within our relationships, our character becomes stronger and our integrity becomes brighter.

Integrity in everyday life is the embodiment of our personal character, the virtue of inner strength in daily decisions and the worthiness we demonstrate in our relationships. It finds expression in the courage to hold firm to our beliefs in times of chaos and social pressure, in balance with the courage to respond to the changing needs of community, as we embrace the well being of the whole. Being consistently ourselves, we stay true to the integrity of our essence by putting what matters to us in a variety of relationships, contexts and situations first. There is a recognizable thread of integrity as we draw upon our unique strengths and our inner wisdom as a father or son, mother or grandmother, employer or employee, at work or at home.

I often observe integrity in action as the horses engage in their herd relationships and as they engage with people. When they experience integrity, it ripples through the herd and influences how they relate. One day, I was supporting a woman who was interested in exploring the felt experience of integrity. She knew what it meant cognitively, but was more interested in feeling the experience of integrity.

Jerry's task was to get to know the horses and to earn their respect by engaging with them with the integrity of respect. She was to take the lead and inspire two very large horses, Bea (our Clydesdale) and Raven (our Frisian), to move forward together as a team within a relatively small space, in a rhythm of integrity. At first, there was chaos; the horses took the lead, running and challenging Jerry's leadership. Jerry stayed calm, kind and focused and within a few minutes, the horses responded to the integrity of her leadership presence by slowing down and moving together around her respectfully in a wide, coherent circle.

"During the chaos," Jerry reported after the experience, "I felt crowded and unsure of myself, but as I learned to literally stand my ground calmly and with purpose and to move decisively, things opened up and there was space for us all. In this uncertain situation, what seemed impossible became possible. I was able to inspire two very big horses to move willingly and coherently forward in the same direction through my actions of integrity. We all moved together, in a space of kindness and trust. How might the world be different if we all walked together with the integrity of kindness and honor, respect and trust, and collective purpose?" she asked.

We all experience moral dilemmas as a part of our everyday life. How we face, manage and resolve these dilemmas has everything to do with maintaining our integrity. Sometimes we respond from our heart with a quick and intuitive response while other times we ponder the dilemma with a more cognitive thought process and reasonable response. Most of the most difficult moral and ethical decisions that challenge our integrity are not good verses bad but good verses good or doing the least harm and the most good. These dilemmas provide opportunities to be the kind of person we strive to be and to confront the integrity of our character in our everyday interactions.

Horses can be amazing guides as we find our way through life's moral dilemmas and challenges to our integrity. Though it may seem strange to consider horses moral beings they demonstrate their integrity; in being sensitive to the difficulties of others, in their respect of social order and expected behavior, in managing their behavior and in peacemaking for the good of the herd. Much like integrity in our human herds the horse herd responds best through reciprocal relationships and shared values for the greater good of the community. This good spirited way of being and responding is the essence of integrity.

Horses can help us create the best possible conditions to discover our integrity and to resolve the moral dilemmas w have within our selves, in our relationships with others and within in all life. Horses offer us the field conditions and a supportive relationship that is conducive to moral decision-making and to the alignment of our integrity. Horses offer to us; a quiet place of honesty, a fair place of non-judgment, a compassionate place to consider our options. They provide a courageous place from which to explore life's choices and to determine actions that are aligned with our values.

In the presence of the horses people have been better able to prepare to confront a wrong doing in the workplace, to have a difficult conversation with a loved one, or to make a challenging life decision that is in alignment with their nature and moral perspective.

Our personal integrity is a body, mind and spirit experience. Our embodied presence grounds us in reality and sense-ability allowing us to know when we are losing our footing on the path. Our hearts, when open and loving, choose only what is good and just. Mindful thought leads to an awareness of our values and the spiritual wisdom that is held within the vessel of our temporal human bodies. Integrity in action is found in every step we take when we are in harmony within ourselves, and with the world around us.

> *"To be in harmony is to live the great integrity.*
> *To live the great integrity is the ultimate wisdom…*
> *Great acts are made up of small deeds….*
> *A journey of a thousand miles*
> *begins with a single step."*
> —Lao Tzu, Tao Te Chin

The Great Integrity is a concept that comes from the Tao Te Chin, which was written in the sixth century by Lao Tzu, a Chinese spiritualist. The pathway to integrity is one of harmony and wholeness, of individual uniqueness and collective unity. The Great Integrity, however, is more than individual integrity; it is a field of integrity, holding the whole of life together.

The pathway of the great integrity is expressed in our spiritual traditions through sacred text and is shared by teaching stories passed down around a campfire. In oral traditions and sacred teaching stories and through spiritual texts such as Kabala, Koran, Torah and Tao, sacred knowledge is shared. The living concept of creating a field of Great Integrity is a call to action for justice, generosity, wisdom and loving kindness in all we are and all we do. It is a living pathway to our authentic presence leading us deeper toward our virtuous humble selves and our dances with destiny.

The field of great integrity holds the pure potential of creativity, healing and well-being. The concept of the field of great integrity is elusive to define, but we know it when we experience it.

The great integrity is experienced when we are in harmony with each other, with the environment, with all life and with ourselves. The pathway of integrity requires that we release the mindless, empty-hearted doing that keeps us from that harmonious state; we let go of all that is unimportant to us, open our minds to be free of judgment, release our hearts from unkindness and ourselves from perceived fear. We can then ascend to our highest aspirations.

Gathering the Sparks of Integrity

In my Jewish tradition, the great integrity is revealed in the concept *tikkun olam* ("repairing the world"); it is about gathering the sparks of the sacred into a unified whole. *Tikkun Olam* is a Jewish concept defined by acts of kindness performed to perfect or repair the world. This tradition teaches that in the beginning, a fragile vessel was shattered, spilling and scattering sparks everywhere. Each person has the gift and responsibility of finding and gathering those sparks of light and love. Each of us can do our part in repairing the world and returning it to sacred wholeness. Gathering the sparks, we discover the pathway of the great integrity is one of being in rhythm with nature and our authentic human nature, rather than doing what is against our authentic nature.

The Field of the Great Integrity

The responsibility of *tikkun olam*—returning the world to wholeness—like the responsibility of the Great Integrity, is an individual one, challenging us to bring loving kindness into the world, each in our own way and according to our destiny. It becomes a collective responsibility of integrity as communities of humanity gather the sparks of light and love for the dignity of all life, not just human life, through the generations.

> *"Do not be daunted by the enormity of the world's grief. Do justly now. Love mercy now. Walk humbly now. You are not obligated to complete the work but neither are you free to abandon it."*
> —Talmud

Section IX—The Path of the Great Integrity

Pause, Reflect and Respond

Reflect on a moment in your life when it was a challenge to be honest and tell the truth and you faced a deeply felt moral dilemma. What was the situation? Who was involved? What were the competing values? What choices did you make in leadership and/ or in daily life?

What did you learn by facing your challenge with integrity?

What is one modest deed that benefits both yourself and others that you can do today to live and lead with integrity?

Take several index cards and write a word or phrase and an image that came from your reflections on each individual card.

Save these cards, as you will be reflecting back on them.

X

The Journey to Your Spirit of Authentic Presence

Chapter 20
Bringing It Together and Bringing It Home

> *"Instructions for living a life.*
> *Pay attention.*
> *Be astonished.*
> *Tell about it."*
> —Mary Oliver

If anyone is going to live my life, I want it to be me. I believe the most important journey to learn from is our own. I trust that the most important story to tell is ours. I believe that Love is the most precious resource on life's journey.

It is love that inspired me to write this book and love that carried me through the often challenging journey of telling my story; love of family, love of the horses and all nature, love of friends and community, and love of life.

I am including one last horse story as a tribute to the horses and all who have learned with them. It is a true love story that unfolded here at the ranch a few weeks ago.

A young couple that had been together a few years, Maria and Christian, came to the ranch for a retreat to better understand themselves and each other and to deepen the intimacy of their relationship. They were in love and wanted to strengthen their commitment through marriage and yet they were struggling to set the date and plan their wedding. Each time one of them brought the calendar to the table to decide on a date for the wedding, the other had a reason why the time was not right. They not only had difficulty deciding when, but where and how the marriage would take place, and they stressed over who would be invited and who would be in the bridal party. Maria and Christian agreed they wanted to get married but could not understand why they were having so much difficulty getting it to happen. They spent two days and evenings in the quiet of the forest reflecting and then engaging together in important conversations about their upcoming marriage and life journey. Through this process they deepened their love, intimacy and commitment to marriage but were no closer to unraveling the mystery about their lack of agreement around the actual details of the ceremony and movement toward getting married.

On day three of their couples retreat, Maria and Christian decided that they would like to engage with the horses to see if they could gain more clarity on the situation. The morning was hot and the flies bothersome. The horses were standing still, half asleep in front of their fans, lazily swishing flies with their tails. The herd seemed completely disinterested in us as we approached their horse area, a large tent-like cathedral. I was certain the horses would be reluctant to leave their fans and expected they would mostly ignore us or treat us like bothersome flies by flicking their tails in irritation at us. Much to my surprise when we entered, the horses turned towards us with ears forward and looked at us with curiosity. Within a few minutes, each of the horses came over to warmly greet Maria and Christian who were standing close together with their arms around each other. All the horses approached the loving couple except Holly the zebra who stood by the doorway looking out at the pasture seemingly ignoring them, her hind tail end strategically facing toward them.

Maria and Christian were excited that all the horses had come over to be with them and believed that each horse in its own unique way had blessed their relationship; Bea blessed them with honesty, Silver with strength, Tess with playfulness, Bud with compassion, Toby with calm, Spirit with passion, Raven with loyalty. They were touched by the magic of the horse blessings and at the same time, disappointed that Holly had not approached them. They had hoped that she would come over to them or at least acknowledge their presence.

Letting go of the expectation that Holly would befriend them and feeling well blessed, Maria and Christian stood quiet-ly holding hands, smiling and breathing in the love around them from the horses and the love within them for each oth-er. Sometimes letting go of expectation, disappointment and the fear that what we most want won't come to us, a place opens within us for something wonderful and extraordinary to come. Within moments, to their surprise and delight, Holly the zebra turned and walked toward them. As Holly came closer and closer, the couple, facing one another and holding hands, slowly lowered themselves to the ground and onto their knees. Christian, being a tall, professional basketball player did not want to tower over Holly, and Maria had joined Christian in moving closer to the ground. Holly wandered over and with sweet zebra breath, she gave Christian a zebra kiss on the back of his neck and rubbed her velvet nose gently along his back just behind his heart space. Holly then approached Maria and gently nudged her on the back by her heart space. Holly the holy zebra then slowly circled around them three times, much like the circling ritual found in a Jewish wedding ceremony, weaving the couple together.

Maria and Christian slowly stood up still holding hands and faced one another. Holly took her place about two feet in front of them looking directly at them. All the other horses began to slowly move into a formation of sacred geometry. Bea, Raven, Toby and Spirit lined up on the right side of Holly and the couple and stood at quiet attention, also looking directly at them. Little Tess and giant Bud, our romantic horse couple, stood close together at attention to the left of the couple. The herd looked at Maria and Christian with soft eyes and gentle hearts. Holly, still standing close to and in front of the couple, began to move her lips as if giving sage advice and offering a marriage blessing to Maria and Christian.

I took in, with awe and amazement, the whole and holiness of the scene within the sacred shelter of the horse cathedral tent. The horses had arranged a wedding and Holly was officiating. Tess was maid-of-honor, Bud the best man, and Bea, Spirit, Raven, Silver and Toby served as the bridal party.

The ceremony completed, Holly nodded her head and walked back to her position guarding the doorway. The horses all shifted position and resumed their places dozing in front of the fan.

Maria and Christian laughed and said together, "I think we were just married by a zebra." They bowed to the herd, walked hand- in hand out of the horse cathedral and found a place to rest under the shade of a tree to take in what had happened. Blessed by the horse herd and married in their hearts by Holly the holy zebra, they began to plan with ease their human wedding.

A zebra officiating a marriage, a pony as a maid-of-honor, horses helping people listen within and know what's in their hearts, a herd living free—just another day at Pebble

Ledge Ranch. Opening to the unexpected, to love, and to everyday miracles, we can shift our perspective of reality beyond what we expect, and invite a reality far beyond what we believe is possible.

Choosing the Path of Authentic Presence

> *"Ah, but I was so much older then,*
> *I'm younger than that now."*
> —Bob Dylan

For each one of us there are moments in our lives when our older youthful self meets our younger elder self and embraces both the past and future in the heart of the present. Looking back with compassion and forward with optimism we can journey beyond what had been possible in our leadership of our lives. Following the authentic truth of our inner nature we can better connect to what has meaning and purpose and discover the life that is ours to live. We all have the ability and responsibility to choose our own paths of authentic presence. Not choosing is a powerful way of choosing and it has direct consequences in where our journeys take us. Our lives depend on it.

Each day, with each sunrise and sunset, is a fresh opportunity to awaken and reflect on the everyday choices we make to determine the identity and integrity of our authentic presence. We can begin every morning with a positive perspective of our selves and life. We can awaken and reflect on important life questions. How can we today be most ourselves at our best? Who and for what are we grateful this morning? What random act of kindness might we offer to someone today? How might we be more patient and compassionate with ourselves? What is one dream we can follow beginning today?

> *"It is sometimes easier to make the world a better place than to prove you have made the world a better place"*
> —Amos Tversky, cognitive and mathematical psychologist

As the sun sets or in the darkness as our day closes, we have an opportunity to reflect on and appreciate the best of our day and find peace and rest within the spirit of our authentic presence. What do we value and appreciate about the day we just experienced? How did we strengthen our authentic presence through challenges? What was one heartfelt moment we experienced? Listen to the quiet wisdom within and give the day a title as if it were a book or movie that reflects the meaning or purpose of the day's journey. What decisions and actions did we take to enliven the spirit of our authentic presence to make a positive difference in the world?

In my personal journey and through writing this book I reflected on eight pathways that contributed to the spirit of my authentic presence. We each have our own pathways. Yours might be similar to mine or yours might be one inspired by music or computers or racecars or goldfish. How might we each explore our own paths with curiosity and courage or venture down a path not yet taken? How might we all live with courage and care and a sense of wonder for life's daily gifts and miracles?

We are not alone in this journey. Like the horses in their herds we can create our place of belonging.

Engaging with horses and listening with an open heart to what they have to share with us, we gain access to collective wisdom, which is around us and within us. Connecting with horses we can see things more clearly and turn toward what is true for us, accepting it just as it is. Horses offer fearless com-

Bringing it Home

passion, honest communication and a welcoming community for us in which to learn, evolve and accept the responsibility of our humanity.

We are part of a collective, a tribe, a network to which we contribute and within which we thrive. Connecting with an extended family of like-spirited people in uncertain times and times of celebration, in moments of grief and moments of joy, we can more than survive; we can thrive.

Our human nature as part of Mother Nature is born capable of love. Her lessons of restless change teach us to live each day anew. As we discover our place in the family of nature and a love of the wild, our purpose becomes clearer, our inner nature more known, and we find a path that knows peace.

How we embody ourselves—our embodied physical presence—is our experience of ourselves, others and the world around us. Sensing the world through our embodied selves provides moment-to-moment information and insight guiding our way to live in harmony and balance according to our most authentic nature. Using our senses and placing our awareness in what is happening without judgment or interpretation or "old story," and listening for the best possible result in the present, leads to our best possible future. Going to our learning edge, stepping beyond our comfort zone and approaching challenge with support, we can create the conditions for something better to happen and can achieve more than we expect. Our bodies keep us grounded in the reality of the situation and centered within our own sense of self. Paying attention to our embodied presence and acting with intention—being intentional—gives us the consistency, not of doing the same thing over and over, but of responding consistently to what is called for through the wisdom of the body.

Positivity expands the power of our authentic presence with resiliency and optimism and the ability to dream. The courage to release limiting thoughts and patterns of behavior opens the path to a more meaningful, joyful life. The journey is taken not to change ourselves to be something we are not, but to change to being more of who we are. Life experienced through positivity takes us to our best selves and engages the best in others. A positive life is vibrant, fiercely alive and allows us to dare to dream and to trust in the unknown.

Accessing a full range of our many forms of intelligence offers the possibility to expand our perception of reality and range of choice in behavior and actions. The diversity and inclusion of multiple perspectives expands what is possible. Accessing the full range of our intelligence contributes to more meaningful relationships, provides critical information in situations of challenge and opens a path to realizing our potential.

Our Indigenous culture as members of a tribe, herd, community or family provides the foundation for our most precious identity and our best, authentic selves. The confidence we gain in being part of a larger collective expands our ability to inspire others to join us in creating positive change. Our connection to each other, our ancestors and the natural world offers wisdom essential to living a meaningful, purposeful and moral life for the higher good of all.

Each footstep we take upon the earth can be a blessing. One forward step at a time, we approach a future that is waiting to greet us. The everyday choices we make walking along this journey can guide our personal destination and determine our collective destiny. Our relationship with nature and the wild awakens our most precious and authentic human nature. The sacred ground under our own feet inspires the only steps we can call our own, the wind at our backs moves us bravely forward, guiding us through the forest or desert into the life meant only for each of us.

The path of great integrity is an honest and humble journey of great humility. Being present and aware with exquisite attention to ourselves and others, the consequences of our choices are experienced from within. Listening to our internal authority we can take responsibility for our behavior as part of our moral identity. We need not do anything but humbly be in integrity in each moment, in each relationship. In each blessed choice we make on our journey of authentic presence, we become the change that changes the world into the world we want to create.

> *Even*
> *After*
> *All this time*
> *The sun never says to the earth*
> *"You owe me."*
>
> *Look*
> *What happens*
> *With a love like that.*
> *It lights the whole sky."*
> —Daniel Ladinsky (inspired by Hafez)

In telling our stories and listening to the stories of others, the stories carried by dancing wind, whispering horses in the mist, by the waters of ocean and clouds and tears, from the still voice within, we begin to know what we could not know before. Gathering courage from the stories we can live more intentionally and love more fully. As leaders in the world or as leaders of our own lives, we can begin to authentically know things as they are, know who we are, and maybe even know what is invisibly waiting for us beyond what we can see.

The power of our authentic presence, in tandem with attention and intention, can transform our lives and the lives of others for the greater good of humanity, and for all those with whom we share this amazing planet Earth. The word power contains within it a map to our authentic presence, the treasure of our true self at its best:

The **P** in power reminds us to pause and prepare: slowing and quieting, grounding and centering and listening through all our senses to the territory around us and within us.

The **O** calls us to open and observe: releasing past judgments, disappointments and assumptions to notice with present clarity the reality and resources in the now.

The **W** invites us to wander and wonder: experiencing the present moment from an expansive and curious perspective creating a larger field of choice.

The **E** guides us to enter and engage: stepping beyond our habits and familiar patterns to connect with ourselves and others and the life around us through honest communication, compassion and trustworthy relationship.

The **R** in power expects us to reflect and respond: that we may act with integrity and with the awareness of our way of being, acting and leading for the well-being of "all our relations" for seven generations to come. The power and pathway of authentic presence is already in our compassionate hearts, in our creative minds and in our capable hands.

Bringing it Home

> *"Just do right. Right may not be expedient, it may not be profitable, but it will satisfy your soul. Take up the battle. Take it up. It's yours. This is your life. This is your world."*
>
> —Maya Angelou, American author and poet

There are many diverse pathways to authentic presence, to the heart of human kindness and to just "doing right." My invitation to you is to join the adventure and follow your own path to your best self and authentic presence within the experience of being human in a more than human world.

Collectively we can build communities that embody equal empowerment, creative collaboration and inspired innovation generating the conditions for all life on Earth to thrive.

Writing this book was a way for me to tell some true stories about courage and compassion and the importance of connection. I am grateful for the pathways that opened to me and for the inner journey that writing this book provided. I am grateful for family and friends and horses and home. I am grateful for the guiding light of laughing and loving along this wandering path of authentic presence. I am simply grateful.

Section X—The Journey to Your Spirit of Authentic Presence

Pause, Reflect and Respond

Reflect on a time, place and situation when you experienced the real you, true to yourself and behaved in alignment with your virtues and most authentic self.

What were the strengths you drew upon and the challenges you faced as you acted from your higher nature? How did this benefit you and how did it benefit humanity?

Take all your index cards from all the sections and spread them out in front of you.

Notice words or phrases or images that seem to appear more often than others.

What are the themes that appear and how might they inform the direction of your life journey?

For what are you simply grateful?

Notes

Chapter 1 A Journey to Authentic Presence

"Live Like Horses," lyrics by Elton John and Bernie Taupin From the album The Duets, recorded by Luciano Pavarotti and Elton John, 3.

Chapter 2 Eight Paths to Authentic Presence

Peter Senge, Senior Lecturer MIT
Peter Michael Senge is an American systems scientist who is a senior lecturer at the MIT Sloan School of Management, co-faculty at the New England Complex Systems Institute, and the founder of the Society for Organizational Learning. Known for his work on Systems Thinking, he is the author of *The Fifth Discipline* and *The Necessary Revolution*, 13, 27, 270, 300 (see also Notes Chapter 13, Systems Thinking).

Thomas Malone, MIT
Thomas W. Malone is an American organizational theorist, management consultant, and the Patrick J. McGovern Professor of Management at the MIT Sloan School of Management. He is the author of *The Future of Work* and many other management books,18.

Clarissa Pinkolas Estes is an American poet, Jungian psychoanalyst, post-trauma recovery specialist, a spoken word artist and the author of *Women Who Run With the Wolves*, 20, 254, 279, 295.

David Abram is an American philosopher, cultural ecologist, and performance artist who lectures and teaches widely on several continents and is founder and Creative Director— The Alliance for Wild Ethics. He is the author of *Becoming Animal: An Earthly Cosmology* (Pantheon, 2010), 22.

Friedrich Wilhelm Nietzsche was a German philosopher, cultural critic, composer, poet, philologist, and Latin and Greek scholar whose work has exerted a profound influence on Western philosophy and modern intellectual history, 22.

Martin E. P. Seligman is an American psychologist, educator, and author of self-help books. Since the late 1990s, Seligman has been an avid promoter within the scientific community for the field of Positive Psychology. He is Director of the Penn Positive Psychology Center, Zellerbach Family Professor of Psychology in the Penn Department of Psychology, and Director of the Penn Master of Applied Positive Psychology program.

    Dr. Seligman's books have been translated into more than twenty languages and have been best sellers both in America and abroad. Among his better-known works are *Flourish, Authentic Happiness, Learned Optimism, The Optimistic Child, Helplessness, and Abnormal Psychology*, 25, 298.

Notes

Chief Seattle, 1780-1866
Chief Seattle, a poet and spokesperson from the Suquamish Tribe was an important leader among his people.
    The Indigenous Way of Life is based on a holistic worldview that sees everything—the land, the people and all living things—as vitally connected. The fundamental purpose of this way of life is sustainability. Indigenous social, political and economic models are designed to keep our families, communities, and natural environment in balance, not just for the present, but also for generations to come, 28, 378.

Rainer Maria Rilke was a Bohemian-Austrian poet and novelist, was one of the most lyrically intense German-language poets. He is well known for his book *Letters to a Young Poet*, 33, 232, 303, 398.

Lao Tzu, the *Tao Te Chin* is a Chinese classic text traditionally credited to the sixth-century BCE sage Lao Tzu who was an ancient Chinese philosopher and writer. He is known as the reputed author of the *Tao Te Chin*, and the founder of philosophical Taoism, 32, 33, 447.

Chapter 3   **Meet the Herd: The Heart of Collective Wisdom**

Mary Oliver is an American poet whose poetry has won numerous awards, including the Pulitzer Prize and the National Book Award, 39, 455.

Maya Angelou is an American poet, author, songwriter, performer and civil rights activist, 43, 401, 465.

Thomas Kibble Hervey was a British poet, critic, and editor in the 1800s, 61.

Chapter 7   **Human Guests in a Herd of Horses**

Margaret Mead, an American author, speaker and a respected anthropologist, approached entering an indigenous culture by respecting its inherent integrity, 200.

James Kepner is a psychologist and author of *Body Process: A Gestalt Approach to Working with the Body In Therapy* and *Healing Tasks: Psychotherapy with Adult Survivors of Childhood Abuse,* 212.

Arawana Hayashi is a choreographer, performer and educator through collaborative improvisation. Hayashi's pioneering work as a choreographer, performer and educator is deeply sourced in collaborative improvisation. She currently heads the creation of Social Presencing Theater (SPT) for the Presencing Institute where she guides people in tapping into the body as a primary resource in gathering essential data, 213, 271.

Notes 473

Chapter 8 **Nature and Human Nature**

Paul Hawken is an author, environmentalist, and entrepreneur. His books include *Blessed Unrest*, and many others, 252.

Albert Einstein, A German physicist, considered the most influential physicist of the twentieth century; he developed the theories of relativity and was awarded the 1921 Nobel Prize in Physics, 223, 315, 339, 424.

John Muir was a naturalist, environmental philosopher, writer and advocate for the preservation of the wilderness, 228.

Rainer Maria Rilke was a Bohemian-Austrian poet and novelist, 232 (see Notes Chapter 2 for more information).

Ralph Waldo Emerson was am American lecturer, essayist and poet, 234, 235.

Chapter 9 **Listening to the Genius of Nature**

Janine Benyus is the co-founder of Biomimicry 3.8. She is a biologist, innovation consultant, and author of six books, including *Biomimicry: Innovation Inspired by Nature*, 237.

Ralph Waldo Emerson was am American lecturer, essayist and poet, 238.

M. Thomashow, *Voices of Ecological Identity*, 1996 a preeminent educator, shows how environmental studies can be taught from different perspective, one that is deeply informed by personal reflection, 239.

Theodore Roosevelt Jr. was an American statesman, author, explorer, soldier, and naturalist, who served as the 26th President of the United States. Some of Roosevelt's most effective achievements were in conservation. He added enormously to the national forests in the West, reserved lands for public use, and fostered great irrigation projects, 246.

Chapter 10   **Nature and the Wild Path to Authentic Presence**

Clarissa Pinkolas Estes, Author, *Women Who Run with Wolves*, 254 (see Notes Chapter 2 for more information).

Chapter 11   **Embodied Presence–The Vessel of Our Humanness**

Ron Kurtz, *The Body Reveals: What Your Body Says About You*. Kurtz developed Hakomi Therapy, a blend of western and eastern psychology, integrating mindfulness and somatic techniques, 261.

Notes 475

Peter Senge, Senior Lecturer MIT, 270 (see Notes Chapter 2 for more information).

Clarissa Pinkolas Estes, Author, *Women Who Run with Wolves,* 279 (see Notes Chapter 2 for more information).

Richard Boyatzis, Distinguished University Professor, Departments of Psychology, Cognitive Science and Organizational Behavior, Case Western Reserve University, Adjunct Professor of People and Organizations, ESADE, co-author with Dan Goleman and Annie McKee of the international bestseller, *Primal Leadership* and co-author, *Becoming a Resonant Leader: Social and Emotional Intelligence* was developed by Richard Boyotzis, among others, and his colleagues at CWRU and Daniel Goleman and his colleagues. It is an approach that focuses on developing the capacity to bring out the best in the relational realm and achieve desired outcomes in social transactions through emotional competency, 299, 321.

Arawana Hayashi is a choreographer, performer and educator through collaborative improvisation, 271 (see Notes Chapter 7 for more information).

Gabrielle Roth is an American dancer and musician in the world music and trance dance genres. She created the 5 Rhythms approach to movement, which is now taught worldwide, 271.

Peter Drucker is a management consultant, educator, and author, whose writings contributed to the philosophical and practical foundations of the modern business corporation, 275.

Chapter 12 **Embodied Ways of Being**

Martha Graham, was an American modern dancer and choreographer, a world leader in dance bringing the innovation of improvisation to modern dance, 281.

Mark Walsh is an Embodied Training Manager. His company "Integration Training" teaches embodiment to coaches, manager and leaders, 285.

Chapter 13 **The Positive Approach to Leadership and Life**

Mahatma Gandhi was the primary leader of India's independence movement against British rule. His nonviolent philosophy of passive resistance taught a new way to change the world. Gandhi was loved and known by his followers as Mahatma, or "the great-souled one," 293.

Anne Frank wrote *Diary of A Young Girl*, a collection of writings kept while in hiding with her family for two years during the Nazi occupation of the Netherlands during WWII. Anne Frank died in the Holocaust at age thirteen, 293.

Notes 477

Clarissa Pinkolas Estes, Author, *Women Who Run with Wolves*, 295 (see Notes Chapter 2 for more information).

Martin E. P. Seligman is an American psychologist, educator, and author of self-help books, 298 (see Notes Chapter 2 for more information).

David Cooperrider, Professor in Appreciative Inquiry and Organizational Behavior Case Western Reserve University, is best known for his original theoretical articulation of A.I. or Appreciative Inquiry, a strengths-inspired approach to change being practiced extensively in the corporate world. He has served as an advisor to prominent leaders in business and society, including projects with five presidents and/or Nobel Laureates such as William Jefferson Clinton, His Holiness the Dalai Lama, Kofi Annan, and Jimmy Carter, 299.

Systems Thinking, developed by Peter Senge, reminds us that we are part of the system in our families, communities and institutions creating both desirable and undesirable consequences. Systems Thinking engages the dynamic interrelationship of all the parts of the whole to better understand how it operates leading to appropriate positive action for all parts of the system and the system as a whole. Theory U, designed at Presencing Institute, MIT by Otto Scharmer, Peter Senge and Joseph Jawarsky, proposes that the quality of the results that we create in any kind of social system is a function of the inner quality of awareness, attention, or consciousness within the system from which we operate, 298, 300.

Roger Saillant, Ph.D. is a past Executive Director at the Fowler Center for Sustainable Value at the Weatherhead School of Management, Case Western Reserve University.

He served as President and Chief Executive Officer of Plug Power, Inc. from December 2000 to April 2008. Dr. Saillant joined Ford Motor Company in 1970 as a Research Scientist. He is currently a board member at Cloud Institute for Sustainability Education, 300, 302.

Peter Senge, Senior Lecturer MIT, 300 (see Notes Chapter 2 for more information).

Rainer Maria Rilke was a Bohemian-Austrian poet and novelist, 303 (see Notes Chapter 2 for more information).

Chapter 14   **The Collective Wisdom of the Eight Intelligences**

Albert Einstein, A German physicist, considered the most influential physicist of the twentieth century, 315, 339 (see Notes Chapter 8 for more information).

Dr. Evelyn B. Hanggi is president of the Equine Research Foundation, 318.

Richard Boyatzis, Distinguished University Professor, Departments of Psychology, Cognitive Science and Organizational Behavior, Case Western Reserve University, 321 (see Notes Chapter 2 for more information).

Notes

Franklin Delano Roosevelt, known as FDR, was an American statesman and political leader who served as the 32nd President of the United States, 324.

———————————————————————————

Steven Paul Jobs was the chairman, chief executive officer, and co-founder of Apple Inc. He is known as an American entrepreneur, business genius and inventor, 332.

———————————————————————————

Mother Teresa, Saint Teresa of Calcutta, was an Albanian-Indian Roman Catholic nun and missionary. She is remembered and revered for her unconditional loving kindness and compassion, 337, 403.

———————————————————————————

Ralph Waldo Emerson was an American lecturer, essayist and poet, 337*.

*Different iterations of this quotation have been credited to Oliver Wendell Holmes, Henry Stanley Haskins, and Henry David Thoreau.

———————————————————————————

Deepak Chopra is an American alternative medicine advocate, author, and public speaker, 338.

———————————————————————————

Helen Keller was the first deaf-blind person to earn a Bachelor of Arts degree. She was an inspiring American author, political activist, and lecturer, 338.

———————————————————————————

Chapter 15   The Wisdom of Our Indigenous Way of Being

First People's World Wide is an organization that facilitates the use of traditional Indigenous knowledge in solving today's challenges, 361.

Margaret Wheatley is an author, global speaker, and consultant to leaders and their organization and communities, 374.

John Welwood is an American clinical psychologist, psychotherapist, teacher, and author. He integrates psychological and spiritual approaches. He has published books and articles on relationship, psychotherapy, consciousness, and personal change, 378.

Chief Seattle, 1780-1866 was a chief to the Duwamish people. A prominent figure among his people, he is famous for having made a speech that was in favor of being responsible to the environment and demanding respect of the land rights of his people, 378 (see Notes Chapter 2 for more information).

Chapter 16   Cross Cultural Guide to Authentic Presence

This medicine wheel is based on one of the Medicine Wheels from the Lakota traditions, 390.

Notes

Rainer Maria Rilke was a Bohemian-Austrian poet and novelist, 398 (see Notes Chapter 2 for more information).

Nelson Rolihlahla Mandela was an inspirational South African political leader and anti-apartheid revolutionary who was President of South Africa from 1994 to 1999, 400.

Maya Angelou is an American poet, author, 401 (see Notes Chapter 3 for more information).

Mother Teresa, Saint Teresa of Calcutta, was an Albanian-Indian Roman Catholic nun and missionary. She is remembered and revered for her unconditional loving kindness and compassion, 403

Martin Luther King Jr. was an African American Baptist minister and human rights activist who was an inspirational spokesperson and courageous leader in the civil rights movement. He preached hope and led non-violent protests. He was an exemplary human being in his integrity, demand for justice and compassion, 405.

Crazy Horse, Sioux Chief was a Native American leader of the Oglala Lakota in the nineteenth century. He led his people in battle against the United States federal government to fight against encroachment by white American settlers and to preserve his culture and traditions, 406.

Chapter 18   The Collective Wisdom of the Emerging Future

Lee Smolin is an American theoretical physicist, 424.

Albert Einstein, A German physicist, considered the most influential physicist of the twentieth century, 424 (see Notes Chapter 8 for more information).

Maria Augusta von Trapp. Maria Augusta von Trapp was the stepmother of the Trapp Family Singers. She wrote *The Story of the Trapp Family Singers*, published in 1949, 431.

Lao Tzu was an ancient Chinese philosopher and writer, 447 (see Notes Chapter 2 for more information).

Chapter 20   Bringing It Together and Bringing It Home

Mary Oliver is an American poet, 455 (see Notes Chapter 3 for more information).

Dr. Amos Tversky is a mathematical and cognitive psychologist who changed the way experts in many fields think about how people make decisions about risks, benefits and probabilities. He was the Davis-Brack Professor of Behavioral Sciences at Stanford University, 460.

Notes

Daniel Ladinsky, *The Gift: Poems by Hafiz* (1999), p. 34. This is not a translation or interpretation of any poem by Hafez; it is an original poem by Ladinsky inspired by the spirit of Hafez in a dream, 463.

Maya Angelou is an American poet and author, 465 (see Notes Chapter 3 for more information).

Author Contact Information

jacalynstevenson@gmail.com
www.spirit-of-leadership.com

About the Author

Jackie Stevenson is the founder and CEO of Spirit of Leadership LLC providing coaching, leadership and team building training and seminars for corporations and non profit organizations. Some of Jackie's coaching clients include leaders and managers and people invested in personal discovery. She coaches at her Ranch and internationally via Skype with clients from New Zealand, Belgium and Dubai.

Jackie Stevenson teaches at Case Western Reserve University Weatherhead School of Management Executive Education Program and the Mandel School of Applied Social Sciences. She is on the Weatherhead School of Management coaching staff and the ICF Gestalt Institute of Cleveland Coaching Program. She is a Board Certified Coach (BCC).

Jackie is also the past Director of the Mandel Jewish Community Center of Cleveland and past Clinical Center Director of the Gestalt Institute of Cleveland. She teaches and lectures within the U.S., and in Turkey, Israel and Mexico.

She is the founder of "Wolf Creek," a wilderness-based leadership and personal development training program for women. Over 100 women have participated in this yearlong training program exploring the teachings of nature and the power of personal presence and what is possible when creating community.

She is founder and director of the "Experiential Learning with Horses: Developing Human Potential for Positive Change" certificate program preparing people to integrate their work with horses into their professional work with people, and for people who want to develop their professional and life skills by engaging with horses.

Jackie's work is unique to each client. The coaching process is grounded in well-accepted practices and focuses on a strength-based approach of "what's working" and "what needs to change" perspective. As an executive coach, she is a champion of authenticity and character and "doing well by doing good." Incorporated in her coaching is the development of embodied leadership presence, focusing on body language and the alignment of mission, goals and action. Jackie specializes in unique coaching sessions and leadership and team building retreats through experiential learning with horses and nature.

From the Author

I have been privileged to follow my professional interest and passion for engaging people in personal discovery and development for almost forty years. For the last thirty years, I have integrated into my coaching and consulting work my personal respect and passion for nature, horses, the intelligence of our bodies and experiential learning.

I bring this approach to my work and the work of my clients at a time when we struggle with the changes brought by a highly evolved technological culture and a less evolved relational culture.

About the Author

My clients include a diverse population drawn from individuals, families, groups, organizations and communities. I have worked with kids from the inner city, parents and children, family businesses, professional men and women embarking on their careers, individuals challenged with demanding leadership responsibilities, teams struggling to succeed, CEOs questioning "For the sake of what do I go to work each day?"

We all struggle with day-to-day challenges, trying to earn a living and do productive work while living our dreams and destinies. We seek meaning and identity in our lives and in our life's work and strive for purpose in our endeavors. Being physically, emotionally and mindfully present provides the wellspring for meaningful relationships and the courage and creative energy to inspire greatness in ourselves and others.

My hope is that this book empowers you to achieve your best purpose and to enjoy well-being in service of the whole.

—Jackie Stevenson